Robert Cooper is the Curator of the Scottish Masonic Museum and Library at Freemason's Hall in Edinburgh, a position that affords him privileged access to rare Masonic documents and artefacts. A world authority on Freemasonry, he is a member of numerous Masonic organizations, including the Great Priory of Scotland, the Ancient and Accepted Rite for Scotland, the Supreme Grand Royal Arch Chapter of Scotland, the Royal Order of Scotland and the Grand Imperial Council of Scotland. He has appeared many times in the media, and lectures internationally on the history and ethos of the Craft.

By the same author:

The Voyages of the Venetian Brothers Nicolo and Antonio Zeno (ed.)
History and Origins of the Order of Free Gardeners
The Genealogie of the Sainteclairs of Rosslyn (ed.)
The Illustrated Guide to Rosslyn Chapel etc. (ed.)
An Account of the Chapel of Rosslyn (ed.)
Freemasons, Gardeners and Templars
The Templar Church of London (ed.)
A Winter with Robert Burns (ed.)
The Rosslyn Hoax?

CRACKING THE FREEMASON'S CODE

UNDERSTANDING THE LOST SYMBOL OF THE FREEMASONS

Robert L. D. Cooper

RIDER BOOKS
RIDER
LONDON · SYDNEY · AUCKLAND · JOHANNESBURG

1 3 5 7 9 10 8 6 4 2

First published in 2006 by Rider, an imprint of Ebury Publishing,
A Random House Group Company

This edition published by Rider in 2009

The Random House Group Limited Reg. No. 954009

Addresses for companies within the Random House Group can be found at
www.rbooks.co.uk

A CIP catalogue record for this book is available from the British Library

The Random House Group Limited supports The Forest Stewardship
Council (FSC), the leading international forest certification organisation.
All our titles that are printed on Greenpeace approved FSC certified paper carry
the FSC logo. Our paper procurement policy can be found at
www.rbooks.co.uk/environment

Printed and bound in Great Britain by
CPI Cox & Wyman, Reading, RG1 8EX

ISBN 978-1-8460-4246-1

To

Richard F. Driver of Phoenix, Arizona,

a friend and Brother.

CONTENTS

LIST OF FIGURES

ACKNOWLEDGEMENTS

My thanks to the present Grand Secretary of the Grand Lodge of Scotland, David M. Begg, and his immediate predecessor, C. Martin McGibbon, for all their encouragement. There are very many other people I would like to thank, but as the list is immense and I would surely forget one or two important names if I attempted to include everyone who deserves a mention, I must simply say a great big thank you here to all who have assisted, encouraged and talked to me about this project – in particular to my wife Yvonne who, above all others, has been my greatest supporter throughout the preparation of this work.

INTRODUCTION

What is Freemasonry? I've lost count of the number of times I've been asked that question. I've also lost count of the number of times that I've jokingly replied: 'I'm sorry, I can't tell you – it's a secret!' It's not a secret, but the question – simple though it seems – is actually a very difficult one to answer. This book will reveal that Freemasonry is not as secretive as it might first appear by explaining the history, heritage and ethos of the Craft (as it is often called). In so doing, it will become clear why there is no single answer to that oft-repeated question.

When it comes to defining Freemasonry, the essential difficulty lies in the fact that no one person or group of people can speak for the Craft. Certainly people who are very involved in Freemasonry, such as me, can offer their views and opinions as to what it is, what it does and what it means. But these are all personal, and other Freemasons – quite a number, I am sure – would disagree. I don't mind that at all. Indeed, one of the attractions of Freemasonry is that it can mean many things to many men. It is also one of the root causes for the confusion that surrounds the Craft today, so let me emphasize the point in another way. Because Freemasonry is a fragmented organization in the sense that it does not have a single 'head office' and has nothing in its structure akin to bishops or pastors, or even a CEO at an international level, there is no one person, or even group of people, who can speak for Freemasonry in its entirety. Confused? Well, aren't we all – and I'm not just talking about non-Freemasons!

The purpose of this book is therefore to give some insight into the world of Freemasonry primarily from a personal point of view, but with a strong emphasis on its history. Whilst I offer this personal perspective, I would like to think I am in a slightly more privileged position than most to access unique material (especially historical source material) and provide important evidence alongside a valid interpretation of it, if simply by dint of my occupation as Curator of the Grand Lodge of Scotland. This does not mean, however, that the views of others are invalid.

The contents of this book are laid out in a manner that reflects my personal understanding of Freemasonry and my views on the order of importance of certain subjects. When trying to define a group or organization connected to Freemasonry, I will often refer to its origins or history. However, I am reluctant to describe Freemasonry as a whole as an organization, for to do so might suggest certain characteristics associated with organizations that are in fact missing from Freemasonry. Simple questions such as when was it founded, who by, how did it develop and what does it offer or 'sell' cannot be answered as easily as for organizations such as Rolls-Royce or Microsoft. This does not mean that I will not attempt to address them, merely that the answers in this book are based upon my own findings and therefore some of my colleagues and fellow historians will agree with them whilst others will not.

Cracking the Freemason's Code will briefly examine the principal theories of the origins of Freemasonry and explore their relative strengths and weaknesses. Having sketched the various theories, I will be looking at the development of Freemasonry across the world. (Because Freemasonry has been exported to most other parts of the world I have highlighted a specific incident relating to Scottish Freemasonry and a particular event in the USA in Chapter 11, which readers may find particularly fascinating.)

A comparison between the Craft and other organizations serves to highlight the differences between them and modern Freemasonry, giving an insight into the workings of other 'secret societies'. Inevitably I will also be considering the position of Freemasonry in modern society and its relevance today; to do otherwise would be to suggest that there are no problems in this area. However, at the risk of repeating myself, I would like to emphasize that these are my personal views and must not be taken to represent the views of my employer, the Grand Lodge of Scotland, or of any Masonic bodies of which I am a member. Whilst I am at liberty to talk about Freemasonry in general, the issue here concerns being unable to speak collectively for individual bodies that have their own rules and regulations, and their own methods of electing (and occasionally expelling) members. My thoughts on matters of religion and Freemasonry, politics and Freemasonry and society and Freemasonry are therefore mine and mine alone!

Because the earliest records of the organizations (the incorporations and Lodges) and the rituals that play an integral part in Masonic history are to be found in Scotland, I will argue that modern Freemasonry has its origins there. As I live and work in Scotland as a 'professional' Freemason, the discussion in this book is inevitably grounded in my knowledge and experience of Scottish Masonic history and culture. It is not possible in a work of this size to explain in detail the differences between Scottish Freemasonry and the various forms of Freemasonry that are practised elsewhere. However, it is, in my opinion, extremely important to bear this Scottish perspective in mind when reading not only *Cracking the Freemason's Code* but also other books that discuss and comment on Freemasonry.

The welter of books published in the public domain that touch upon Freemasonry in some way (indeed, some of which are almost entirely about Freemasonry) is not a new phenomenon. In fact, non-Masons have been writing about Freemasonry since at least 1730, when a booklet by Samuel Prichard entitled *Masonry Dissected* was published in London for sale to the public. This was what is known in Masonic circles as an 'exposure': the printing for sale of the Masonic ritual, usually said to be done to 'protect' those who might be tempted to join Freemasonry. The fact that the exposures are sold for profit is not mentioned.

I take the opportunity to 'expose' the oldest known Masonic ritual in the world in these pages! But I do so for a different motive: historical clarification. Understanding the origins of Freemasonry is crucial to dispelling the myths that have grown up around the Craft. 'Of course,' I hear you say, 'it's included in a book that comes at a price!' I take your point. I am therefore quite happy to supply free copies of the oldest Masonic ritual in the world if you contact me by e-mail with your request – providing that's all you ask for!

Closely associated with Masonic ritual are Masonic symbols. This is a most fascinating aspect of Freemasonry and well worth studying in more detail than these pages will allow. However, I have provided some important examples that may whet your appetite to learn more.

Some of the subjects discussed in this book have already been well researched by other authors. I have therefore added a short Suggested Reading list, but have tried to be selective about the titles that I've included. Modern writers on Freemasonry often claim to give some sort of exclusive insight to the Order that no one has provided previously. In fact this is very rarely the case and many of these authors merely reproduce ideas offered by previous generations of writers on the subject. I have no doubt they all add their own personal 'twist', but rarely are any of the latest theories regarding Freemasonry truly original. This is probably one of the reasons why Freemasonry is not widely studied in the academic world, where it is considered to be something of an odd subject. This is rather sad because, as has been demonstrated by Professor David Stevenson, Freemasonry as a cultural and social phenomenon has much to offer the student of history.

It is my sincere belief that Freemasonry has much to offer society today, as will become clear in the following chapters.

Robert L. D. Cooper
Curator
Grand Lodge of Scotland Museum and Library
June 2006

1

FROM STONEMASONS TO FREEMASONS

The true origins of Freemasonry are obscure and belong to a period when the academic discipline of history was not nearly as rigorous as it is at present, with the consequence that over the years a considerable number of different theories have been put forward regarding the beginnings and history of the Craft. The earliest records relating to a body of men with clear links to modern Freemasonry occur in Scotland during the late sixteenth and early seventeenth centuries. Some of these men began to speculate regarding the origins of the Lodges and organizations of which they were members, and as they did so the early Freemasons came up with an unusual way of speculating about the past and about life in general. That unusual method of exploration is the basis of modern Freemasonry. What it is, what it means and what it does is the subject of this book, but let us first consider the beginnings of Freemasonry itself.

The Knights Templar

There can be no doubt that the most dominant theory regarding the origins of Freemasonry current at the time of writing is the claim that modern Freemasonry derives directly from the medieval Order of the Poor Soldiers of Christ and Solomon's Temple, founded about 1118 and more commonly known as the Knights Templar. The Order's country of origin was France, where it owned the most property and where the

Knights Templar were most numerous. The Order was monastic in that its members lived in closed communities and followed the Rule of the Cistercian Order, another monastic order of the Church.

When the Order was first established, its members were given quarters on the Temple Mount in Jerusalem on, or very near to, the original site of King Solomon's Temple. Mysteriously, within a few years the Order became incredibly wealthy and it was claimed that whilst stationed on Temple Mount they had excavated down to the foundations of King Solomon's Temple, where they had found something that made them not only wealthy but enormously powerful. So powerful did they become that they were answerable only to the Pope himself. They were excused all taxes and were independent of all Church authority – in other words they could do pretty much whatever they liked.

But what had the Knights Templar discovered in the foundations of King Solomon's Temple? What was it that made the Pope the only one who could command them? And what was it that attracted so many people to join them? There have been many rumours, speculations and suggestions: the Holy Grail, the Ark of the Covenant, the secret teachings of Jesus Christ or perhaps something else altogether – something called Solomon's Key.

The Order continued to grow and become even wealthier as more and more people donated land and money. It owned land in every part of Europe and recruited people from all walks of life, although only knights could become full members. The knights had to take vows of chastity, obedience and poverty, and were therefore in this respect monks much like any others. They differed from monks in that they were authorized to fight non-Christians, especially those who occupied the Holy Land (modern Palestine), because that was the birthplace of Christianity. According to their principles, the Holy Land had to be freed from the infidel and re-Christianized. They were therefore Warrior Monks – Knights of Christ. The Knights Templars' training and fanaticism caused their fighting abilities to become legendary, and they were a major element of the crusading forces in the Holy Land. Their rivalry with the Knights of St John (the Knights Hospitaller) was fierce, which would ultimately contribute to their undoing, as would the Order's wealth.

The Knights Templar invented international banking. Because they owned property throughout Europe, it was possible to deposit money in one of their preceptories, on receipt of which they would prepare a note to be sent to another preceptory, where the creditor could collect the money. This meant that large sums of money no longer needed to be transported through dangerous country. Needless to say the Order charged a fee for this service.

After the fall of the last Christian outpost in the Holy Land, at the Battle of Acre in 1291, the Knights Templar retreated to Cyprus, where they established their new headquarters. With the loss of the Holy Land, the Knights Templar had effectively lost the justification of their existence, but this did not prevent them from becoming arrogant and self-indulgent, and openly flaunting their wealth.

Figure 1 A medieval Knight Templar.

Philip the Fair and the Fall of the Knights Templar

The theory that modern Freemasonry is directly descended from the medieval Order of the Knights Templar concerns Machiavellian intrigue and the affairs of both Crown and Church. As we have seen, the Knights Templar had strong links with France, a country that relentlessly promoted the belief that the monarchy, their monarchy, was divinely ordained. Philip the Fair (1268–1314), so called because of his complexion, not his disposition, had been King of France since he was seventeen years old and ruled with a rod of iron. He was the eleventh Capetian King of France and came to a throne burdened with huge debts as a consequence of previous wars; he owed money to just about anyone who would lend it to him. The Jews, the Lombards (a people originally descended from North European tribes) and the Knights Templar were major creditors.

Philip struggled to free himself from debt but could never quite manage it: he either could not raise enough, or spent too much, or both. He introduced special taxes on certain businesses, licences on exports and forced loans. He also introduced special taxes on Jews, Lombards and the Church, which brought him into direct conflict with the Pope, Boniface VIII, a conflict that only ended with the Pope's death shortly after Philip had had him kidnapped. Benedict XI, who followed Boniface, died in mysterious circumstances after only nine months as Pope, following a series of arguments between him and Philip. The election of the French Pope Clement V (1264–1314) in 1305 was supported by Philip and these two characters were to play a central role in subsequent events concerning the Knights Templar.

In the 1290s Philip had devalued the coinage to the extent that after ten years it was only worth a third of its original value. This temporarily increased income for the Crown but also reduced the amount received in taxes. In June 1306 Philip declared that the value of money would return to the level that had existed prior to the devaluations, which meant prices, and therefore taxes, would triple overnight. The people of Paris rioted and Philip was forced to flee to a Knights Templar preceptory for protection. It is known that a few years previously he had applied to join the Order and had been rejected. It must have therefore been especially galling for the King of France to ask for protection from an organization that had not wanted him as a member, but during the three days he was under its protection he studied the Order, how the preceptory operated and what its fortifications and security were like. After the riots a new strategy was necessary, and on emerging from the protection of the Knights Templar, Philip moved quickly. Secret orders were issued and on 21 June 1306 every Jew in France was arrested and all their property stolen, thereby eliminating one of the King's major creditors.

In 1306 Pope Clement V called a meeting to discuss a possible amalgamation of the Knights Templar with the Order of St John (the Knights Hospitaller). The Grand Master of the Knights Templar, Jacques de Molay (c. 1244–1314), travelled from Cyprus to France for the meeting, accompanied by a large retinue of sixty knights and a baggage train loaded with gold and jewels of an immense but unknown value. However, the Grand Master of the Hospitallers, William de Villaret, replied that he could not attend because he was overseeing the transfer of the Order to Rhodes.

The Hospitallers had reinvented themselves. They had become a powerful naval force continuously engaged in keeping the Mediterranean sea lanes clear of infidel pirates and were therefore perceived as still performing their main function. In complete contrast, the Knights Templar had changed hardly at all, having failed to recognize that the world and their role in it was changing, especially after Christians had been ejected from the Holy Land sixteen years earlier. Their failure to acknowledge the changing times was owing to their fixed belief that there would be another crusade; it was not a question of 'if', but 'when', and this was exactly what de Molay proposed to set in action when he arrived in France early in 1307.

He did not go directly to Poitiers, where the Pope was residing, but instead went to Paris to deposit the treasure he had brought with him into the Knights Templar preceptory. He was received by Philip at the royal court and, with all seeming well between the Order and the monarch, de Molay travelled on to Poitiers, unaware that Philip had already informed the Pope that the Knights Templar were indulging in heretical and abominable practices in the secrecy of their preceptories.

As the Order was part of the Church and answerable only to the Pope, nothing could be done to follow up the allegations against it without his permission. The Church had no army of its own, relying on the secular authorities, so if the allegations had any basis in truth, Clement would have to ask Philip to arrest the Knights Templar and the Church would investigate. Clement was therefore in a very difficult position. He knew that he had been made Pope with Philip's help and he was also aware of how Philip had treated his two predecessors. The Pope that Philip had made could just as easily be unmade. It seems that Clement adopted the tactic of simply delaying making a decision until Philip finally resolved to take action himself.

Up to the very last minute de Molay was lulled into a false sense of security. On 12 October 1307 he was accorded the honour of being a pall-bearer at the state funeral of Catherine of Valois, Philip's sister-in-law. But Philip had secretly instructed his officials to arrest every Knight Templar in France, and the very next day, Friday 13 October, nearly every one of the estimated five thousand Knights Templar in France was duly arrested.

Until this juncture, the Knights Templar theory about the origins of Freemasonry repeats accepted historical facts. However, it has been claimed, especially in recent years, that some Knights Templar were warned of their impending or imminent arrest, and that they fled to the Atlantic port of La Rochelle, where Templar ships lay at anchor. These knights escaped the clutches of the rapacious King of France and allegedly sailed to Scotland, specifically to the west coast of Argyll, where they went into hiding, taking with them their treasure from the preceptory in Paris.

The French Knights Templar and Robert the Bruce

The argument continues that the surviving Knights Templar chose to go to Scotland because Robert the Bruce (1274–1329) had been excommunicated the previous year by Pope Clement V, following the Bruce's killing of John 'the Red' Comyn in the Greyfriars' church in Dumfries. For this reason, it is said, papal authority did not apply in Scotland and, of course, Robert the Bruce would have welcomed the arrival of tried-and-tested knights during his struggle against English forces to obtain independence for Scotland. At the Battle of Bannockburn on 24 June 1314, just as the battle could have swung for or against the Scots, the story goes that there suddenly appeared on the field an unknown force whose unexpected appearance struck fear and terror into the hearts of the English knights. The English turned and ran, and were slaughtered by the pursuing Scots; the King of England, Edward II (1307–1327; b. 1284), barely escaped capture after this terrible defeat. The cream of English knighthood died but Scotland's independence for the next four hundred years was secured.

Victory may have been his, but Robert the Bruce wanted his newly independent country to be re-admitted to Western Christendom. However, he faced the twin problems of having been excommunicated himself and of having heretic Knights Templar in his army. In the event, his excommunication was revoked shortly after his death, but in the process of trying to rejoin the Church whilst he was alive, he first had to assure the Pope that there were no Knights Templar in Scotland. To achieve this, he resorted to subterfuge and invented the Order of Freemasonry into which the Knights Templar who had helped him defeat the English were quietly integrated. He could now inform the Pope that Knights Templar did not exist in Scotland. Moreover, by his actions Robert the Bruce rewarded the fugitive Knights Templar for assisting him in defeating the English army and also protected them from the Church. The Knights Templar under another name – Freemasonry – simply continued to exist as they had before 1314.

Evidence of the Knights Templar who came from France is said to be found in the graveyards of Argyll, where there is a large number of anonymous Knight Templar graveslabs. There is a range of additional evidence to prove the continued existence of the Knights Templar after 1314, including charters and other documents that mention the Order by name. It is known that members of the St Clair (Sinclair) family were Knights Templar; according to this theory, the family built Rosslyn Chapel in 1446 in order to provide a secret sanctuary for the Knights Templar treasure. The head of the Sinclair family was always hereditary Grand Master of the 'masons' of Scotland. The Freemasons today are therefore direct descendants of the Knights Templar who came from France in 1307. They possess the secret knowledge and treasure of the Knights Templar, which they protect in a hidden location known only to the highest initiates of the Order.

When I first heard this fascinating story it stood my understanding of history on its head. It was only after I had become a Freemason myself that I discovered that this completely different, secret version of history existed. Throughout my education I had been taught the standard version of history, such as the events surrounding the Scottish wars of independence, including the Battle of Bannockburn and the reign of James II (1437–1460, b. 1437), during which the building of Rosslyn Chapel was begun. However, it is important to realize that only certain parts of Scottish Freemasonry contain this secret version of Scottish history. It was some years after I had joined a Masonic Lodge that I learned of the alternative history described above – when I became a Knight Templar.

The 'Underground Stream'

Some theories, like the Knights Templar account described above, are fairly specific, but there are others that are rather vague and contain little factual evidence. One of these I shall call the theory of the 'underground stream', and it's probably the vaguest theory of them all. It is relatively simple and supported by hardly any factual material; it conjectures that 'the knowledge of the ancients' originated on the fabled island of Atlantis and that this knowledge has been passed down to us today by a variety of means, principally by certain elites. After the destruction of Atlantis this knowledge was transferred to ancient Egypt, whose high priests preserved it within their religion before it was passed on to Greece, then on to Rome. There, with the fall of the Roman Empire, it became restricted to only an extremely few people. Some say that it was preserved by the Celts, and particularly through the Druid priesthood, before it was transferred from them to the court of King Arthur.

There was another route allegedly taken: it flowed from the ancient Egyptians to the court of King Solomon, where it remained hidden in the foundations of Solomon's ruined temple until it was discovered by the Knights Templar in the early twelfth century. Whether it was discovered by the Knights Templar in Jerusalem or passed on to the court of King Arthur, some commentators point to the fact that both the Templars and the Knights of the Round Table became incredibly powerful and wealthy. This, it is claimed, was owing to their possession of the secret knowledge of the ancients, whatever that may have been. Both routes lead to Britain, and so Britain is the place were the knowledge now remains and is where all those who seek it must look. The supposed involvement of the Knights Templar means that this theory links with the Knights Templar theory considered above, connecting at the point where the Knights Templar came to Scotland from France in 1307. It similarly continues thereafter with the idea that Robert the Bruce created Freemasonry in order to disguise the existence of the Knights Templar. The theme of the court of King Arthur, without the involvement of the Knights Templar, suggests that the secret knowledge was transferred from them to unknown others before finally being passed to the Freemasons of Scotland.

The problem with this theory is that 'the secret knowledge' is never explained. Consider the theory in this light: a variety of writers describe, often in great detail, the various stages through which the knowledge is passed from group to group, yet no one provides any details of the nature of the knowledge itself.

The Stonemasons of King Solomon's Temple

The next theory is based entirely upon biblical evidence: that is, specifically the building of King Solomon's Temple as described in the Old Testament books of Kings and Chronicles. This theory claims that the stonemasons who built the Temple must have possessed secret knowledge, but whether this was transferred to them from Atlantis via ancient Egypt and Greece as described above is not clearly stated. It is occasionally hinted that the 'secret' was the knowledge of building in stone itself, a knowledge that only stonemasons possessed and that came directly from Yahweh. In any event, King Solomon's Temple, constructed to contain the Ark of the Covenant and as a place of residence on earth for the God of the Jews (Yahweh or Jehovah), clearly contained special and secret building techniques known only to those stonemasons.

By contrast, the Tower of Babel was a sinful building – an attempt by man to reach heaven by his own devices. This was an affront to God, who destroyed it and caused mankind to speak in many different languages so that people could no longer communicate to build the tower. As an unholy building, the tower was not suitable for the stonemasons to use as an example of their special, unique and God-given abilities. Moreover, the Tower of Babel was built out of brick and would therefore not have involved them. It was definitely not a worthy example of their knowledge and skills.

According to the King Solomon's Temple theory, since the time of King Solomon the special knowledge possessed by the first stonemasons was transferred, generation after generation, to other stonemasons through ceremonies that were only accessible to those in the craft. Those in possession of the secrets, sometimes called the knowledge of Sacred Geometry, were able to build some of the world's most awe-inspiring structures, such as the medieval cathedrals of Europe: the patrons who commissioned them were at a loss to explain how such humble men could erect such tributes to the glory of God. When nearly everyone lived in small crude dwellings, when only nobles owned anything much larger than a hut, imagine the impact it must have made to round a bend or top a hill, and suddenly come upon an incredibly huge structure that was God's House! The theory suggests that the secret knowledge that originated with the building of King Solomon's Temple now lies with modern Freemasons.

From Incorporations to Masons: the Transition Theory

This brings me to the most commonly accepted and historically credible theory of the origin of Freemasonry, which lies with the stonemasons of the medieval period and most particularly the stonemasons of Scotland.

Incorporations

This theory argues that Freemasonry begins with the political and social climate of medieval Scotland itself. In Scotland in the Middle Ages there existed 'burghs', essentially walled towns,* administered differently to the countryside which, with the exception of the Highlands, was governed feudally. A royal burgh was even further

* Edinburgh (originally Eden Burgh) is a good example as remnants of the old city walls remain extant.

removed from the control of feudal barons: it was created by the monarch and was therefore answerable – and paid taxes – directly to the Scottish king or queen.

Associations of tradesmen such as bakers or stonemasons occupied an important place in the life of the burghs, but even collectively these tradesmen were not at first as powerful – economically or politically – as the merchants. Unlike the merchants they did not belong to guilds, but they were sufficiently well organized that their influence could not be completely ignored. The various trades agitated increasingly for recognition by the establishment and, on the basis that it is better to have potential troublemakers inside the establishment (where some control can be exercised over them) than outside the system, the burgh town councils eventually granted them charters. In Scotland such a charter is known as a 'Seal of Cause'.* The burgh establishment granted this new kind of status to the most important town trades, which were by this process 'incorporated' into the burgh's political and economic life.

The nine Incorporated Trades of Edinburgh and the date of their Seal of Cause

Baxters (bakers)	1456
Bonnet makers	1473
Skinners	1474
Masons and wrights (carpenters)	1475
Wobsters (weavers)	1476
Hammermen (blacksmiths etc.)	1483
Fleshers (butchers)	1488
Coopers (barrel-makers)	1489
Cordiners (shoemakers and leather-workers)	1510

In granting tradesmen a charter, the town council conferred certain rights such as limited representation on the town council, but expected certain responsibilities in return. The newly established incorporations agreed to keep their houses in order by controlling their members, and regulating their wages, working practices and arrangements for apprenticeships, and even their moral welfare. The incorporations became the point of contact between the tradesmen

* It is not unreasonable to consider incorporations as a very early form of trade union.

Figure 2 An engraving of the Incorporated Trades of Edinburgh. Note the long aprons. (From *The Master Masons to the Crown of Scotland*, Edinburgh, 1893.)

they represented and the town councils, thereby developing an economic and political role. In effect, to become an incorporation was to make a public announcement that a trade was respectable and had some status within the burgh.

The Incorporation of Wrights and Masons

For our purposes, the foundation of the Incorporation of Wrights and Masons in 1475 marks a key moment. The incorporation became the focal point of the wrights' and masons' economic activities and it was here that they agreed the rules to govern their craft, such as how long someone would serve as an apprentice and what conditions had to be met before he was allowed to become a full member of the trade. It was here also that they formulated tactics for negotiating with their employers and established funds for each other's financial assistance.

As the economic cycle rose and fell the Incorporation of Wrights and Masons came to include trades that were not directly connected with building work, such as coopers (barrel-makers), and others that were indirectly connected with erecting buildings, such as plumbers. These trades probably became members because of the need to maintain membership numbers and thereby the income of the incorporation during difficult times. This created tensions within the incorporation and between the various trades in their efforts to create a united front to their employers, i.e. the town council and to a lesser extent the Church and private individuals.

Incorporations created monopolistic conditions for each trade within each town. This enabled the wrights and masons to exert economic pressure by maintaining a high income and high wage structure. However, the civic authorities retaliated by creating laws to curb the incorporations' high wage-demands and this occasionally led to violence. Again the wrights and masons were not unusual in attempting to maximize their income when they had the economic ability to do so. Other incorporations did exactly the same.

However, the masons were not concerned solely with maximizing income, although this was clearly important; they were also interested in the spiritual welfare of their members, an indication of which lies in the manner in which they often paid for the maintenance of a specific aisle for their own place of worship.

As a mark of their newfound respectability in 1475, the Edinburgh stonemasons were granted the use of the aisle of St John the Evangelist within St Giles' Cathedral. In return, the incorporation maintained the aisle by donating candle wax and paying the officiating priest, who said prayers and masses for the souls of deceased members. This link with the aisle in St Giles' Cathedral is why the patron saint of Freemasonry in Scotland is St John the Evangelist (feast day 27 December), whereas virtually everywhere else in the world it is St John

Figure 3 A stonemason at work.

the Baptist (feast day 24 June).* The stonemasons also ensured the burial of deceased members when their families could not do so, and looked after their widows and orphans.

Lodges

There was yet another aspect that made the stonemasons of Scotland different from any other trade or incorporation. They had a secret level of organization that did not exist elsewhere: the lodge.

Exactly why they deemed it necessary to form a separate organization is not clear. One reason may be that, because the Incorporation of Wrights and Masons had from time to time included other trades in addition to those of carpentry and stonemasonry, the stonemasons wished to have a meeting place that was exclusive to their particular craft. As it would not have been necessary to create a lodge of stonemasons in order to discuss matters that were already the responsibility of the incorporation (to do so would have be repetitive rather than constructive), the stonemasons must have had unique business of their own that they did not wish to share with non-stonemasons.

That masons had meeting places known as 'lodges' is confirmed by a document dated 1491 and entitled 'statue anent [about or concerning] Masons of St Giles'. The document stipulates the hours to be worked by 'master masons' and states that they are allowed 'to get a recreation in the common lodge'. This demonstrates that the stonemasons' lodges were not simple huts for the storage of working tools but were structures large enough to be used for recreational purposes; in other words, they were places where stonemasons could congregate privately. And, as will become clear, the lodges became important centres where stonemasons could perform ceremonies in order to convey their special esoteric knowledge from generation to generation.

The lodges must have appeared fascinating to outsiders, in awe of the stonemasons' abilities. Non-stonemasons were intrigued and slowly, even reluctantly, the stonemasons of Scotland permitted a few of them to join their lodges, passing on to them the secrets that had only ever been in the possession of the stonemasons themselves. What attracted these non-stonemasons to the lodges was most likely simple

* The aisle still exists although no doubt considerably changed. It is now named the Chepman Aisle.

curiosity, the mystique created by rumours of the existence of secrets, and perhaps they were even happy to slum it occasionally with their social inferiors, experiencing the thrills of social voyeurism.

The Survival of Lodges

When considering the history of Freemasonry, it is worth remembering that until the early eighteenth century Scotland and England were separate countries: the Union of the Crowns in 1603 gave them a single monarch but the parliamentary systems remained separate until 1707. The conditions in one country were not the same as in the other; laws enacted in Scotland had no effect in England.

This is one reason why the Scottish incorporations survived the Reformation in 1559, unlike the English merchant and craft guilds, which were suppressed in 1540 as superstitious foundations. Indeed some Scottish incorporations still exist and possess continuous written records that date from medieval times, although they are now charitable institutions.

There is every reason to believe that, like incorporations, the stonemasons' lodges also survived. In fact there is evidence to support the view that pre-Reformation lodges have a continued existence to the present day. Admittedly the evidence is scant until the end of the sixteenth century, but there is circumstantial evidence for their existence before and after the Reformation. Indeed, in the sixteenth, seventeenth and early eighteenth centuries, the Lodge was the only 'unit' of Freemasonry.

Prior to the late sixteenth century, lodges are very occasionally mentioned in town-council records. Lodges themselves did not maintain written records at first, but by the end of the sixteenth century things were set to change, as will become clear in Chapter 2. As there are no known records of Lodges in England before 1716, the focus here must be on what records there are, and these are only to be found in Scotland. It must be made clear, however, that lack of records does not mean that there were no Lodges in England prior to 1716: merely that we know virtually nothing about them.*

* The principal exception is the admission of Sir Elias Ashmole to a Lodge in Warrington in 1646. It is often incorrectly claimed that Sir Elias was the first known Freemason, and his connection to Warrington is a problematic reference.

What happened in the stonemasons' lodges of Scotland during the fading years of the sixteenth century had an impact that allows us to contrast them with the institutions that pre-existed them and to make some educated guesses as to what they did and why they developed into modern Masonic Lodges. This 'before and after' comparison can only take place in a Scottish context as material of the same nature simply does not exist in any other country, and it is partly for this reason (there are others discussed below) that we can confidently claim that modern Freemasonry originated in Scotland.

The Transition

Eventually, over a period of approximately one hundred years, from the start of written records in 1599, many lodges came to include a large number of men who had no connection to the craft of stonemasonry whatsoever. This gradual change from stonemasonry to Freemasonry can only be traced within Scotland and is known as the 'Transition theory'. The 'transition' from stonemasons' lodges to modern Masonic Lodges is witnessed within the written records of the Scottish lodges themselves.

One strand of the Transition theory suggests that English gentleman visitors to Scotland decided that Freemasonry looked to be a pleasant pastime and decided to create Lodges of their own on their return south. An alternative suggestion is that Scottish stonemasons seeking work in England created Lodges there, admitting anyone in order to establish them quickly, which meant that from the outset the Lodges created in this way were not strictly speaking stonemasons' lodges. Be that as it may, the main point is that by one means or another Freemasonry spread from Scotland to England.

With the spread of Freemasonry inside and outside its borders, three different types of Lodges now existed within Scotland. There were the traditional stonemasons' lodges, such as those at Kilwinning, known to be in existence in 1599. There were lodges of mixed membership, such as that of Aberdeen, which was probably founded in about 1670. And there were Lodges that had no connection with stonemasonry whatsoever, such as the one founded in 1702 in the hamlet of Haughfoot in the Scottish borders.

A form of 'Speculative Freemasonry' developed in some new Lodges in both Scotland and England. It was 'speculative' in the sense that the Lodges themselves were established by men who had no direct connection with stonemasonry; its members were not stonemasons and so were therefore 'speculating' about what stonemasons did in their lodges, what their secrets were and where their knowledge had originated.

In Scotland, the development of different Lodges, and with them different forms of Freemasonry, led to a curious situation. When the Grand Lodge of Scotland was founded in 1736 it was a speculative body. The majority of lodges that had been in existence for the last hundred and forty years wanted nothing to do with its newfangled Masonic 'system'. Some saw no point in becoming part of a new 'speculative' system when theirs was a lodge of stonemasons; others did not see the need for a Grand Lodge given that they had managed independently and quite happily for more than one hundred years. Many remained independent until they ceased to exist or until they eventually joined the new Masonic system more than a hundred years later. But one or two strands still survive today (see Chapter 9).

The Big Bang Theory

The last remaining theory of origin that I wish to discuss very briefly is known as the 'Big Bang theory', which proposes that a small number of Freemasons existed in secret in London, but decided to 'go public' in 1717 by forming a Grand Lodge. This Grand Lodge, the first in the world, was formed by four Lodges, which had apparently only been in existence for a short time.

In this respect, English Freemasonry was created without a connection with any other group such as stonemasons. The purely speculative form of Freemasonry thus created could therefore have been moulded by its creators into whatever form they wished. This would not have been possible in Scotland, where non-stonemasons had joined an existing organization that was not theirs to shape. Untangling precisely how and when the English Lodges first came into being and for what purpose is difficult, but it is not impossible that there was some synthesis with what was taking place in Scotland.

2

THE FATHER OF FREEMASONRY AND THE FIRST MODERN FREEMASON

There may be various theories as to the origins of modern Freemasonry, but there is one individual who stands out as its architect.

William Schaw, the King's Master of Works

In 1583 William Schaw of Sauchie (c. 1550–1602) was appointed the King's Master of Works, the King being James VI of Scotland (1567–1625, b. 1566). James VI of Scotland became James I of England in 1603 and reigned for almost twenty-two years. In his capacity as the King's Master of Works, William Schaw was responsible for overseeing the repair, maintenance and new building work of all palaces, castles, hunting lodges and other buildings that might be used by the royal family. He was therefore a civil servant and a member of the royal court.

The First and Second Schaw Statutes

Schaw's duties in dealing with the buildings used by the Scottish royal family meant that he was in regular contact with stonemasons, who were responsible for carrying out his instructions. In fact there are records of the transactions he made with masons and other tradesmen who carried out work for him.* In 1598 and again in 1599 he wrote what are now called the First and Second Schaw Statutes (see Appendix 1). These documents were sent to every known stonemasons' lodge in Scotland and detailed the rules and regulations that Schaw expected them to follow from then on.

When reading Schaw's statutes, it becomes clear that there's a great deal of practical guidance in them. There are rules regarding working conditions but the majority deal with the internal relationships between stonemasons, such as master masons and apprentices. Some of the terminology is very interesting: for example, when a youth was apprenticed, typically at the age of fourteen, his name was to be entered in the lodge records; in other words he became an entered apprentice, which is now the first degree in modern Freemasonry (which will be discussed in more detail later). Rules were also provided for the running of the stonemasons' lodges themselves. For instance, no one could be admitted to a lodge unless there were at least six masters and two entered apprentices present.

Much of what Schaw wrote was pretty similar to the by-laws of any voluntary body, but there are a couple of items that suggest that there may have been more going on here. The very first 'rule' reads:

> First that they obserue and keip all the gude ordinanceis sett doun of befoir concerning the priviligeis of thair Craft be their predicessors of gude memorie,
> And specialie
> That they be trew ane to ane vother and leve [live] cheritablie togidder as becumis sworne brether and companzeounis of craft.

This, the very first instruction Schaw gave to the lodges (and it is important to bear in mind that copies of these statutes were sent to *all* known lodges in Scotland), reveals some important facts. Schaw notes that the stonemasons had good ordinances that had been set down by their predecessors and that they should continue to observe them. He makes one special instruction: 'That they be true to one another and live charitably together as becomes sworn brethren and companions of

* See *Accounts of the Masters of Works for building and repairing Royal Palaces and Castles. Volume 1: 1529–1615* (Edinburgh, 1957), pp. 319–23.

craft'. This shows that the stonemasons had 'sworne' – that they had taken an oath or obligation – and that Schaw was emphasizing that this act made them special; that it meant that they had particular responsibilities to each other. In an age in which there was no social welfare system, family and friends were often the first to be approached in times of trouble. However, as workers in general, and tradesmen in particular, organized themselves into incorporations or lodges, they became one of the most, if not the most important, part of a stonemason's support network. Such a network was based on mutual defence and support. Trust in one another was essential for the system to work and an oath or obligation reinforced that trust.

The fact that Schaw places the instruction to be true to each other first in the statutes suggests that he believed it to be one of the most important aspects of the lodge. It is probably no coincidence that 'bonding' of this type is known in Scotland as *brithering* (brothering). Modern management techniques that involve creating a team ethos, with all the team members relying on and trusting each other, are really nothing new! The creation of a Masonic esprit de corps is one of the functions of Lodge ritual and ceremonial to this day. This continuity with the past, a past that stretches back over hundreds of years, is one of the enduring features and, indeed, attractions of Freemasonry.

This instruction tells us something very important: Schaw did not 'invent' lodges nor did he invent the oath that stonemasons took to look after each other. All of this was already in existence by the time he became Master of Works. Taking this into consideration together with all the other rules in Schaw's First Statutes, it would appear that he was intent on formalizing an existing but loose and informal association of Scottish stonemasons and their lodges.

The question must be asked: but why did he bother? The stonemasons were his social inferiors and they were obliged to do what he instructed. It may have been that Schaw was a genuinely good man who used his position to assist those less fortunate than himself. He may also have believed that formalizing the existing arrangements of the stonemasons would make them more efficient and therefore whatever work they did for him would also be of a better quality. The fact that he was a civil servant may also have meant that he simply could not bear to see stonemasons working without written rules and regulations! That said, the statutes do seem to suggest that he had more than a mere passing interest in the stonemasons, a notion that is reinforced when we consider the Second Statutes of 1599.

The Precedence of Lodges

As we have seen, the First Statutes were sent to all lodges in Scotland, but they provoked a strong reaction from one lodge in particular: Kilwinning. This lodge, situated near the west coast in Ayrshire, sent Archibald Barclay to Edinburgh, where he was received by William Schaw and the members of the lodge of Edinburgh on 27 and 28 December 1599. This meeting resulted in the Second Statutes and the contents reveal why he had been sent to Edinburgh on behalf of the lodge.

The very first item of the Second Schaw Statutes deals with the method of electing the Warden of the lodge and declares that the result of that election must be notified to the 'generall warden', i.e. William Schaw. He makes it immediately clear who the boss is. Moreover, these statutes are addressed directly to the Kilwinning Lodge, presumably so that they can be in no doubt as to whom he is speaking.

Very early in the statute Schaw deals with the matter of precedence of lodges. It seems that one of the main points (probably an actual complaint) made by Barclay to him was the matter of Kilwinning's position in his plans. The First Schaw Statutes had not mentioned precedence of lodges and this had perturbed Kilwinning to the extent that they probably hoped that by sending Archibald Barclay to see him, he would declare theirs to be the premier Lodge of Scotland. If so, they were disappointed. He described the Kilwinning as being *'the heid* [head] *and second ludge of Scotland'* but Edinburgh as being *'the first and principall ludge in Scotland'*.

We cannot be sure now exactly what took place at their meeting, but it is not unreasonable to conjecture that Schaw did not realize the depth of the Kilwinning Lodge's feelings on this matter. The First Statutes were written in Edinburgh, the capital of the country and the place of the royal court, and it probably simply did not occur to him that a lodge in another part of the country might be older than that in Edinburgh. But what was he to do? He had probably already acknowledged the lodge of Edinburgh as the head lodge when along came another lodge out of the blue to challenge that claim. No matter what he did, he was going to upset one lodge or the other. His solution was to try and fudge the issue in true civil-service style! Kilwinning became the Head and Second Lodge and Edinburgh the First and Principal Lodge. It seems that Kilwinning saw through the subterfuge, as we know they were not involved any further in Schaw's plans. The consequence of this continues to have an impact on Scottish Freemasonry today.

Despite the problems leading to the Second Schaw Statutes, the contents of the documents contain details of great importance for our understanding of the origin of Freemasonry. The Second Statutes, like the First, contain guidance for the lodges and their activities. One instruction in particular is very revealing:

> That ye [the] warden of ye lug of Kilwynning, being the second lug in Scotland, tak tryall of ye airt of memorie and science yrof [thereof], of everie fellowe of craft and everie prentice according to ayr of yr vocations; and in cais yat [that] yai [they] haue losy ony point yrof dvied to thame To pay the penalie as followis for yr slwethfulness [slothfulness], viz., Ilk fallow of craft, x x s [20 shillings] Ilk prentess x s [10 shillings] and that to be payit to ye box for ane commoun weill [common good] zeirlie [yearly] & yat conforme to the commoun vs and pratik [use and practice] of the commoun lugs of this realm.

Here the lodge is being instructed to 'test' – '*tak tryall of ye airt of memorie and science yrof*' – the members of the lodge once a year on their ability to remember 'something'. There are to be no exceptions; the warden of the lodge is to test every member of the lodge: '*everie fellowe of craft and everie prentice*'. As there would be little point in conducting an annual test on something that was common knowledge, this test suggests the existence of a shared body of knowledge known and special to the stonemasons alone. Unfortunately the 'something' to be memorized is not specified, but, as we shall discover in Chapters 3 and 4, educated guesses can be made as to the ceremonial performed within the lodges and the nature of the stonemasons' secret knowledge.

But why an annual *memory* test? The answer must partly be

because the majority of stonemasons were illiterate. Had they been able to read and write there would be no need to memorize 'something'. It's obviously not short or simple: '*in cais yat yai haue losy ony point yrof dvied to thame To pay the penalie as followis . . .* '. Failure to remember every point incurs a penalty. Here then is someone who, in creating these statutes, knows his fellow countrymen very well indeed: for how do you get a Scotsman to do something he really doesn't want to do? Threaten to take money off him, of course! Schaw obviously knows that the lodge members require an incentive to memorize the 'something' and a system of fines is his answer. By introducing this system he has told us something very important: the 'something' is not just a word, a handshake or a particular movement. In those particular instances there would no need for detailed instructions such as these; instead, there is substantial matter to be memorized here. I would therefore argue that Schaw is referring to the stonemasons' secret ceremonies, including all the words, handshakes etc. (There is further evidence in support of this argument, which will be discussed in the section on Hermeticism in Chapter 3.)

It is very clear that, for one reason or another, William Schaw, Master of Works to the King, took a great deal of interest in the internal lodge activities of the Scottish stonemasons. As has been suggested above, it may simply have been a matter of his assisting those less well organized, or an instance of good administration. But whilst this might be true, it does not explain why he would go to such lengths. For instance, why does he want the stonemasons' special knowledge preserved? He seems to be almost fearful that the stonemasons are incapable of preserving their own traditions and lore. But how did he know it was worth preserving?

I think the answers lie in the fact that William Schaw was a member of a lodge and that he simply could not abide the casual, unrecorded, unregulated methods then used by stonemasons. For Schaw to have known that the stonemasons' esoteric knowledge was worth preserving *he* must have been in possession of that knowledge. This claim is, I confess, based on conjecture because there are no written records to show he was a member of a lodge. This may be one of the quirks of history: written lodge records did not come into existence until after Schaw had instructed lodges to keep them. If he was a member of a lodge then that was another reason for the statutes themselves to be written.

There is one further piece of evidence in support of this assertion. The First Schaw Statutes are dated 28 December 1598. We know that Archibald Barclay was present at a meeting of the Lodge of Edinburgh held on 27 and 28 December 1598, and that the Second Schaw Statutes are dated 28 December 1599. As mentioned in Chapter 1, the patron saint of Scottish stonemasons was (and is) St John the Evangelist, whose feast day is 27 December – a day on which nearly all Scottish Lodges held, and many continue to hold, their Installation or Annual General Meeting.

It is inconceivable that Schaw, an able administrator, would write a document the day after the AGM of the principal lodge of Scotland (or what he believed to be the principal lodge) in the knowledge that a full year would elapse before discussing it at its next AGM. Schaw had probably joined the lodge earlier, perhaps even on 27 December 1598, and the very next day wrote the first statutes telling all the lodges what had been decided (principally by him) at the AGM of the lodge.

If this is true then William Schaw is the first known Freemason, but here we come to one of the major problems regarding the definition of a Freemason. Scottish stonemasons worked as stonemasons during their normal working lives, but they did not work as stonemasons within their lodges. Let me emphasize this point. At work during the day stonemasons cut, carved and dressed stone in order to build. In their lodges in the evening they did not. They did not build anything there, or at least they did not build anything physical. Their lodge activities seem to have been entirely devoted to ceremonial – ceremonial by which means esoteric knowledge was discussed, elaborated and transferred to other members.

Schaw's Legacy

Schaw's lasting impact was to formalize a pre-existing, probably very casual, system of stonemasons' lodges that were already in possession of a number of traditions, lore, ceremonies and a system of esoteric knowledge. In doing so he began a process that would ultimately lead to modern Freemasonry. His statues meant that lodges had for the first time to keep records, which is why the oldest lodge records in the world exist in Scotland. Aitcheson's Haven's records commence on 9 January 1599, followed by those of the lodge of Edinburgh on 31 July 1599.

With these formalities the organization (and I use the term 'organization' in its loosest possible sense) slowly began to acquire all the trappings of a permanent institution. Whereas before the time of Schaw the stonemasons' meetings had probably been held as and when necessary, the new formal requirements to keep written records, gather and record money collected and spent etc. meant that the proceedings began to become more regular, more fixed. Many of the aspects introduced by Schaw are still to be found within modern Freemasonry. These include records of meetings and proceedings, as well as the terminology used, a few examples of which are: the craft, cowan, entered apprentice, fellow craft, master, warden, lodge, mark and deacons.

It seems obvious that by putting his statutes in place, Schaw was attempting to create a national organization with himself at its head. If this is correct then it is unfortunate that its exact shape and purpose is unknown. Schaw died in 1602 but he had begun another initiative involving the stonemasons which introduced the St Clair family into the history of Freemasonry. Moreover, the Second Schaw Statutes even imply that Schaw was attempting to involve the King in his plans, but whether this was in order to seek the King's permission to establish the stonemasons as a national body is also frustratingly unclear. In any event, the King did not become involved – again for reasons unknown. It is possible that, in attempting to promote his plans, Schaw knew he was dying and was worried about how the stonemasons would manage after his death.

With Schaw's death the lodges did indeed lose their central 'guiding hand'. Over the decades, attempts were made to find a replacement for him (the first of which had been instigated by Schaw himself when he was still alive), but without success. The lodges therefore appear to have relied on the statutes as their only solid form of guidance. For this reason they were extremely important and this was recognized by the lodges themselves, some of which included them in their minute books. It was not until almost one hundred years later that the first lodge ritual, the Edinburgh Register House MS (1696), was committed to paper (see Appendix 1).

Schaw's Final Testament

Schaw was certainly a man admired by many, including the stonemasons. The epitaph on his tomb makes powerful reading:

WILLIAM SCHAW, Live with the Gods, and live for ever, most excellent man;
This life to thee was labour, death was deep repose.
To his most upright Friend,
ALEXANDER SETON, Erected DEO OPTIMO MAXIMO
(To God the Best and Greatest.)
This humble structure of stones covers a man of excellent skill, notable probity, integrity of life, adorned with the greatest of virtues – William Schaw, Master of the King's Works, President of the Sacred Ceremonies and the Queen's Chamberlain.
He died on 18 April 1602.
Among the living he dwelt fifty-two years; he had travelled in France and other kingdoms for the improvement of his mind; he wanted no liberal training; skilful in architecture; was early recommended to great persons for the singularity of his mind; and was not only unwearied and indefatigable in labours and but constantly active and vigorous, and was most dear to every good man who knew him. He was born to do good offices and thereby to gain the hearts of men; now he lives eternally with God.
Queen Anne ordered this monument to be erected to the memory of this most excellent and most upright man, lest his virtues, worthy of eternal commendation, should pass away with the death of his body.

By anyone's standards these are powerful words, words full of admiration and loss.

Schaw's tomb still lies within Dunfermline Abbey. Each stone used in its construction bears a heavily incised mason's mark:

Figure 4 The mason's mark on William Schaw's tomb in Dunfermline Abbey.

It has been thought that this may be the mark of William Schaw himself. However, this mark is repeated so prominently on the tomb it may instead be the mark of the stonemason responsible for its construction. Marks were a form of shorthand devised because many stonemasons could not write, and were used by them to identify their work and receive the correct payment due. They were personal to their owners and when non-stonemasons joined their lodges they too selected a personal mark. These were incorporated into an esoteric element within Freemasonry – an element that exists to this day.

The mark that appears on Schaw's monument is very similar to that belonging to a stonemason by the name of David Skowgall (Scougall), who worked in Crail, Fife. He may also be the same David Skowgall mentioned as a member of the Lodge of St Andrews in the St Clair 'Charter' of 1601. Was this the stonemasons' secret way of paying tribute to one of their own on a very public monument?

The Father of Freemasonry

Whether Scotland was the last outpost in post-Reformation Europe to retain a secret system of esoteric knowledge or whether Schaw reshaped it we are unlikely to know for certain; but Schaw was certainly the catalyst for a more formal organization that eventually evolved into modern Freemasonry. It is for this reason that, in Scotland at least, he is known as the Father of Freemasonry. It will no doubt come as a surprise to a great many to learn that William Schaw, the Father of Freemasonry, was a Roman Catholic.

The St Clair Family and the 'Masons'

Before his death in 1602, William Schaw drafted the First St Clair Charter in 1601. The timing implies that Schaw was making long-term plans for the stonemasons in whom he was so interested. The term 'charter' is unfortunate as it suggests that it is something that it is not; it is in fact a letter addressed to William St Clair of Rosslyn, signed by Schaw and representatives of five stonemasons' lodges, Edinburgh, St Andrews, Haddington, Aitcheson's Haven and Dunfermline. Kilwinning is noticeable by its absence, further evidence of the rift between Schaw and that lodge.

The charter commences by stating that the masons (that is, the stonemasons) have always considered the St Clair family to be their 'Patrons and Protectors' and acknowledges that, through the stonemasons' negligence, the association has been allowed to lapse. The letter is an attempt to re-establish that relationship.

From the outset it is the stonemasons, not the St Clair family, who claim the family to be their hereditary patrons. (The fact that this patronage had been allowed to lapse, assuming that it ever existed, perhaps demonstrates the importance placed on it in the past by both parties!) For reasons which will become clear, the stonemasons accept the blame for the failure of the relationship and, through a combination of flattery, 'history' and self-effacement, they hope to entice the household of St Clair into accepting their proposal.

The stonemasons' real motives for approaching the St Clair family become apparent: the stonemasons are so poor that they cannot afford to go to court to have their disputes resolved and, even if they could, the legal system is too slow for their needs. In other words, the stonemasons are asking William St Clair to become the arbitrator of their internal disputes and *nothing else*.

Many authors today cite the charter as proof that the St Clair family were hereditary grand masters of the 'masons' (stonemasons) of Scotland. But the letter to St Clair makes no mention of this, even though it explains its purpose in some detail. The stonemasons seek St Clair's involvement in a very limited way: to become the arbitrator of their disputes.

Their entreaty uses flattery and an appeal to the past in order to encourage him to accept the position. He is *not* asked to become a member of a lodge and he is *not* asked to become a Grand Master. The stonemasons are not even going to pay any expenses he may incur! This document is Schaw's attempt to seek someone of a certain social position to help the stonemasons with their internal disputes. It suggests that internal arguments were a fairly common occurrence and required someone on standby whenever needed. It also indicates that Schaw, perhaps for reasons of ill health, did not anticipate fulfilling that function for much longer.

The choice of patron and protector turned out to be disastrous. St Clair was a Roman Catholic who made no secret of his faith and was constantly fighting with the Protestant authorities. Following an extramarital affair with a miller's daughter he ran away to Ireland and there is no trace of him doing anything of note to assist the stonemasons.

The death of Schaw and the disappointment of St Clair must have been major blows to the stonemasons of Scotland. Their employer and champion was dead, and their so-called patron and protector a failure. All they had to fall back upon were Schaw's statutes, but the guidance in them caused the lodges some problems. Before they had been put in place, the lodges had convened in secret, with meetings called by word of mouth and no records taken. To keep written records as demanded by Schaw meant the lodges could no longer enforce the level of secrecy they had enjoyed. Written records meant that activities such as the collection of money and fines and the annual testing of members were to be recorded for posterity. There are no indications that there were any public concerns about the lodges' activities (in fact the contrary can be inferred: decades of lodge activity had attracted no adverse comment or criticism from potential detractors), but all was not well within the craft and in 1628 the stonemasons decided once more to seek a patron and protector.

A second letter, c. 1628, was dispatched to the son (also named William) of the St Clair addressed in the first 'charter'.* This letter essentially takes the same form as the first document, although it is considerably longer owing to considerable repetition. The central theme remains that the stonemasons consider the Sinclair family to be their 'Patrons and Protectors'. The stonemasons once again accept the blame for the break between them and the family, which they claim is owing to their negligence. The letter is an appeal to re-establish the connection. It also demonstrates that the first attempt was a failure.

The second letter makes two 'new' claims:

> Like our predecessors we obeyed, revered and acknowledged them [the Sinclair family] as patrons and protectors thereof [who] had letters of protection and other rights granted by his Majesty's most noble progenitors of worthy memory together with sundry others of the Lairds of Roslin his writings were burnt in a flame of fire within the Castle of Roslin in an [sic] . . . . [blank].†

* The St Clair Charters are the property of the Grand Lodge of Scotland.

† Quoted in Father Richard Augustin Hay, *The Genealogie of the Santclaires of Rosslyn* (William Anderson & Sons, 2002), p. 159.

Here, and for the first time, the Scottish monarchy, masons (stonemasons) and the St Clair family are linked together. Most importantly, it is claimed that rights were originally granted by the King to the family. But once again it is stonemasons, *and no one else*, who allege such an association. More specifically it is in this second letter that the stonemasons claim an unnamed king actually issued letters of 'protection and other rights' to the Sinclair family over Scottish stonemasons. It is in this document that these letters of protection are first mentioned – the same document that goes on to claim that they were lost in a fire at Roslin (Rosslyn) Castle. The monarch is not named, the nature of the 'rights' over stonemasons are not specified and even the space for the date of the fire at Roslin Castle has been left blank. The historian Father Richard Augustine Hay, who was related to the St Clair family and is the most single important source of information about them,* reports that such a fire took place in Rosslyn Castle in 1447,† but also states that the family chaplain saved all the manuscripts.‡ Unlike his father, this William St Clair was much more interested in the activities of the stonemasons and in response to the second St Clair 'Charter' decided to exercise the rights that the stonemasons claimed he had as patron and protector.

The stonemasons and the St Clairs probably came into contact in the early 1620s, during the course of building living accommodation at Rosslyn Castle. William Schaw, as King's Master of Works, promoted the involvement of the St Clairs in the affairs of the stonemasons whereas his successors did not. Times had changed since Schaw's death: James VI had gone to London in 1603 and the second 'charter' referred to Charles I (1625–1649, b. 1600) for royal approval. He was inclined to grant it, at least initially.

Before Charles I would do so, the authorities in Edinburgh were asked to confirm that granting St Clair the 'rights' in the 'charter' would not interfere with the existing Scottish system of government. Almost immediately there was a reaction. The King's Master(s) of Works object-

* He became a member of the St Clair family when his mother married the widower St Clair. He had access to all the family documents and, as we shall see, became the single most important source of information about the family.

† See the *Genealogie*, p. 28.

‡ The castle was again set on fire in 1544 by the Earl of Hertford during the so-called 'rough wooing' of Mary Queen of Scots and these charters again survived.

ed to St Clair's encroachment into their area of responsibility. The two Masters of Works were Sir James Murray (? – 1634) and Sir Anthony Alexander (? – 1637); they held the post jointly, although Murray was senior and so on his death Alexander became the sole Master.

After almost a decade of wrangling over precisely who had jurisdiction over the stonemasons of Scotland, Alexander emerged victorious over St Clair. Intriguingly, on 3 July 1634, Alexander, his elder brother Lord Alexander and Sir Alexander Strachan of Thornton (Kincardineshire) were admitted to the lodge of Edinburgh.* It is likely that this probably took place after the death of Murray that year and looks as if Alexander was consolidating his position as the King's Master of Works (he is recorded with this title in the lodge minutes of that date), although why his brother and a friend accompanied him is unclear. What must be significant is that he joined a stonemasons' lodge whereas his rival William St Clair did not.

Ironically, whilst Alexander is one of the first known non-stonemasons to join a stonemasons' lodge, and can therefore rightly be described as the first Freemason of the modern sort, and, moreover, had jurisdiction over all stonemasons, he is almost entirely forgotten, whereas it has subsequently been claimed that William St Clair, who was not even a member of a lodge, was the Grand Master over the very same stonemasons.

It is known that Alexander had an interest in architecture and had travelled to other countries to acquire knowledge of the subject. Unlike his predecessor, William Schaw, his motives for joining the lodge may well be considered dubious – he even tried to get the lodges to pay him a fee for every new member they admitted.

The dispute between Alexander and St Clair ended as the country entered civil war. But the fact remains that the St Clair family most emphatically did *not* become 'Patron and Protector' of the stonemasons, despite Sir William's willingness and the stonemasons' own desire for him to do so. A government official, the Master of Works, was confirmed as having jurisdiction over stonemasons instead.

This dispute may seem to have been a very small and curious matter to preoccupy the King of Great Britain and numerous officials

* Joseph E. McArthur, *The Lodge of Edinburgh (Mary's Chapel), No. 1 – Quatercentenary of Minutes 1599–1999* (The Lodge of Edinburgh, 1999), p. 6.

for such a long period of time. However, it was not the issue of jurisdiction over the stonemasons that was important; the real issue was a power struggle within the court. St Clair had married the daughter of John Spottiswoode (1565–1639), Archbishop of St Andrews, and he was Chancellor to the King. On the other side was Sir Anthony Alexander's father, the Earl of Stirling, and he was the King's secretary. It has been adroitly explained: 'The chancellor controlled the seals through which Alexander's grant had to pass, but the secretary controlled the king's correspondence which gave orders as to what should pass the seals!'*

Most importantly of all, perhaps, is that the St Clair family's claim to possess hereditary rights over the stonemasons was noted if not granted. King Charles, angry at St Clair's interference, wrote of him: 'pretending ane heritable charge of the Maissones of our said kingdome [Scotland], though we [the crown] have nevir gevin warrant for strengthning of aney heritable right.'† Thus the ultimate authority in such matters, the King, denied that the St Clair family ever had any hereditary rights as claimed.

Sir William St Clair died in 1650, having never obtained the official sanction for the second St Clair 'Charter'. His battle shows that not only did he want these vague and allegedly hereditary rights, but also probably believed that his family had at one time actually possessed them. In this sense at least the stonemasons of Scotland succeeded in creating a 'history' for themselves which continues to have repercussions for Scottish Freemasonry to the present day.

It is because of a particular document dating to c. 1628 that much subsequent speculative writing on the origin and development of Scottish Freemasonry, together with even earlier alleged connections with the St Clair family, is based. That inaccurate interpretation of these documents continues to be repeated today: 'To his son William were granted the charters of 1630 from the Masons of Scotland, recognising that the position of Grand Master Mason of Scotland had been hereditary in the St Clair family since it was granted by James II 1441.'‡

* For a detailed analysis and discussion of the rather complex issues surrounding the second 'charter' see David Stevenson, *The Origins of Freemasonry – Scotland's Century 1590–1710* (Cambridge University Press, 1988).

† Ibid., p. 64.

‡ The Earl of Rosslyn, *Rosslyn Chapel* (Rosslyn Chapel Trust, 1997), p. 46.

Reading the actual document, it can be seen that this is simply not so. James II is not mentioned, there is no date provided (although it is claimed to be 1441) and the term Grand Master Mason is nowhere written. The date 1441 was first used by James Anderson in his *New Constitutions* of 1738 in relation to the building of Roslin Chapel (see Chapters 8 and 9). Alexander Lawrie, in his 'history' of 1804, states:

> The office of Grand Master was granted by the crown to William St Clair, Earl of Orkney and Caithness, Baron of Roslin, and founder of the much admired chapel of Roslin. On account of the attention which this nobleman paid to the interests of the order, and the rapid propagation of the royal art under his administration, King James II. made the office of Grand Master hereditary to his heirs and successors.*

and:

> In Hay's Manuscript [Father Hay] in the Advocates' Library, there are two charters granted by the Scottish Masons, appointing the Sinclairs of Roslin their hereditary Grand Masters.†

and:

> It deserves also to be remarked, that in both these deeds [the St Clair 'Charters'], the appointment of William Sinclair, Earl of Orkney and Caithness, to the office of Grand Master, by James II. of Scotland, is spoken of as a fact well known and universally admitted.‡

The modern quote above dates from 1997 and is merely a repetition of Lawrie's (and others') inaccurate reading of the St Clair 'Charters' – charters which he reproduces in his book! It can be conjectured why Lawrie offered such an inaccurate interpretation. The building of Rosslyn Chapel commenced, according to Anderson, in 1441 when James II was king. To Lawrie, this made it clear that it must have been, could only have been, James II who made William St Clair, Earl of Orkney and Caithness, hereditary Grand Master because the 'Deed of Resignation' signed in 1736 by William St Clair 'proved', to Lawrie at least, that the family *were* hereditary Grand Masters. Lawrie, however,

* Alexander Lawrie, *The History of Free Masonry* (Lawrie, 1804), p. 100.
† Ibid., p. 102.
‡ Ibid., p. 103.

makes some elementary mistakes. The St Clair 'Charters' make no mention of the Earl of Orkney and Caithness, a Grand Master (hereditary or otherwise) or James II. The alleged involvement of the St Clair family with Freemasonry is therefore based not on the actual documents, charters etc. but on grossly inaccurate interpretations of them, Lawrie's being the prime example. It is this error which is being perpetuated today.*

Figure 5 William St Clair of Rosslyn, the first Grand Master Mason of the Grand Lodge of Scotland (1736–1737). (From *The History of Free Masonry and the Grand Lodge of Scotland*, Edinburgh, 1859.)

* This is not surprising given that no popular author has been to Freemasons' Hall to read the original documents.

3

THE MYSTERIES OF THE MASONS

It is clear that the stonemasons' lodges have long been associated with systems of esoteric knowledge or a secret 'code' such as that which William Schaw seems to have formalized with his statutes. The Masonic link with secret knowledge may indeed date back as long ago as the building of King Solomon's Temple itself, as some theories suggest. Be that as it may, a form of esoteric 'mystery' was certainly an integral element of the early lodges, beginning with the incorporations from which they are descended.

The Mysteries of the Masons

Medieval crafts had 'Mysteries', systems of esoteric knowledge appropriate to each trade, and they used their working tools – the items with which each member was intimately acquainted – as visual aids to teach the trade's particular moral lessons. Obviously such knowledge was restricted to members.

Each incorporated trade also had its own patron saint and an appointed aisle in which to worship. It's not surprising that each trade acted out that part of the biblical narrative that was particularly relevant to it or which it favoured. This acting out may have taken place in public on special occasions, for instance in the performance of mystery plays, which normally took place annually on the feast of Corpus Christi (the Thursday after Trinity Sunday), with each craft taking part in a pageant. In Haddington, for example, all the incorporations took part. Such pageants were under the patronage of the Church, which saw them as an additional method by which to educate the laity. Records in Scotland show that master mariners enacted Noah and the Ark, the hammer men performed the temptation of Adam and Eve, the vintners (wine merchants) performed the wedding feast at Cana and the goldsmiths enacted the adoration of the Magi.

Essentially the stonemasons would have been no different from the other trades in their desire to perform their favourite portion of Holy Scripture, which would have expressed an aspect of their trade mysteries and esoteric knowledge. However, if ever there was a pan-European body of esoteric knowledge known to all stonemasons and embodied in the mystery plays (public or private), the Reformation in Europe swept away many of the organizations designed to retain it. In England the trade guilds were suppressed by Henry VIII in 1540; in Scotland the Reformation left in place the incorporations but completely changed the religious observance of the country. From 1559 the incorporations could no longer stage the mystery plays that they had probably enacted for hundreds of years.

The loss of these rich, colourful pageants (as well as a couple of days off work!) must have been quite a blow. Yet there was little that the incorporations could do, as the suppression of their performances was part of a sea-change across Scotland that was enforced by religious as well as civic authorities.* However, one group of men had a secret organization that no other incorporation had and that would help it to keep its mysteries alive: the stonemasons had, of course, their lodges.

Secret Performances

We have seen previously that the stonemasons were clearly using lodges for more than storing their working tools, although frustratingly it is not known exactly what motivated them to form these private organizations. But imagine for a moment that you and your workmates have been forced to abandon a pastime that you thoroughly

* I appreciate that this is to make a complex situation appear simple but in essence this is what happened, although it took many years.

enjoyed, something that makes you feel special, such as an activity that no one else experienced, and that it used to be a highpoint of your working life? If you and your workmates were already doing something in secret, something reserved only for you and your fellow stonemasons, what would you do? It can only be speculation – some might say wild speculation – that the stonemasons added what they would otherwise have lost to their secret ceremonies within their lodges.

But what was it that the stonemasons might have lost with the Reformation? Again, it is a matter of conjecture. As we have seen, trades enacted the 'mysteries' from the Bible that had a particular relevance to them. These events took place at a time when the ordinary man had access to only one book for guidance in all matters such as history, religion and morals: the Bible. What is the first stone building in the Bible? King Solomon's Temple, of course. Imagine the pride the medieval stonemasons must have felt in the belief that their predecessors had built the first major stone building in the world!*

The imagery of King Solomon's Temple plays an important role in Masonic ceremonies today, yet there are other mysterious elements in the ceremonies and symbolism of Freemasonry that may have their roots in equally intriguing esoteric sources.

The Hermetic Element

As the Middle Ages gave way to the Renaissance, there was some overlap between preoccupations of the two eras. The Renaissance of the fourteenth to sixteenth centuries was marked by cultural advancement in a number of areas such as art, literature and architecture under the influence of classical models. Of particular interest for the understanding of Freemasonry are Renaissance developments in architecture and most especially the revival of interest in the work of the ancient Roman architect Marcus Pollio Vitruvius, who lived in the first century BC (c. 75 to c. 25). Little is known of his life, although he was probably a free citizen of Rome and may have served in the Roman army under Caesar, and he was also the author of *De Architectura*, a

* The Tower of Babel (Gen. 11:1–3) comes before King Solomon's Temple but, as explained in Chapter 1, it was built of brick not stone and so would have had little resonance for Scottish stonemasons.

work in ten volumes.* *The Ten Books of Books of Architecture* by Vitruvius are the only books on architecture of any consequence to survive from classical antiquity. In them, he emphasized that any building must have three main attributes: strength, usefulness and beauty. This statement has a resonance with modern Freemasonry in respect of the attributes of the 'three who rule a Lodge' (i.e. the master and the two wardens; see Chapter 5, page 81). It is not unreasonable to think that Vitruvian concepts entered Freemasonry through the 'filters' of Renaissance Hermeticism (see below) and Schaw's stonemasons' lodges.

Basing his work on Vitruvius's writings, Andrea Palladio (1508–1580) designed numerous houses and palaces around Vicenza, as well as several churches in Venice. His style attempted to revive Roman architecture by using classical Roman forms, symmetry and proportion. Others interested in Vitruvius's work included Donato Bramante (1444–1514), who designed the Tempietto in Rome on the site where tradition has it St Peter was crucified, basing his plans on Vitruvius's explanation of the Doric order.† But this interest was not limited to architects. Leonardo da Vinci followed his description of the proportions of the human body:

> The navel is naturally placed in the centre of the human body, and, if in a man lying with his face upward, and his hands and feet extended, from his navel as the centre, a circle be described, it will touch his fingers and toes. It is not alone by a circle, that the human body is thus circumscribed, as may be seen by placing it within a square. For measuring from the feet to the crown of the head, and then across the arms fully extended, we find the latter measure equal to the former; so that lines at right angles to each other, enclosing the figure, will form a square.

In many respects, the Renaissance was essentially a rational movement, with Vitruvian architecture an obvious and prominent

* The adoption of Vitruvius's work as the 'gospel' of architecture was not immediate as it was hampered by the fact that the text was not supported by illustrations. An illustrated edition was published by Giovanni Giocondo (c. 1433–1515) in 1511. The version translated into Italian by Daniele Barbaro (1513–1570) in 1556 and illustrated by the architect Andrea Palladio (1508–1580) was reproduced numerous times and became for many the inspiration for Renaissance, Neo-classical and some Baroque architecture.

† Doric is one of the five classical orders of architecture, the others being Ionic, Corinthian, Tuscan and Composite, and which play a part in modern Masonic ritual.

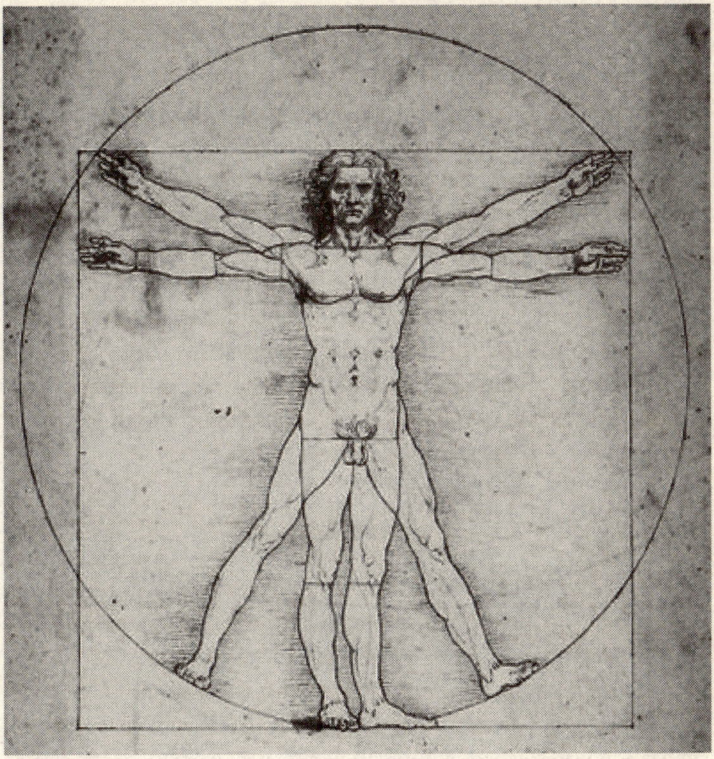

Figure 6 Leonardo da Vinci's drawing 'The Proportions of the Human Figure' (1485–90).

manifestation of that quality. However, the Renaissance was underpinned by many elements that may not appear to be particularly rational to us today, including astrology, magic, alchemy and Neoplatonic philosophy. The part played by these seemingly non-rational factors is being reassessed by some historians, as when considering the Renaissance the emphasis has long been on the progressive, rational elements that – it is claimed – prepared the way for the modern age. Certainly, during the Renaissance these other seemingly non-rational elements were held to be essential methods whereby to understand the world and the universe.

Neoplatonism

Neoplatonism underpinned these non-rational elements of the Renaissance and can be considered as the 'umbrella' under which the other elements operated. According to this philosophy, the cosmos is an organic whole in which each part is connected to all the others. The borders between matter and spirit are indistinct. Earth and everything in and on it are alive and animate and the divine imbues all matter. Man, the microcosm, is linked to the macrocosm, the universe, by an enormously complex system of spiritual influences, relationships, forces and connections. An example of how this works is the belief that the planets and stars affect the activities of man through a variety of occult forces. There is also a strong emphasis on the properties of symbols as keys to the spiritual world.

Hermeticism

As many leading lights of the Renaissance believed that antiquity had been humanity's high point spiritually, and therefore materially, they actively sought to revive it: Renaissance means Rebirth.* The interest in Vitruvius is but one example of that process in action.

The reverence accorded antiquity meant that the ancient Egyptian civilization was deemed by some to be the most worthy for the simple reason that it was the oldest known civilization during the Renaissance. There was therefore a great deal of interest in Egyptian culture and artefacts. The Neoplatonic preoccupation with the potential of symbols led to a fascination with Egyptian symbols and hieroglyphs: as Egyptian symbols were the oldest then known, it logically followed that they must be the original and the best. That these ancient symbols or hieroglyphs could not be readily interpreted merely confirmed to many that the ancient Egyptians had a special, secret means of communing with the occult world of the macrocosm. This was entirely in accordance with the Neoplatonic belief system and the opaque quality of Egyptian hieroglyphs only added to their mysterious allure. It became a challenge to break the 'code' of the ancients. This challenge fuelled the movement known as Hermeticism.

* The term was first used in 1550.

Hermeticism is wide in its scope and contains numerous diverse strands, including the concepts of cause and effect, reincarnation, duality and the central maxim 'as above, so below'. Hermetic belief cannot be explained with absolute accuracy because it can be interpreted differently by each individual. Like Freemasonry it had, and has, no 'head office' nor does it have detailed and generally accepted beliefs.* In other words there is no dogma. What can be said is that Hermeticism is panentheist (all-in-God), that there is one God, one great cause, of which every human being is part, in which respect it is well suited to the Neoplatonic theories prevalent in the Renaissance.

During the Renaissance period, Hermeticism was primarily viewed as a form of magic. Hermeticism itself is generally accepted to be a set of religious and philosophical ideas and beliefs drawn from writings attributed to one Hermes Trismegistus (Thrice-Great Hermes).† He was, allegedly, an Egyptian priest who was also the head of a secret religion followed by the intellectual elite of ancient Egypt. He is considered by many to be a fusion of the Greek god Hermes, the messenger of the gods, and the Egyptian god Thoth, the god of wisdom and magic.

One of many agents of Cosimo de' Medici, known only as Leonardo, had been sent to seek out ancient lost texts and in 1460 he brought a copy of the *Corpus Hermeticum* to Pistoia. The Hermetic revival during the Renaissance can be traced to a Latin translation of 1471 entitled *De potestate et sapientia Dei* by Marsilio Ficino, who was a member of the de' Medici court.

There were other Hermetic writings in a range of languages and they contain a wide range of subject matter. Alchemy, magic and similar concepts are discussed in the form of dialogues. Other dialogues debate matters reminiscent of Gnosticism and even Neoplatonism, suggesting another reason for the interest they generated. Hermes Trismegistus, the Thrice Great, derives his title from his claim in *The Emerald Tablet of Hermes Trismegistus* to know the wisdom of the whole universe, which comprises three parts: alchemy, astrology and theurgy.

* Manly P. Hall claimed that Hermeticism gave rise to Freemasonry in *The Hermetic Marriage* (nd.)

† Hermeticism is based on a number of Greek texts brought together as the *Corpus Hermeticum* during the Italian Renaissance.

Alchemy – the Operation of the Sun

The word 'alchemy' conjures up images of a medieval laboratory in which attempts were made to turn lead or other base metal into gold. This process could only be achieved by securing the philosopher's stone (*philosophi lapis*), a mythical substance that could supposedly transmute base metal into gold. The philosopher's stone could also be used as, or to create, an elixir that could make people younger. The search for it was one of the major preoccupations of the Renaissance until about 1630.

Our modern-day appreciation of this search for the philosopher's stone is likely to be misguided with respect to the Renaissance alchemists themselves, as we may tend to dismiss their quest as merely a materialistic and selfish attempt to gain wealth and immortality. However, the genuine Renaissance alchemist was motivated by far higher aspirations: the desire to improve the spiritual state of mankind. The popular depiction of the alchemist as a sort of medieval scientist is actually allegorical and originally intended to be understood only by those in the know. The use of a base metal is an excellent metaphor for the state of mankind's moral and spiritual nature, which the alchemist attempts to transform into a purer, higher, better state: the moral equivalent of gold. This alchemical process has interesting parallels within Freemasonry. In Masonic ritual, the rough ashlar represents the rude matter – i.e. the non-Mason – which, through the medium of Freemasonry, is transformed into a smooth, or perfect, ashlar.

But to return to the Renaissance: through his work, the alchemist was attempting to tap into the hidden spiritual forces that connected everything, to 'move' from the microcosm to the macrocosm. This would lead to an understanding of how these occult forces worked, which, once understood, could be – or at least had the potential to be – manipulated by the alchemist. Spiritual perfection was a highly desirable aim because in achieving it, not only would the successful alchemist become one with the divine essence that imbued everything; he would, through his own improvement, improve the spiritual well-being of the whole of mankind.

Yet all this had to be achieved in secret. It was believed that the search for the philosopher's stone could only be undertaken by individuals or groups of a few adepts; secrecy was necessary because the majority were simply not capable of understanding – even though they would be, unknowingly, beneficiaries of the alchemist's endeavours. Secrecy was also necessary so that the knowledge held, and searched for, by these individuals and groups would not be diluted as it would be if it were to become common knowledge. This legitimate prerequisite for secrecy ensured that there were throughout Europe an enormous number of secret societies.

Tapping into the occult world could only be achieved through using some kind of intermediary, some means by which the unknown might be revealed and studied. In alchemy, symbols became the stepping stones. As we have already seen, in Neoplatonic thought symbolism was irrevocably bound up with an understanding of the world, with the concepts of the macrocosm and the microcosm. Although I will discuss symbolism more specifically in relation to Freemasonry in Chapter 7 it is worth mentioning here that Neoplatonists viewed symbols in a slightly different manner than we understand them today. Because symbols could simultaneously reveal and conceal the divine essence, they could never be fully understood by the use of mere words, whether written or spoken. Therefore, not only did alchemists meet in secret but their language of symbols was secret in the profound sense that, in common with other Neoplatonist symbology, it could not be reduced to a common language for others to understand (assuming that the alchemists would even have wished that to be the case). In other words, alchemists sought secrets, in secret, using secrets!

Astrology – the Operation of the Moon

The writings of Trismegistus state that the ancient Persian prophet Zoroaster was the first to understand the movements of the celestial bodies and that he passed this knowledge on to the rest of mankind. The Hermetic belief was that the movements of heavenly bodies had meanings beyond those of their observable orbits. It was believed that, although the stars and other planetary bodies had an impact on the affairs of mankind, they did not dictate but influenced individual actions. This influence worked through a variety of unseen occult forces, and knowledge of those forces and their associations, the relationships and interconnections between them, allowed them to be manipulated, thereby offering insight and wisdom. The influence of these forces could only be accurately interpreted by astrologers.

This knowledge of the universe was not merely to be exploited at an individual level by, for instance, having an astrologer interpret the occult forces and draw up a person's horoscope. It was believed that tapping into the spiritual forces using a variety of conduits, primarily magic and alchemy, would produce spiritual benefits for the whole of mankind as well as for the individual.

Theurgy – the Operation of the Stars

Theurgy means 'the art of divine works' and is considered to be the practical aspect of alchemy. It involves the use of ritual, particularly magical ritual.

During the Renaissance, magic was considered to be composed of two parts.* Goëtia, or black magic, was the attempt to communicate with and control demons and other evil spirits. If control was not possible an alliance was the best alternative. Theurgy was the exact opposite, and might be described as 'divine magic', which attempted to create an alliance between the alchemist and divine spirits, such as angels, archangels and ultimately God. It would not be strictly correct to describe it as 'white' magic. The use of ritual magic, theurgy, is the key by which the alchemical endeavours are brought to fruition, the aim being to achieve *theosis* – unity with the Godhead – thereby perfecting oneself and improving the spiritual stock of all mankind.

The Three Parts of Wisdom and Freemasonry

These three parts of the wisdom of the whole universe – alchemy, astrology and theurgy – are often Hermetically described as the 'operations' of the Sun, the Moon and the Stars. This has a resonance within Freemasonry, which makes use of symbols representing these three types of heavenly bodies.

A Hermetic Magus

Hermeticism is closely related to occultism (the study of hidden knowledge) and it too was conducted in secret but for a different

* As defined by Giovanni Pico della Mirandola (1463–1494) in his *Apologia* (1489).

reason: to avoid persecution. The Renaissance was not a good period in which to digress too far from orthodox religious views, and the open study of God, alchemy, astrology and theurgy would have attracted attention. It is for good reason that the term 'hermetically sealed' derives from the secretive nature of the Renaissance Hermeticists.

The Church and civic authorities were aware of the views of the Neoplatonists and their study of the Egyptian mysteries, but because it was claimed (with considerable justification) that the Egyptian religion foretold the coming of Jesus Christ and had some parallels with Christianity it was accepted as a form of proto-Christianity. That was the public explanation. What the Neoplatonists said and did as Hermeticists in their private meetings may well have been quite different.

The best-known Hermetic magician, or magus, of the Renaissance was Giordano Bruno (1548–1600). He entered the Dominican Order and was ordained priest in 1572 but was excommunicated as a heretic. He then became a Lutheran and was excommunicated by them allegedly for promoting the ideas of Nicolaus Copernicus (1473–1543). He then became a Calvinist. He wrote more than twenty books during his lifetime, including several about mnemonic techniques (aids to memory), and it has been claimed that these works were disguised Hermetic texts; others were explicitly Hermetic in content.*

Bruno was especially prolific when in France from 1579 to 1586, where he enjoyed the protection and patronage of a number of powerful members of the aristocracy, and of Henry III (1574–1589, b. 1551). Bruno visited England between 1583 and 1585, carrying letters of recommendation from Henry III with the intention of obtaining a teaching position at Oxford. Having offended his hosts, he failed to obtain a post and so returned to France. Within a year he had become embroiled in another argument and left for Germany, where he moved between Marburg, Wittenberg, Prague, Helmstedt and Frankfurt.

After an absence of more than ten years Bruno returned to Italy and by 1592 was teaching in Venice. Perhaps he thought that the lapse of time might have afforded him protection, but it was not to be. He was denounced to the Inquisition and sent for trial in Rome. Held in prison

* See Francis A. Yates, *The Art of Memory* (Routledge and Kegan Paul, 1966).

for six years, he refused to fully recant and in 1600 was hung upside down, naked, and burned at the stake.

Bruno had adopted an extreme position of which he made no secret. As a Hermeticist he claimed that because the Egyptian religion was the oldest and purest, Christianity must consequently be a debased, corrupt, form of it. Bruno clearly did not follow other Neoplatonists in assuaging the Church authorities by claiming that the Egyptian religion was a form of proto-Christianity.

The Hermetic Legacy

As we have seen in our study of the operations of the sun, the moon and the stars, Freemasonry makes use of symbolism similar to that of Hermeticism. By the time William Schaw was drafting his statutes, and thereby shaping the destiny of Freemasonry in Scotland, the ideas and preoccupations of the Renaissance had spread from northern Italy and were colouring the intellectual and social fabric of Western Europe. Schaw's interest in Renaissance thought will become even more evident as we move on to consider another important concept from the Renaissance.

The Art of Memory

In rediscovering material from ancient Egypt, Greece and Rome, the Renaissance also revived the 'method of loci' or *Ars memoriae,* the art of memory. Its roots lie in ancient Greece, although much of what is known about it comes via the Renaissance from Roman sources. At its simplest, the art of memory was a technique to assist in the memorizing of long speeches, and was used by many politicians in the ancient world. In an age long before printing was invented and before manuscript books circulated in any number, anything that could assist a person to remember large tracts was welcomed.*

The Technique

The technique required the individual to visualize a building, particularly the rooms within it, with which he was familiar. In each room he

* Johann Gutenberg developed the first printing press in the Western world in Mainz, Germany in 1440.

'placed' or pictured mentally articles that prompted an associated idea or image. A horse might indicate travel, wine a festival and so on. In order to imprint the image of the object more forcefully on the mind of the individual, the object selected would often be striking in some way – grotesque, crude or rude, brutal or erotic as best suited the subject matter of the speech he was to give. The actual building may have existed in reality but the objects that the person placed in the rooms were his own invention and therefore of no significance to anyone else. The longer and more complex the piece to be memorized, the more objects (and eventually more rooms) were required to be visualized.

To deliver a speech the person would mentally enter the building and 'walk' through the rooms on a predetermined route. For example, this might mean visualizing a walk clockwise round the ground-floor rooms in a certain sequence, noting the object(s) in each room. The object would prompt the speaker to recall the next part of his speech.

This memory technique enabled speakers to deliver very complex and lengthy orations. The Romans developed the art to such an extent that every word of a book could be recalled by this method. In today's world we may think this technique strange, even absurd, as the amount of time and effort required to remember the imagery of building, rooms and objects seems inordinate for the end result. However, the amount of material that comes down to us from the Roman period shows that the technique worked well and was widely used.

The success of the technique might owe much to the fact that the human mind is not always logical in the way it processes information, and in order to understand how it worked, it may be useful to divide memory into two types, natural and artificial. Natural memory is untrained and almost unconscious, whereas artificial memory is trained and tends to have had thoughts, ideas and facts more forcefully ordered within it. Learning multiplication tables by rote is one way of forcing material into the artificial memory. Mentally walking round a building noting a variety of diverse, apparently unassociated objects is another.

The Hermetic Twist

In reviving the art of memory, the Hermeticists of the Renaissance added an entirely new twist. In their attempts to achieve *theosis*, oneness with the divine spirit, they harnessed the art of memory as a means of contacting the occult world.

The Hermeticist Giulio Camillo (1480–1544) produced a Memory Theatre made from wood. This large model allowed an individual to walk into it to view a Roman amphitheatre.* In addition, Camillo's theatre had a number of biblical and Hermetic influences. The auditorium had a standard layout, but on each step or level there were figures or objects placed on the rising steps between the seven 'planets' then known: Sun, Moon, Mercury, Venus, Mars, Jupiter and Saturn. True to the art of memory, these depictions were intended not only to remind the viewer of the planets important in astrology, but to indicate the seven essential measures or first causes of creation from which all other things derive. The 'highest' level in height and importance is the seventh, which is devoted to the art.

Camillo had therefore taken the imaginary building used in the art of memory and given it a physical form. Unlike the objects that the Greeks and Romans visualized mentally in buildings, he endowed the objects in his system with Hermetic meanings. In effect, they became talismans through which mankind might attempt to gain an understanding of occult influences.

William Schaw, Hermeticism and the Freemasons

Our good friend William Schaw, the Scottish Father of Freemasonry, lived against this Renaissance intellectual background all his life. With this in mind, let us return once more to consider the question partly answered in Chapter 2: why was he so interested in the stonemasons of Scotland?

It is known that he travelled to France and Denmark and 'other kingdoms for the improvement of his mind'. Unfortunately it is not known exactly when he was in France. To suggest that it was at the same time as the Hermetic magus Bruno, between 1579 and 1589, is pure speculation, but we do know that Bruno was in England from

* *L'idea del Theatro* (1550) briefly explains its function and construction. Frances Yates also showed that it was based on classical Roman theatre designs as described by Vitruvius. See *The Art of Memory*, op. cit., pp. 129–59.

1583 to 1585 and that his third work was published there in the year of his arrival.*

This work aroused great controversy and it is significant that his staunchest defender was a Scot, Alexander Dicson (Dickson) (1558–c. 1604). Dickson was born in Perthshire and studied at St Leonard's College, St Andrews (graduating in 1577); he moved to England, but maintained close contact with Scotland. His first defence of Bruno was in the form of a critique of Bruno's work on memory, *De umbris idearum*, published in 1582 in Paris. A second defence followed under a pseudonym.† Bruno was clearly aware of Dickson's support and, even if the two never met in person, Bruno considered him to be a disciple, describing him as such in later works.

Importantly, Dickson's own first work places his description of the classical art of memory in a very obvious Hermetic Egyptian setting, and in this respect outdid Bruno himself. That Dickson had a clear grasp of the classical art of memory and the new Renaissance Hermetic version is demonstrated by the fact that he is known to have taught the technique to a variety of students for a fee. He was also involved in various shadowy pursuits which may have included paid work as a spy.

By 1592 he was back in Scotland and at the royal court, which worried the English agents monitoring his activities, who described him as a 'Master of the Art of Memory'. His adherence to the Church of Rome and his close contact with the Catholic earls of north-east Scotland (for whom he may have undertaken missions overseas) ensured that he was always regarded with some suspicion. His lack of discretion regarding his religion brought him into conflict with the reformed Church of Scotland which, on one occasion, had him imprisoned. Eventually he was accepted at court, becoming a servant of James VI.

As we know, William Schaw was appointed the King's Master of Works in 1583. He was of a similar age to Dickson and worked at the royal court in which Dickson circulated. But Dickson was not the only

* *Ars reminiscendi et in phantastico compo exarandi, Ad plurimas in triginta sigillis inquirendi, disponendi, atque retinendi implicitas nouas rationes & artes introductoria; Explicatio triginta sigillorum* . . . (nd.) Quoted in Francis A. Yates, *Giordano Bruno and the Hermetic Tradition* (University of Chicago Press, 1991), p. 205.

† *De umbra rationis & iudicii, sive de memoriae virtute prosopopaeia* (London. 1583/4), quoted in Francis A. Yates, *The Art of Memory*, op. cit., p. 266 et seq., and *Giordano Bruno and the Hermetic Tradition*, op. cit., p. 199.

individual at court who had an interest in the art of memory. William Fowler (c. 1560–1610) graduated from St Leonard's College the year after Dickson. He wrote a treatise on the art of memory and also appears to have taught the technique to his king, James VI. Schaw was Queen Ann's chamberlain at the same time that Fowler was her secretary. Although the personal relationship of these two men is unknown they were well known to each professionally and both accompanied James VI to Demark during 1589 and 1590.

This was the background against which Schaw lived and worked, but what effect did the influences in his surroundings have upon his dealings with the Scottish stonemasons and their lodges? As discussed in Chapter 2, in his statutes Schaw instructed the lodges to ensure that all their members took part in an annual memory test and instituted a system of fines, with specific sums applied to every point of failure. Although it is possible that stonemasons used the art of memory before Schaw became involved in their activities, it is certain that he formalized its use by the Scottish lodges.

However, the question remains as to what form of the art of memory was being used. If Schaw had learned the Hermetic form adapted from the classical type during the Renaissance and practised by Bruno, Dickson and others, the conclusion is inescapable: he chose to introduce Hermetic elements to the lodges. If it was simply the practical antique technique as an aid to memory then any inclusion of Hermetic elements would have been accidental.

Freemasonry and the Art of Memory

It appears that by operating in secret, the stonemasons' lodges were safeguarding a special knowledge that was unique to them, thereby protecting their 'intellectual property' in the best way they knew how. Even if the stonemasons were not all illiterate, much of their esoteric knowledge would not have been committed to paper, in order to keep it secret. (In fact this may well be proved indirectly by the absence of any written evidence of ritual for almost one hundred years, with the appearance of the Edinburgh Register House MS.) The art of memory would therefore have been very suited as a tool to keep certain knowledge secret from non-stonemasons and as an efficient aid to its memorization.

There remains another reason why the art of memory was particularly suited to the stonemasons' activities. Imagine a stonemason who has been introduced to the art of memory and who is invited to choose an appropriate building for that purpose: given the central position of King Solomon's Temple in the lore of the stonemasons, as revealed in the earliest known rituals, the choice of any other building is simply impossible. It was virtually inevitable that King Solomon's Temple should be used by the stonemasons as a construct of the mind in order to recall, room by room, step by step, the ritual used in the lodge. The appeal must have been enormous.

Not only was King Solomon's Temple the oldest stone building in the Bible, and was therefore built by the stonemasons' predecessors in the craft, the Hermetic art of memory offered a means by which the stonemasons could seek to improve their mental abilities and their moral and spiritual lives. This means linked the art of memory to the stonemasons' particular lore and made them special and unique in a respect shared by no other craft or trade. Once the ritual and all the associated words and signs of the stonemasons' esoteric knowledge were committed to memory in this way, and passed to each successive generation in this manner, the parts of the ceremonial became fixed, as did their relative importance in relation to one another.

The construct of King Solomon's Temple became absolutely central to all that the lodge did and this, I suggest, is clear from its place in the earliest rituals. The permanence and position of important elements were reinforced once the ritual was committed to paper, especially once the first printed rituals began to appear in the first part of the eighteenth century. However, we are getting a little ahead of ourselves.

The Preservation of Hermeticism?

As we have seen, ideas grouped under the umbrella of Neoplatonism, such as Hermeticism, were tolerated if their expression was not too extreme or too public; to do otherwise could lead to the same fate as poor Bruno suffered.* The principal reason for this tolerance was the widely held belief that Hermeticism was a precursor to the true faith of Christianity, a belief that was strengthened by the fact that there

* An official expression of 'profound sorrow' for Bruno's death was made during the papacy of John Paul II.

appeared to be some parallels between Hermeticism and Christianity. However, this was all based on the supposition that the Hermetic texts originated in ancient Egypt and long predated Christianity.*

In 1614 the scholar Isaac Casaubon (1559–1614) analysed the language used in various Hermetic texts, particularly that in *Corpus Hermeticum*, the most philosophical of the works, which he dated to around AD 300 and certainly no earlier than AD 200.† This destroyed the basis on which Hermetic writing had previously been accepted by regal and Church powers. The parallels with Christianity were now seen to consist of no more than the accidental inclusion of some biblical themes. Hermetic philosophy was shown to derive from various Jewish, Greek and Egyptian ideas that had been in circulation in Alexandria during the Hellenistic period in particular.

Hermeticism was discredited just before the rise of scientific investigation in the seventeenth century, but if some strands of Hermeticism had already been implanted into the stonemasons' lodges there is the intriguing possibility that Hermeticism, albeit adapted and modified, remains an element within modern Freemasonry. As we shall see, the influence of Hermeticism on Freemasonry does not end here.

* Exact dating was rarely given and the texts were often attributed to 'the time of Moses'.
† *De Rebus sacris et ecclesiasticis exercitiones XVI*. London? 1614.

4

THE EARLIEST RITUALS

Whilst considering the origins and development of Freemasonry, we have circled time and again around one particular question: what did the stonemasons do in the secrecy of their lodges? The answer is that they took part in pretty much the same sorts of activities hundreds of years ago as modern Freemasons do today. There have certainly been a lot of changes along the way, which include additions to the activities and ceremonies, but the kernel of the ritual remains much the same in the Craft Lodges as it ever did. The Craft Lodges are those Lodges that confer the first three 'degrees', which denote the 'status' of a Freemason. (As we shall go on to explore in later chapters, there are other branches of Freemasonry that are additions – some early, some recent – to the Masonic 'family', and these confer further degrees.)

For many Freemasons this continuity from the past into the present is of paramount importance. It means that modern Masons have a direct connection with the hundreds of thousands of Freemasons of previous centuries. As Freemasons still take part in the self-same activities as our Masonic forebears some hundred, two hundred or three or four hundred years ago, it means that a Freemason today shares his experience not only with members of his own Lodge but also with those generations of Freemasons who are no longer with us.

Masonic Morality

In order to understand the significance of Masonic ritual, it is necessary to consider the aims and nature of Freemasonry itself. There is an

American definition which is helpful: 'Freemasonry strives to make good men better. It cannot make bad men good.' It may sound a little trite to British and European ears, and personally I prefer 'A peculiar system of morality, veiled in allegory and illustrated by symbols.' This definition was penned more than a hundred and fifty years ago, but it still holds true today. In order to understand its meaning fully, it needs to be translated into our modern terminology. Today, the word 'peculiar' tends to be used to indicate a quality that is odd, strange or not quite right. However, when originally written the word meant 'special' or 'unique'.

The 'system' that the maxim refers to is, of course, that of the three degrees, which we shall be considering in more detail in Chapter 5, on pages 83–87. The whole Masonic system is veiled in allegory; that is, disguised in the time-honoured way of using, or saying, one thing in order to indicate another. Finally, the whole package is illustrated using symbols, whose potential potency we have touched upon in the consideration of Hermeticism in Chapter 3.

Using more modern terminology, Freemasonry might be described in this manner:

> Freemasonry teaches morality in a special way using allegorical material to highlight specific aspects and with symbols as visual aids.

I acknowledge that this statement might appear too simplistic for some, but it is as good a starting point as any. As I mentioned in this book's introduction, it is worth remembering that Freemasonry cannot be defined absolutely by either me or anyone else; and for many that is one of the beauties of the Craft.

Shared Teachings

Essentially, the ritual and symbolism of Freemasonry took seed within the confines of the Lodge. The primary function of a Masonic Lodge has always been to teach, especially to teach the secrets passed on generation after generation from the distant past when only stonemasons, and no other trade, possessed them. Sharing and teaching remain important factors in Freemasonry.

As to what is taught, let us direct our attention once more to the Lodges of the sixteenth and seventeenth centuries, and to what is known of their activities. Chapter 2 discussed how William Schaw reorganized lodges and provided them in 1598 and 1599 with the two sets of guidelines that are now known as the Schaw Statutes. The Second Statutes included a reference to the art of memory, making it clear that the stonemasons were meant to memorize something important, and suggesting that Schaw may even have introduced Hermetic teachings into the Lodges.

That the stonemasons practised the art of memory is intriguing and frustrating in equal measure: intriguing because it hints strongly at the existence of esoteric knowledge and the method by which it was passed from one generation of stonemasons to the next, and frustrating because the exact nature of the esoteric knowledge thus conveyed is never revealed. However, I think that, as we have seen in Chapter 3, we can now conjecture what that knowledge might have been with some certainty.

The Earliest Masonic Rituals

The earliest known 'ritual' in manuscript form is the Edinburgh Register House MS, which is dated 1696 and is given in full in Appendix 1. Two further handwritten rituals date from soon after the Edinburgh Register House, the Airlie MS (1705) and the Chetwode Crawley MS (c. 1710).

It is significant that these transcribed Masonic rituals began to appear in the 1690s. That they exist at all is a clear reflection of the changes that had occurred during that century. The first ceremonies performed by the stonemasons in their lodges were never intended to be written down: even in the sixteenth century, Schaw required that they be memorized. In any event, there would have been little point in committing the ceremonies to paper, given that the majority of the stonemasons of the period were illiterate. Knoop, Jones and Hamer believed that they 'possibly represent an operative working which existed some decades before the date at which the documents were written'.*

* Douglas Knoop, G. P. Jones and Douglas Hamer, *The Early Masonic Catechisms* (Manchester University Press, 1943), p. 19.

As we see lodges evolving and admitting more and more non-stonemasons, we also begin to see the appearance of written ritual. It seems that although the stonemasons themselves adhered to Schaw's instructions, non-stonemasons either could not or would not do so, and took notes for their own personal use. Perhaps the non-stonemasons felt that they were not bound by Schaw's instructions because they were literate men and therefore thought that the statute's instruction to memorize did not apply to them. The manuscripts may have come into existence simply because these men wished to consider the ceremony in more detail outside the lodge and needed a form of aide-memoire. If the activities of notable Freemasons such as Sir Robert Moray are in any way indicative (see Chapter 7, page 120), perhaps some did indeed want to make a private, personal study of the ritual in their own homes.

Be that as it may, to ignore Schaw's instruction might be considered by some to be an act of arrogance on the part of the writers of these brief rituals, implying these men thought themselves above the rules of the lodges that they had joined. However, from a historical point of view it is fortunate that a few did break the rules. In any event, the relatively uniform content of the various catechisms recorded in the manuscripts suggests that there may have been strict controls as to which aspects were permitted to be put into writing.

The early rituals listed above are very similar in content; any differences are owing to variations in spelling, punctuation, grammar and layout, and copying errors. This last point is important because copying errors (and a couple are very obvious) suggest that there may have been even earlier manuscripts in existence than the three we still possess.

Although we have referred to the practices recorded in the three manuscripts variously as 'rituals', as 'catechisms' and as 'aides-memoires', each of these terms alone is inadequate in that it only describes one aspect of the practices' function. All three manuscripts contain two sections: a series of questions and answers, and a description of the actions required to give and to receive the 'mason word'. The first part consists of a catechism: a series of sixteen questions and answers, which, once written down, became an aide-memoire. The second part describes the ceremonies of being made an apprentice and a fellow craft.* Unlike the modern system of the three degrees (see Chapter 5, page 83–87), it is clear that originally there were only these two ceremonies. The first was for giving and receiving the individual words of the entered prentice and the second was for giving and receiving the individual words of the fellows of craft – there is no mention of a master mason's degree. Finally, the manuscripts contain hints of the ritual or ceremony during which the 'mason word' was imparted. The catechism format implies that it was intended to prompt certain physical responses as well as verbal ones.

All three manuscripts are headed similarly. The Edinburgh Register House MS reads: 'Some questions that Masons will put to those who have ye word before they will acknowledge them.' Right away we can see that the purpose of the questions is one of recognition: the method that Masons once used to identify themselves to each other.† However, although this may have been the primary purpose, the number of questions is too great for that purpose alone. When the content of the catechism is considered it is obvious that it serves another purpose: education.

The Oldest Masonic Ritual in the World

Let us focus on the catechism part of the Edinburgh Register House MS, the oldest Masonic ritual in the world, whose questions and answers are listed below. The document is written in a language known as middle Scots. At the time the document was created, the Anglicization of the language was well under way, but strong Scottish elements were still evident in it, and bearing this in mind, and that more than three hundred years have gone by since the document was written, it is hardly surprising that some of the words and phrases in it may sound odd to us today. The passage of time is also the reason why the catechism shown below has changed almost beyond recognition in its present form in modern Freemasonry, but the core elements remain.

* The two parts are reversed in the Chetwode Crawley MS.

† The fact that this ritual has been committed to writing strongly suggests that non-stonemasons were entering stonemasons' lodges in numbers, and so were Freemasons in the modern sense.

In reproducing the Edinburgh Register House, I have kept the spelling and punctuation as near to the original as possible.

> Question 1
> Are you a mason. Answer yes

Blunt and to the point: if the answer was 'no', then there was no need to ask the next fifteen questions!

> Question 2
> How shall I know it? Ans: you shall know it in time and place convenient. Remark the forsd answer is only to be made when there is company present who are not masons But if there be no such company by, you should answer by signer tokens and other points of my entrie.

This question asks how the individual can prove that he is a Mason. There are two answers: one for when it is known that non-Masons are present and one for when only Freemasons are in the company. When non-Masons are present the question is skirted: 'you shall know it in a time and place convenient'. If there are only Freemasons around, the proof is as obtained during the initiation ceremony: a sequence of signs, tokens and other matters is exchanged.

> Question 3
> What is the first point? Ans: Tell me the first point ile tell you the second, The first is to heill and conceall, second, under no less pain, which is then cutting of your throat, For you most make that sign, when you say that.

Here the questioner is being tested in the sense that he must offer some information that serves to prove that he too is a Freemason. There are two points or parts.

The first is to 'heill and conceal' and here we find the use of an old Scottish word *heill*, which means 'to keep secret'. It is immediately followed by the words 'and conceal', which means the same thing and this tells us something very important. Catechisms were essentially verbal exchanges between two people and, as we have seen previously, the people taking part in Masonic rituals would, in the earliest times at least, often have been illiterate. Here, the catechism has been committed to writing and has therefore been recorded by, and for, someone literate. By the time the manuscript came to be created, the spoken word *heill* has become sufficiently obscure that the writer feels obliged to clarify its meaning by adding 'and conceal'. In this way he has not changed the catechism, but added to it. When these rituals, or their descendants, reached the United States of America the word *heill* was considered to be an error and was changed to 'hail'. The logic was understandable, but it shows that the Scottish origins had been lost or forgotten.

The second point in this exchange involves the use of a sign: that of cutting one's throat. That sign has been used to hound Freemasons almost ever since the ritual first became known to others outside the Craft. It is sufficient here to note that the use of a word also required a sign to be given, and that two elements were needed to identify the candidate as a Freemason.

> Question 4
> Where wes you entered? An: At the honourable lodge.

This seems to be an innocuous question but it is important nevertheless. There is evidence to suggest that some people were made Freemasons 'irregularly', i.e. not in a genuine Masonic Lodge. Someone initiated in this way might not realize the correct answer is 'At the honourable lodge'.

> Question 5
> What makes a true and perfect lodge? An: seven masters, five entered apprentices, A dayes Journey from a burroughs town without bark of dog or crow of cock.*

Here I think that we are beginning to see the educational purpose of the catechism. Only a Freemason regularly initiated in an 'honourable Lodge' would know what constituted a regular (honourable)

* Although there were only two ceremonies for stonemasons, the terms Fellow Craft and Master Mason were used interchangeably within the lodge. The terms appear to have had different applications in a working environment in that a master mason could employ others whereas a fellow craft could not.

Lodge. The answer also reminds all present of the rules for holding a Lodge meeting. Twelve men were required: seven masters and five entered apprentices. (As suggested by the ritual itself, at this point in time masters were 'fellows of craft' and the two descriptions were used interchangeably.) This number was probably to ensure that there were sufficient knowledgeable Freemasons present to conduct the ceremony correctly, to form a 'true and perfect Lodge'. This would have been especially important at a juncture when meetings were held infrequently and members of a Lodge could come from a wide area.

The second part of the answer reveals that the Lodge meetings were private affairs: a day's journey away from any town and out of earshot of any farm. As this would have been rather difficult to achieve in a country that was still largely rural, it is unlikely that this requirement was intended literally and is more likely have been to emphasize the private nature of Lodge meetings.

Question 6
Does no less make a true and perfect lodge, An: yes five masons and three entered apprentices &c.

This question asks what happens if the numbers to form a 'true and perfect Lodge' are unavailable. The answer is, rather reluctantly, that a Lodge meeting can be held if there are five master masons (fellows of craft) and three entered apprentices present.

Question 7
Does no less. An: The more the merrier the fewer the better chear [cheer]

The question asks what happens if even five masters and three entered apprentices cannot be found for a meeting. The answer is that no meeting can be held but instead some socializing is OK!

Question 8
What is the name of your lodge An: Kilwinning.

Being asked the name of the Lodge would almost certainly catch someone out who had not been initiated regularly, for he would be highly unlikely to give the correct response even if he knew the name of a Lodge at all. However, that aside, the fact that all these early rituals give the name of the same Lodge as an answer is most interesting. As discussed in Chapter 2, Kilwinning is one of the oldest Lodges in the world. The fact that it is this Lodge and no other that is consistently mentioned in these rituals indicates that it was widely accepted that Kilwinning was the most important and oldest Lodge, regardless of whether or not this was accurate. It also confirms the Scottish origin of these early rituals.

Question 9
How stands your lodge An east and west as the temple of Jerusalem.

The question 'How stands your lodge?' is intended to elicit one reply only and this is the direct comparison of a Masonic Lodge to King Solomon's Temple – *the* temple of Jerusalem. Notice, however, that there is no suggestion that a Masonic Lodge is the same as King Solomon's Temple: only the orientation, east and west, is the same for both.

Question 10
Where wes the first lodge. An: in the porch of Solomons Temple

As question 8 cites the Lodge at Kilwinning, which is known to be one of the oldest and most established in the world, it might be assumed that the correct answer to question 10 would also be 'Kilwinning'. Instead, the answer is 'in the porch [entrance] of Solomon's Temple'. This shows that, having been of paramount importance to the stonemasons, Solomon's Temple was equally important to the non-stonemasons (Freemasons) who subsequently joined their lodges. The fact that it is mentioned twice, in questions 9 and 10, demonstrates just how central it is to Freemasonry.

However, it is worth noting that the first lodge was not in King Solomon's Temple itself: it was located in the porch or entrance. This is probably the origin for calling Masonic Lodges 'temples', as it is easier to say 'temple' than 'the entrance to the temple'!

Figure 7 A seventeenth-century imaginative view of King Solomon's Temple, showing the porch. (From *Orbis Miraculum or the Temple of Solomon Portrayed by Scripture Light*, London, 1659.)

> Question 11
> Are there any lights in your lodge An yes three the north east. sw, and eastern passage The one denotes the master mason, the other the warden The third the setter croft [fellow craft].

Here we see that 'lights' in a Lodge were two things. Firstly, they were passages in the north-east, south-west and east. These are, therefore, positions within the Lodge. Secondly, they were officials of the Lodge (known as 'office-bearers' in Scotland and 'officers' in England).

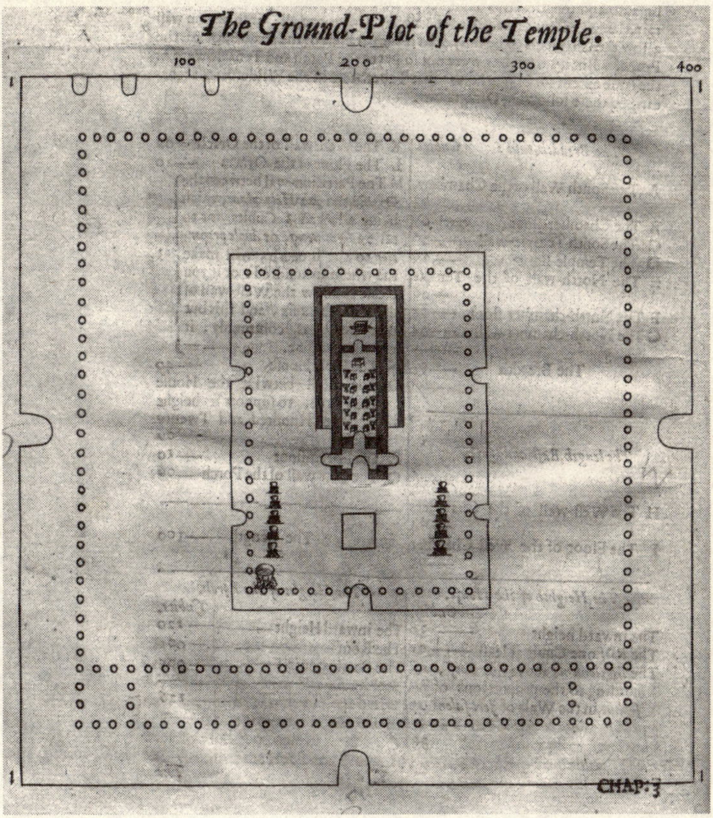

Figure 8 An eighteenth-century ground plan of King Solomon's Temple. (From *The Temple of Solomon*, London, 1725.)

It seems reasonable to assume that the officials were placed at these 'passages'.

There is very little to go on here but it may be that this was how a stonemasons' lodge was originally laid out; a layout that was subsequently changed following the influx of non-stonemasons, along with the elaborations, additions and inventions that they introduced to what took place there. In modern Freemasonry, the lights, for, example are no longer passages or these three particular officials. The lights have in fact been developed into three 'Great Lights' and three 'Lesser Lights', of which more later.

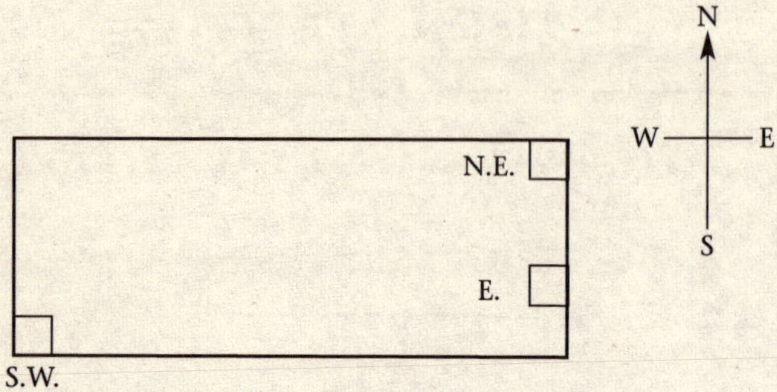

Figure 9 The layout of the Lodge according to the oldest ritual.

Question 12
Are there any jewels in your lodge An Yes three, Perpend Esler a Square pavement and a broad ovall.

Like the lights of a Lodge, the 'jewels' now have a different meaning within modern Freemasonry. However, in this original context, they refer to three objects associated with stonemasons, two of which are still in use. A 'perpend esler' is a perpendicular ashlar, a dressed (i.e. prepared by a stonemason) upright stone. A square 'pavement' is a square floor or, more often in Freemasonry today, a square carpet. In Scotland, a 'pavement', especially in a church, was made of square stone slabs dressed and laid by the stonemason. The 'broad oval' has long been something of a puzzle to Masonic historians, but, given the two previous items' direct relevance to the work of stonemasons, it seems likely that this is a stonemason's maul or mell, which was used to strike a chisel.* Another alternative is that 'broad ovall' is a corruption of 'broached ornal', a facing stone that has been worked with a chisel to carry diagonal or horizontal furrows. If the latter is accepted then the three elements, all of stone, could be interpreted as representing the interior of a Lodge: its floor and walls. More likely, they refer to rough and smooth ashlars placed on a square chequered carpet, as is still common in ceremonies performed in the majority of Lodges outside the USA.

* The Airlie MS has 'brobid ornall'. The Chetwode Crawley MS uses the term 'Broked-mall'.

Question 13

where shall I find the key of your lodge, yes [Ans] Three foot and an half from the lodge door under a perpend esler, and a green divot. But under the lap of my liver where all my secrets of my heart lie.

Here we reach clues that imply the existence of esoteric content in the stonemasons', and thereby the Freemasons', rituals. The use of the word 'key' suggests that there is a secret to be unlocked, but is it the Masonic secret? Something that is locked away can only be discovered by the use of a key. The finding of the key is therefore of paramount importance as nothing else can be done without it. Given the previous allusions to Solomon's Temple, there is the distinct possibility that what is being asked for is the whereabouts of Solomon's Key.

The answer given to that question is obscure and open to some interesting interpretation. The first part of the answer, 'Three foot and an half from the lodge door', shows that the key to 'your' Lodge's secrets lies outside the Lodge; to be precise, three feet six inches from the Lodge door. As we have seen, 'under a perpend esler' must refer to a dressed perpendicular stone. Next we are told: 'and a green divot'. So, the Key of Solomon as understood by these stonemasons and Freemasons is located outside the Masonic Lodge, under an upright dressed stone and under green grass – in other words, in the grave. Although the secrets belong to the Lodge, or to Solomon's Temple, there is only one place that you will find them outside a Masonic Lodge, and that is in the grave of a Freemason: he takes *his* key of the Lodge with him to the grave. This is an important point and worth further thought. The question being asked is 'Where are the keys to *your* lodge?', not 'Where are the keys to *the* Lodge (i.e. Freemasonry)?' This is a personal question asking for a personal response. I believe that it comes down to the point that I have emphasized earlier: that much of what Freemasonry contains is subject to personal interpretation, admittedly with some guidance.

The second part of the answer is equally fascinating: 'But under the lap [lobe] of my liver where all my secrets of my heart lie'. This too has had Masonic historians wondering. At a simple level the answer may be taken to mean that all secrets, especially Masonic ones, are to be carefully guarded from the outside world. However, I believe this part of the answer provides us with some insight into the possible influence of Hermeticism on early Freemasonry.

Claudius Galen (c. 130–c. 216) was a Greek philosopher and anatomist, whose work, summarizing and systematically presenting all the medical knowledge known to the ancient world, was translated into Latin in 1322 by Niccolo de Reggio, and much of what Galen wrote became a part of Renaissance Hermetic thought. Galen argued that the fundamental principle of life was *pneuma*. This came in three forms with three actions: animal spirit (*pneuma psychicon*), located in the brain, which was the centre of sensory perception and movement; vital spirit (*pneuma zoticon*), which was found in the heart and regulated blood-flow and temperature; and natural spirit (*pneuma physicon*), which existed in the liver and was the centre of nutrition and metabolism. Galen believed that the heart distributed blood through arteries and the liver through the veins in two separate systems. The three most important organs of the body were therefore the brain, heart and liver.

In the medieval period the belief that the body operated in this way led to the conviction that the Black Death (which reached England in 1349 and Scotland the following year) was caused by infected vapours entering the body and carried by the blood to the brain, heart or liver. Each of these organs had a corresponding excretory duct. For the brain, this was the ears or throat; the heart's was the armpit and the liver's the groin. Buboes in those areas indicated the organ affected and determined the treatment, which usually involved bloodletting or cauterization. Bloodletting was necessary to balance the humours of the body, the humours being a concept that dated from the time of Pythagoras and which comprised four components: phlegm, blood, choler (melancholy) and bile.* For good health these four had to be in balance.

In the early seventeenth century, William Harvey (1578–1657) discovered the true circulation of the blood, proving that the heart was a 'muscular pump' and that blood flowed in one direction only.† Although several of Harvey's precursors had agreed with Galen's

* These were also closely associated with earth, air, fire and water, from which the ancient Greeks believed everything was made.

† *Exercitatio anatomica de motu cordis et sanguinis in animalibus*, Frankfurt, 1616.

notion that the liver was a centre of circulation, Harvey's work dispensed with that once and for all. From then on the liver ceased to be considered as one of the three principal organs of the body. Yet here it pops up in the first known Masonic ritual of 1696. Even after Harvey had discredited the liver's role, the ritual still referred to it in the same breath as the heart, as the place where the secrets of the heart were stored. But why?

The emphasis on the 'lap of my liver' suggests a link between the answer to question 13 and the Renaissance period, when the views of Galen had been incorporated into those of the Hermeticists. It implies that there is a connection between the answer and Hermetic notions concerning the influence of the occult world on the body. This possible link between Freemasonry and Hermeticism, via the stonemasons' lodges, may indicate that the ritual (or catechism) is much older than previously thought.

Question 13 and its answer are all about secrecy, the need to take Masonic secrets to the grave rather than divulge them. And there is one further thought: according to Galen's theory, the liver's excretory gland was in the groin, which is surely one of the most secret parts of the human body and therefore particularly well suited to meet the esoteric needs of those who created and used this ritual.

> Question 14
> Which is the key of your lodge. An: a weel hung tongue. where lies the key. Ans: In the bone box.

This question refers once more to a key and again suggests the existence of something locked away from others. The respondent is asked 'which' key, implying that there is more than one. As the question is asked of an individual, could it be that each member of the Lodge has his own key? The first part of the answer might well be taken to support that view: a 'weel hung', or well-held, tongue is that of someone who does not talk out of turn, who does not indulge in loose talk.

A second question is asked in the Edinburgh Register House and an answer is provided.* The question returns to where the key might be found and again indicates that there is a search taking place. The answer

* The Airlie and Chetwode Crawley MSS make this a separate question.

is intriguing: 'In the bone box.' The previous answer revealed that a tongue was the key to 'your' Lodge and so there appears to be the strong possibility that the bone box refers to the skull, wherein lies the tongue. The stonemasons may be indulging in a little word-play here. We have noted that there has been an earlier reference to a grave. What kind of box goes into a grave? A coffin. Perhaps the stonemasons are emphasizing that the key, the secret, Solomon's secret key lies in the grave?

There then follows a short address to the candidate:

> After the masons have examined you by all or some of these Questions and that you have answered them exactly and mad[e] the signes, they will acknowledge you, but not a master mason or fellow croft [craft] but only as [an] apprentice, soe they will say I see you have been in the Kitchine but I know not if you have been in the hall, Ans I have been in the hall as weel as in the kitchine.

This tells us that all the previous questions relate to the entered apprentice ceremony (the first degree) and shows to what lengths Freemasons would go to identify impostors. The fact that they took the opportunity to include educational material shows that some considerable thought, then as now, went into this process.

The Edinburgh Register House catechism requires some explanation. It appears that not all the questions had to be asked and that it was probably only used when the individual was not already well known to the other Lodge members. The answers to the questions had to be accompanied by signs and although more than one sign was involved (the plural is used) surely each answer didn't require a different sign? Another small example of why the study of Freemasonry is so absorbing!

Once the questions had been answered and the correct signs given, the individual being questioned was to be accepted as an entered apprentice, but not as a 'master or fellow croft'. Whilst this distinction explains the need for more questions at a later stage, it is also important because it confirms that 'master' and 'fellow craft' were regarded as one and the same. It confirms that there were only two degrees within Freemasonry at this time.

During the address to the candidate there is a question disguised as a statement: 'I see you have been in the Kitchine but I know not if you have been in the hall', with the answer, 'I have been in the hall as weel as in the kitchine.' This is a fairly obscure reference and at first sight does not seem to make much sense. However, there may be an obvious explanation: a typical rural Scottish home was a simple two-roomed house, sometimes divided by a hall where the outside door was located. Such a home was called (and still is in some places) a 'but an' ben'. The 'but' (or 'butt') referred to the outer room of the house, always the kitchen and always with an outside door, and the 'ben', indicated the best room of the house, a parlour or living room.

This seems to be another example of the writer, or copyist, attempting to clarify the words of the catechism as they were originally spoken by stonemasons in much the same way that the word *heill* in question 3 is explained with the addition of 'and conceal'. This has been done by substituting 'kitchen and hall' for the more colloquial 'but an' ben', but the substitution confuses rather than elucidates the original meaning. When one is aware that 'hall' or 'ha' in Scots also can mean the principal room or 'ben' of an ordinary house, an explanation becomes possible.

Given the position of this injunction (after the catechism questions confirming that the candidate being questioned is indeed a Freemason, but before the questions relating to the Fellow Craft ceremony), it seems clear that in modern English this would translate as: 'I now know that you are an entered apprentice, but I am unsure if you are a fellow craft.' Presumably, if the candidate did not understand the question then the questioner would go no further.

Question 15
Are you a fellow craft Ans yes.

Having obtained the correct response to the question regarding the kitchen and hall, the question is then put bluntly: Are you a fellow craft? This is reminiscent of question 1. If the answer was no, presumably the candidate would be asked no more questions.

Question 16
How many points of the fellowship are ther Ans fyve viz foot to foot Knee to Kn[ee] Heart to Heart, Hand to Hand and ear to ear. Then make the sign of fellowship and shake hand and you will be acknowledged a true mason. The words are in the I of the Kings Ch 7, v, 21, and in 2 chr: ch 3 verse last.

The stonemasons, and increasingly the non-stonemasons who joined them, used this ritual at the end of the seventeenth century and into the eighteenth. It is not known whether this form of ceremonial was used before William Schaw became involved; in any event, it is highly probable that he would have made some changes to whatever existed, if only to formalize the proceedings. Schaw's instruction to memorize the ritual, with the imposition of fines, may have inadvertently ensured that it was written down, even though the ritual itself includes the injunction never to write it in any shape or form!

The Reification of Ritual: Grand Lodges and Rules and Regulations

There is no clear evidence that more than a handful of Lodges existed across Britain (with the majority concentrated in Scotland) at the time that the Edinburgh Register House ritual was transcribed, but with the establishment of the first Grand Lodge the situation changed dramatically. The Grand Lodge of England (now the United Grand Lodge of England) was founded in 1717, followed by the Grand Lodge of Ireland in 1725 and the Grand Lodge of Scotland in 1736. With their creation matters became much better organized. Grand Lodges acted as a form of head office, a central point of contact, to which those aspiring to become Freemasons or to form Masonic Lodges could apply, whereas before Freemasonry had been conducted at a local level.

The Grand Lodge system developed slowly at first, but the appearance of a formal structure ensured that standard methods in all aspects of Freemasonry (such as administration, ritual and conditions for membership) began to be adopted consistently, albeit slowly, by all Lodges. For the first time since the days of William Schaw existing Lodges began to receive central guidance and direction.

The desire to be accepted as a legitimate Masonic Lodge remains strong within Freemasonry. It has always been preferable for a Lodge to be created officially by an existing Lodge rather than by any other means. The earliest example of a Lodge creating another Lodge occurred in 1677, when the Lodge at Kilwinning granted a charter (and recorded the fact in its minutes) forming a Lodge in the burgh of the Canongate, which is now part of Edinburgh. From the late seventeenth century, no Lodge could (nor can) be considered legitimate without a charter. The authority to grant charters ultimately passed to the Grand Lodges, whereby they gained considerable powers to control Freemasonry.

When George Washington became a Freemason in Virginia, in 1752, the Lodge he joined at Fredericksburg possessed no charter or warrant. Today it would be considered clandestine and Washington not a 'real' Freemason, but looking at the membership of Washington's Lodge, one can begin to guess what happened. Because the Lodge contained a lot of Scots, or those of Scots descent, I can just imagine the discussion – 'A charter will cost us five pounds, but what if the Lodge fails in a year or two, what a waste of money!' So the Lodge waited six years to see if it would be successful, and in 1758 its members decided that it was time to become legitimate by obtaining a charter. It is a source of great Scottish pride that the Lodge decided to approach the Grand Lodge of Scotland for such a charter, which was granted that year. George Washington was therefore a Scottish Freemason!

Following the creation of the first Grand Lodges, the first 'rules and regulations' of Freemasonry (as opposed to stonemasonry) were written by James Anderson in 1723, whose contribution will be discussed in more detail in Chapter 8. Anderson was from Aberdeen and had almost certainly been initiated into his father's Lodge there, prior to moving to London in 1710.*

The appearance of Grand Lodges brought about some dramatic developments, certainly in comparison to those of the previous century. There was an explosion of Lodges founded in Britain and Ireland and on the Continent, and it was not long before they appeared in North America too (of which more later). The third or master mason's degree came into existence in the early part of the 1720s, and the first separately printed ritual book, containing all three degrees, was published in London in 1730. Andrew Ramsay's *Oration* of 1737, supposedly to the Grand Lodge of France, almost certainly led to the creation of other branches of Freemasonry (collectively known as *Hauts Grades* – Higher degrees, see Glossary), some of which

* *The Constitutions of the Free Masons* (London, 1723).

continue to exist, although many of the ceremonies have long since disappeared.* Examples of those branches that are still with us and which first appeared after Ramsay's Oration include the Royal Order of Scotland, the Royal Arch and the Knights Templar. Each of these experienced fluctuations in their popularity, occasionally barely surviving, until they became more firmly established in the latter part of the eighteenth and the early part of the nineteenth centuries.

The Importance of Ritual

Freemasonry is all about ceremonies, about ritual. Ritual is the means by which the knowledge, moral lessons, Masonic lore and Traditional Histories are passed to each new Freemason. But although ritual is central it occupies only a small part in a Freemason's life – at least, in terms of time. It is only performed at Lodge meetings and even then not necessarily at every one (some are devoted to Lodge administration). Ritual is primarily important in so far as it is the means by which 'Freemasonry' is explained, although more important is *what* is explained.

We have seen that the earliest ritual was fairly simple but that it contained some profound esoteric messages and lessons from the outset. Over time ritual has become more elaborate and new ones have been added to the Masonic lexicon, but that has not changed the original and fundamental purpose of ritual within Freemasonry. Simply put, without ritual Freemasonry would not be Freemasonry.

* That Ramsay actually delivered the Oration is now considered unlikely, but it was given a wide circulation in printed form and its impact cannot be underestimated.

5

THE MASONIC LODGE AND THE THREE DEGREES

Strictly speaking, a Masonic Lodge is not a place: it is a gathering of Freemasons who have come together to hold a Masonic meeting. With respect to the location itself, the terms 'Masonic Hall' or even 'Masonic Temple' would be more accurate. However, over the years the Lodge gathering has become virtually synonymous with the place in which it meets.

Today, many Masonic buildings are open to the public, with the Grand Lodges of England, Ireland and Scotland providing tours of their buildings that include their meeting rooms. Some Grand Lodges even display photographs of their Lodge rooms on the Internet. There is therefore no longer any secrecy about what a Masonic Lodge room looks like or what it contains. However, confusion may arise if people do not understand what they see there and this may be compounded by the fact that a great deal of Masonic symbolism (discussed in more detail in Chapter 6) can be interpreted differently by individual Freemasons as well as the general public.

Masonic halls come in different shapes and sizes: some are very old and some are brand new, some are set in the countryside and many are in cities. Age, size and place do not define what the space is used for – that is determined by ancient usage and practice, by the members themselves and by the requirements of Masonic ritual. That said, in Chapter 4, when considering question 11 in the catechism of the oldest ritual in the world, we touched upon how a Lodge room may originally have been laid out. It is quite different today.

In the Temple

The Tyler

What, then, will you find in a Masonic hall today? Approaching the Lodge room, the first thing you encounter is its closed door. This will frequently have an imposing knocker on it that the Lodge official, known as the 'outer door guard' or 'tyler' (or 'tiler'), will use to communicate with those inside, most particularly with the inner door guard, by a system of knocks, with different knocks for different situations and circumstances. The tyler is there to ensure that only those who are properly qualified to attend the meeting are admitted. It would not, for example, be appropriate to admit an entered apprentice to a meeting being held in the master mason's degree because an entered apprentice has not yet taken the degrees of fellow craft or master mason that would qualify him to attend. Freemasonry has been called a 'progressive science' and this accurately describes the process of moving through the various degrees.

The tyler is armed with a drawn, unsheathed sword as a sign of his rank, which indicates that he is guarding the Lodge entrance. It is vitally important to remember that much of Freemasonry is symbolic – I have yet to meet a tyler who can actually fence! As is often the case in ceremonial wear, the nature of the artefact itself is unimportant; it's what it represents that counts, and most tylers' swords couldn't cut cheese. I even know a Lodge that use a plastic one because they've lost the real one!

The Pillars

Inside the entrance of the Lodge it is very common to find two large freestanding pillars. These represent the two pillars that stood at the entrance to King Solomon's Temple (see Figure 11, page 82). We have seen that the porch or entrance to King Solomon's Temple was, according to the earliest Masonic rituals, the site of the first Lodge. However, the pillars are not specifically mentioned in the early rituals and this is probably why they are rarely found in Scottish Masonic Lodges. The ritual itself refers to them obliquely by quoting the chapters and verses from the Old Testament in which they are described and discussed (I Kings 7:21 and II Chron. 3:17). The pillars are particularly important in the Fellow Craft degree, where their place in Masonic lore is explained in detail, and they are referred to in the Second degree tracing boards (see pages 93–95).

The Chequered Carpet

The item that dominates the meeting room is usually the carpet or tiled floor, which is made up of black-and-white squares. This is referred to in the Edinburgh Register House MS as a 'square pavement' and was familiar to the working masons of previous centuries. Exactly what significance the 'pavement' had for the early stonemasons is not known, but as their work could often be walked on, great care was taken to ensure that it was level.

In modern Freemasonry the pavement takes a physical form and is the part of the room in which ceremonies are enacted. The new candidate is led to the edge of the carpet, symbolically indicating that he is about to embark on a journey, the same journey that all other Freemasons have taken before him. The black-and-white squares are intended to remind all Freemasons, not just the candidate, that they always have choices in life. Reduced to their simplest form, these choices are good or bad. The carpet therefore instructs the Freemason that throughout life's journey he has to make decisions – for good or ill. Seating for the members of, and visitors to, the Lodge is situated around the carpet or pavement.

The East

When a candidate stands at the edge of the carpet for the first time, he ought to be standing in the west, as explained in the answer to question 11 in the Edinburgh Register House MS (page 62), assuming that the Lodge room is oriented east–west.* This being the case, he will be facing the east side of the Lodge room, where the master of the Lodge is positioned in the centre, often seated in an imposing chair and with a dais before him. The master is usually flanked by some of the senior officials of the Lodge, including any visiting masters from

* It is not uncommon for Lodge rooms not to be oriented east–west, either because the building was not built as a Masonic Temple or if it was then the site would not allow for that layout. Again it is important to bear in mind that it is essential, symbolically, to have the Lodge room arranged this way.

other Lodges and past masters of his own Lodge. Masonic protocol, the number and nature of the visitors, and how much space is available all govern who is permitted to sit in the east.

The master's dais is often equipped with a light, a gavel (much like that used by judges – and for the same purpose), a carafe of water and a glass (some meetings can last several hours) and a copy of the agenda for the business to be conducted at the meeting. As the master is in charge of the Lodge, his dais must always have a copy of the relevant Grand Lodge 'rules and regulations' and copy of the Lodge's own bylaws placed on it. Reference to these is occasionally required and so they must be on hand in case they are needed. It is also common for the Lodge's warrant or charter to be either on the dais or on display nearby. Every Freemason has the right to inspect the warrant or charter in order to confirm the legitimacy of the Lodge.

The master therefore presides over his Lodge from the east, which is the position of power and authority in the Lodge. Because of the proceedings' close connection with the first Lodge, which was located in the porch of Solomon's Temple (see question 10 of the Edinburgh Register House) and which could only have met there with Solomon's permission, the master of a Masonic Lodge is often referred to as 'the humble representative of King Solomon'. Note that he is a representative only and, what is more, only a representative whilst in the Lodge.

The Altar and Oaths

An altar, or dais, is almost always situated at the end of the chequered carpet in the east and is frequently positioned immediately in front of, or is part of, the master's dais. (As with the use of the word 'temple', the use of the word 'altar' has caused some to misunderstand the nature of a Masonic Lodge, but this matter and others of a similar nature will be discussed in Chapter 6.)

The altar is of prime importance as a piece of Lodge furniture because this is where Holy Books are placed, open, during meetings. The Bible is the book most commonly found on altars in the Western world, but increasingly it supports copies of the Torah, the Koran, the Bhagavad Gita, the Guru Granth Sahib and the Tripitaka (the Holy Books of Jews, Muslims, Hindus, Sikhs and Buddhists respectively).

Some Lodges have members of so many different faiths that their altars have to be large enough to carry all these works.

The altar is also where the candidate takes his oath or 'obligation' as a Freemason. I am sure that we have all heard lurid claims about the bloodcurdling oaths taken by Freemasons, and I shall be dealing with that aspect in Chapter 6, but it is worth mentioning that the practice of taking oaths is hundreds of years old and that there is nothing intrinsically sinister about it. In medieval times it was an annual occurrence for vassals to swear an oath of fealty (obligation) to their lord. This oath was given by the vassal placing his right hand on the Bible, or occasionally on a holy relic such as the bones of a saint, and repeating the oath as spoken to him. Oaths were commonplace in the medieval period and were a legally binding means to reinforce the feudal system. Although they were not part of the feudal system in the same way as the rural areas, towns also had a system of oaths. Burgesses (members of the town community who had full municipal rights) were required to take an oath, as were mayors and other officials:

> Burgess' oath, 1346
>
> They are sworn that they shall be at lot and scot in all aids [imposed on] the town of Ipswich whenever and to whatever extent shall be necessary and whenever they are forewarned to contribute to the same by the officers of the town. And that they shall not pretend to be their own the goods or merchandize of foreigners or outsiders. And that they shall resolutely conceal the secrets of the town. And that they shall be obedient to the bailiffs and their [i.e. the bailiffs'] officers and to the coroners of the town who are, or shall be, not causing any dissension or conspiracy to the disturbance of the town. And that each one of them shall have a residence within the town liberties within a year and a day; if not, then the liberties granted to them shall forever be considered void.*

Medieval woodcuts show that these oaths were taken at a gathering of the members of the town council. The mayor or burgess placed his right hand on a Bible and repeated the oath read to him. An official stood nearby with a drawn sword and others were present with a mace or staff of office.

* History of Medieval Ipswich, at http://www.trytel.com/~tristan/towns/ipswich9.html.

Figure 10 The initiation of a Freemason. (From *Hiram: or the Grand Mystery to the Door of both Ancient and Modern Free-Masonry*, 2nd edn, London 1766.)

Today oaths are not used as frequently as they once were, and when they are taken, they tend to be couched in simpler and plainer language. For example, when the President of the United States of America is inaugurated as President he takes the following oath of office:

> I do solemnly swear that I will faithfully execute the Office of President of the United States, and will to the best of my ability, preserve, protect and defend the Constitution of the United States.*

The inauguration takes place out of doors and the President places his right hand on the Bible.

The Bible used by George Washington was a King James Authorized version printed in 1767.† It was provided by St John's Lodge No. 1, New York City, which still owns it. The Bible is offered to each incoming President and many have used it to take the oath.‡ At the conclusion of the oath, George Washington said, 'I swear, so help me God', and this has been part of the oath ever since.

The Masonic oath (or obligation as it is frequently called) is taken on a Holy Book in the same way that it was in previous centuries. The

* Article II, Section 1, of the Constitution.
† Another indirect connection to Scotland – James VI and I was a Scot.
‡ The Bible is usually on display at Federal Hall in lower Manhattan.

reason why this is still done in Masonic Lodges is simply because the use of a holy book adds sanctity to the oath – sanctity in the sense of inviolability. It is also intended to reinforce the serious nature of the oath and thereby the serious nature of the journey that the new Freemason is embarking upon. A long oath taken on a holy book makes an impression on the mind and it is hoped that this will assist all Freemasons to easily recall the lessons the oath contains.

The Masonic oath stands out from all the others because of its content and because it has not changed for hundreds of years. This means that certain elements of it sound decidedly strange to modern ears, owing to our inability today to understand readily what these elements mean, what they stand for and what their purpose is. It is here that we come across the 'rolled-up trouser leg' imagery frequently used to poke fun at Freemasons. In addition to the use of a holy book, the candidate is reminded physically of the oath's serious nature by having his right trouser leg rolled up. He kneels in front of the altar and places his hand (or hands) on the holy book of his faith and then repeats the obligation. The skin of his knee is in direct contact with the Lodge of which he is about to become a member: there is therefore nothing between him and the Lodge when he takes his obligation.

Brothers and Brethren

When the candidate takes his obligation, he makes an oath that offers him membership of a close community. The terms 'Brother' and 'Brethren' have long been used by Freemasons to refer to one another. This is almost certainly because stonemasons also addressed each other in this way. References to 'Brothers' and 'Brethren' appear in the Schaw Statutes of 1598, where the stonemasons to whom the statutes were addressed are described as sworn Brethren, meaning that they have taken an oath and sworn to be Brothers to one another. Today the Masonic meaning of the term is much wider. It is contained within the principal tenets of Freemasonry: Brotherly Love, Relief and Truth. Brotherly Love means love for the whole of humankind, which all Freemasons are taught to consider as one family and therefore treat accordingly.

Rough and Smooth Ashlars

An ashlar is a stone that has been prepared (dressed) by a stonemason and is ready to be used in a building. Question 12 in the Edinburgh Register House MS mentions an esler (ashlar) and, as with other tools and materials used by stonemasons, these have been adopted by modern Freemasons.

When a stone is quarried it is normally quite rough and unsuitable for use in a building. It is the job of the stonemason to transform it into a smooth one, and the process involves repeated exertion and considerable skill. As the stonemason witnessed the stone change from something rough and unusable into something smooth and useful, the process was transferred from the physical to the mental plane.

The candidate is perceived as being the rough ashlar which, through Freemasonry, is improved. (A non-Mason, a potential candidate, may also be thought of as a rough ashlar.) The metaphor implies that, through Freemasonry, the candidate becomes a better person, to the benefit of all. This idea of working at an individual level (the microcosm) in order to improve the rest of humanity (the macrocosm) is very reminiscent of the Hermetic attitude discussed in Chapter 3. This is a typical example of the way that stonemasons and, later, Freemasons adapted everyday work activities and used them for self-improvement in the company of others within the privacy of their Lodges.

The rough and smooth ashlars are normally positioned in the Lodge room so that they are in plain view at all times. This is so that they serve as constant reminders to everyone present of what they were (or perhaps still are!) and what, with some effort, they may become. There is no set position, but it is important that they are clearly visible. I have seen them positioned at the corners of the carpet so that the candidate stands between them, which is another way of demonstrating the potential of the journey through Freemasonry (albeit directionally from north to south). The ashlars are commonly placed in the east, to the right and left of the master's dais, as this is often a space that can be viewed by most, if not all, of those present.

Frequently the smooth ashlar is shown suspended from a rope attached to a tripod known as a 'Lewis'. Although the term is applied to the entire apparatus, strictly speaking a Lewis is the clamp that fits into a hole cut in the stone, which when lifted locks inside the stone. It's used to move heavy stones into their final position in a building, and symbolically the stone in the Lewis indicates the point just before the stone has attainted its ultimate purpose, its near perfect state. The smooth ashlar within the Lewis may be in addition to the smooth ashlar by the master's dais (or situated elsewhere), or it may be a replacement for it. In practice, both ought to be present somewhere in the Lodge room. Although the Lewis is often held to be a piece of Lodge equipment that is present in every Masonic Lodge, whilst it is common throughout England it is rare in Lodges in Scotland and America. This is perhaps owing to the fact that Freemasons in one country may emphasize one particular aspect of the practice, but not another. Indeed, there may be substantial differences between Masonic practice in one county and another.

The Wardens

There are two other daises in the Lodge room, for the senior warden and the junior warden. The structure of the Lodge is hierarchical, ranging from the newest member to the master. The wardens are two of the most senior officials in the Lodge. Part of the ritual explains that 'Three rule a Lodge: the Master and his two Wardens', but in fact the members themselves ultimately make the decisions under the leadership of the master and wardens.

The junior warden is placed in the south and the senior warden in the west. This shows us that the Lodge layout has changed since that described in the Edinburgh Register House MS, as have the titles of the individuals. These changes are probably a reflection of the changes in the ritual after 1717 when Freemasonry began to be 'organized' on a national, rather than local, level.

The Three Columns

Many Lodges have three columns, which are positioned one on each side of the master's and wardens' daises. These columns represent three of the orders of architecture; the Ionic column is placed on the master's dais, the senior warden's has a Doric column and the column for the junior warden is that of the Corinthian order. The three columns represent wisdom, strength and beauty respectively, the

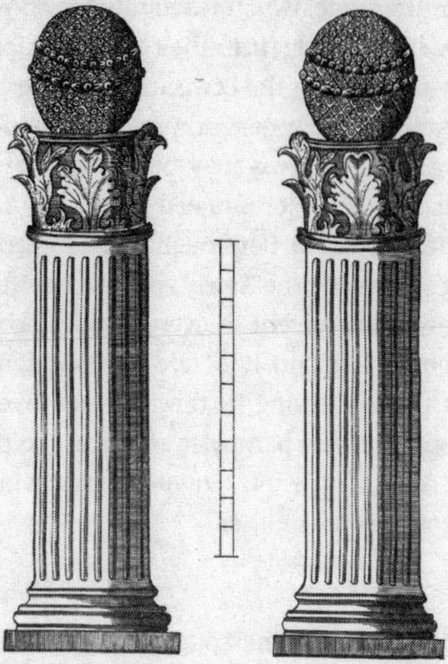

Figure 11 A seventeenth-century engraving of the two pillars, Jachin and Boaz, in the porch of King Solomon's Temple. (From *Orbis Miraculum or the Temple of Solomon Portrayed by Scripture Light*, London, 1659.)

separate attributes that these three individuals ought to focus upon whilst holding their office.

The position of the columns indicates what is taking place in the Lodge room at any particular time: the master's Ionic column is always upright; the senior warden's is laid flat during any adjournments, while the junior warden's is upright during them.

The Keys to the Lodge

The Edinburgh Register House MS and other early rituals refer to the Key of the Lodge, what it is and where it is to be found, making it probably one of the most important esoteric elements of early Freemasonry. The stonemasons clearly enjoyed playing with words and the Key to the Lodge represents another aspect of Lodge activity in which they may have indulged in a bit of wordplay. Before the days of banks, Lodges kept their money in strong wooden boxes that would have two, or more often three, locks and keys. Lodge members paid in money, usually every three months, which was used for various purposes, such as providing charity to the widows and orphans of stonemasons, paying rent and buying food and drink. The Lodge's box could only be opened when all three key holders were present and consented to act together to unlock it. This is tantalizingly similar to the part of the Masonic ritual relating to Hiram Abiff's statement that the secrets of Freemasonry were known but to three in the world, and that each of the three had to be present and to give their consent before the secrets could be spoken aloud. In terms of the stonemasons' love of wordplay, if the key mentioned in the Edinburgh Register House MS unlocks a secret, then the key to opening the Lodge 'bank' would reveal that secret, i.e. how much money they had in their coffers!

Lodge boxes are referred to in numerous Lodge records, some several hundreds of years old. The three who held the keys were known as 'Boxmasters' and can be thought of as the guardians of the Lodge's secrets. So, did the early boxes contain more than just money? If so, what could this have been?

Today Lodges use banks, but it is interesting to note that Lodge cheques still need three (or two) signatures before Lodge funds can be taken out of the bank.

The Degrees

As we saw in Chapter 4, at the time of the Edinburgh Register House ritual in the 1690s, there were two degrees of Freemasonry, entered apprentice and fellow craft, with the third degree, master mason, formally added in the 1720s. The degrees are, in effect, plays in which the candidate is one of the actors, albeit one who has had no rehearsal for his acting part.

This lack of rehearsal is deliberate for two reasons: firstly, it is part of the historical continuity with the past, and secondly, it demonstrates that the candidate trusts those he seeks to join. A candidate seeks to become a Freemason of 'his own free will and accord' and in so doing accepts that he can be told little and experience nothing *before* he becomes a Freemason. In return for his trust, Freemasonry assures the candidate that he will not be asked to do or say anything that might cause him physical or mental pain, nor to break any laws or to experience conflict with his duties as a husband, citizen or employee or as the member of any faith. All this creates a special and unique relationship between the member and the organization. It maintains the mystique. The candidate takes part in each degree in the same way that every other Freemason before him has, and is the first lesson of mutual trust and respect, which the Freemason is taught to extend to everyone, to every other human being.

The Entered Apprentice

The entered apprentice degree is the first of three 'plays' in the craft series and is the candidate's introduction (called an 'initiation') to Freemasonry. Without divulging the details, great care is taken to ensure that the candidate is aware of the nature of the journey that he is about to embark upon. This first degree, like all others, contains moral lessons that are designed to improve the candidate as a human being. These lessons embrace the qualities of, for example, prudence, temperance, fortitude, and especially charity.

The moral lessons are based on an interpretation of stonemasons' working tools: the twenty-four-inch gauge, the mallet and the chisel are delivered to the candidate and an allegorical or traditional history of the Order is narrated. The most elaborate 'visual aid' is the tracing board (see Chapter 6). Tracing boards have been used in Masonic Lodges for hundreds of years and, as Freemasonry is nothing if not traditional, it is likely that they will continue to be used well into the future. There is a different tracing board for each degree, each one depicting a confusing jumble of apparently disassociated symbols (especially in the First and Third degrees). This is deliberate as it requires a knowledgeable Freemason to 'trace' and explain the meaning of the symbols.

The Fellow Craft

The Second, or fellow craft, degree focuses on encouraging the candidate to educate himself daily. A number of different moral lessons are provided, including those of candour, friendship and mercy, to name but three. Working tools are again used as visual aids; in this instance, the square, level and plumb rule. A different tracing board with different symbols, and with different moral lessons associated with each symbol, is used in this degree.

The Master Mason's Degree

The culmination of the three degrees, which must be completed before anyone can be a candidate for any other branch of Freemasonry, is the Third or master mason's degree. This is the most dramatic degree and is also designed to reinforce the lessons of the previous two degrees.

The central character in the degree is now well known to the public: Hiram Abiff. It is important to understand that the Masonic Hiram Abiff is not a real person. The Old Testament mentions an individual of that name; however, although there may be some distant connection to that individual, the Masonic Hiram is involved in activities that are not described anywhere in the Bible.

In Masonic lore, Hiram Abiff is described as being the principal architect of King Solomon's Temple. As such, he was more familiar than anyone else with the design of the temple. He visited it every day at midday, when the workers were having a meal, in order to say personal prayers. This provided an opportunity for three fellows of craft (also known as the three ruffians) to threaten him with death in an attempt to get him to reveal the secrets of a master mason. These fellows of craft were worried that work would finish on the temple before they could be promoted to the degree of master mason, which would mean that they would be denied access to the secrets (and therefore all the privileges) associated with that degree.

Hiram Abiff explained that the secrets were known only to three in the world, the other two being Hiram King of Tyre and King Solomon, and that he had sworn an oath to reveal the secrets only when the other two were present. His refusal led to his death, as the ruffians decided that violence was the only means by which to advance their cause. They stationed themselves at the three entrances of the temple, attacking Hiram at each one. They wounded him in the first two attacks and killed him at the third and last entrance. But Hiram had refused, even at the point of death, to divulge the secrets. The fellows of craft were therefore not only murderers but had gained nothing for their crime. The three fellows of craft placed his body in a shallow grave and attempted to disguise it by covering it with an acacia plant. Then they fled.

The absence of Hiram Abiff was eventually noticed when work on the temple ground to a halt as he was not there to give directions. A roll-call revealed his absence and a search was made for him by three groups of fellows of craft (with fifteen men in each group). One group found nothing. Another accidentally discovered the grave and, after noting its location, returned to King Solomon for further instructions. The third and last group found and captured the three murderers, and the three ruffians were executed for their crime.

The death of Hiram caused a number of problems, including the fact that the secrets (which could only be communicated when the three principal characters were together) had now been lost. King Solomon instructed the group who had discovered Hiram Abiff's grave to return to the site and recover the body. Recovering the corpse, which had by now been buried for some time, was a gruesome task. The fellows of craft used techniques (grips) learned during the course of their work but these failed. A third fellow of craft, who was more knowledgeable, raised the body out of the grave using the five points of fellowship. King Solomon had instructed that they were to note any unusual signs or postures that might be of significance. These were duly noted and later became the substituted secrets of the Third degree until such time as the genuine ones were recovered.

Hiram Abiff could not be laid to rest in the inner sanctum of the temple because he was a mere human but was buried as near to it as the law would permit in recognition of his position and contribution in building the temple.

In the ceremony of the Third degree, the candidate represents Hiram and once the degree has been concluded he is often described as having been 'raised'. This has caused some commentators to suggest that the degree represents a resurrection, perhaps even the Resurrection of the New Testament. As is often the case, they miss the point.

You will have noticed that, in relating Hiram's story, I am only outlining some parts of the ritual. There are several reasons (apart from the confines of space) why I am not willing to provide the ritual in all its detail. Firstly, it is what it transmits that is important, which involves much more than can be conveyed by a written description. Merely reading about a Masonic ritual will not afford a true understanding of it, just as the possession of a book on how to play football does not confer the ability to play the game. Freemasonry is not about words on a page: Freemasonry is a way of life. Secondly, the ritual is private. I don't doubt that you will be able to find details of it if you search for them, but just because someone such as Samuel Prichard (and many others since) stole it and published it 276 years ago does not, in my view, justify my doing so now.

In any event, once the ceremony has been completed and the Third degree has been attained, the candidate is now a full member of the Craft and can participate in nearly all of the Lodge's activities. He has, for example, voting rights and other privileges, such as wearing an apron that shows him to be a master mason (see page 112). The exceptions are, for example, that he cannot become Master of the Lodge, at least not immediately, as he is still too inexperienced and would normally be expected to take on humbler duties first, whilst learning more about Freemasonry.

This Third degree completes the series and many are content to remain at this position within Freemasonry, which is unsurprising given the immense amount of material, lessons, symbolism and Masonic lore that are conveyed during these three ceremonies.

6

TOOLS OF THE TRADE

Words, Signs and Grips

Many people believe that the Masonic secrets take the form of particular words, signs or funny handshakes (known as 'grips'), but in this they are mistaken. Words, signs and grips are simply methods used by Freemasons to recognize each other and to explain where they are in the Masonic 'system'.

Their origins lie with the medieval stonemasons. When they first established their incorporations, every tradesman within a town or village knew all the other members of that trade, and it was impossible to set up shop without the established craftsmen's approval. Before he could earn his living, an up-and-coming craftsman had to pass a test of his ability so that he could be admitted to the appropriate incorporation.

However, unlike those craftsmen who plied their skills exclusively within walls of the medieval burghs, stonemasons were mobile, moving from building site to building site outside the towns of Scotland, wherever work was to be found. In an age when the majority hardly ever ventured beyond the boundaries of their home burgh or village, the stonemasons often had to travel considerable distances.

As we have seen, the evidence suggests that most stonemasons, like most tradesmen, were illiterate. How then to communicate to prospective employers that they were stonemasons and, most importantly, the level of their skill? It would not have been feasible to ask a stonemason to prove his capabilities by working on stone, and some form of 'shorthand' would have enabled him to communicate simply and authoritatively. If apprentices used different signs, words and grips to fellows of craft (which are also different in modern Freemasonry to the master masons'), then any stonemason's level of skill could be determined quickly and easily.

Today, if you are a member of a trade union, you will have a membership card to prove it, and without the card you can't attend meetings or use the union's services. The majority of modern Freemasons, however, have kept to the traditional methods of using signs, words and grips.* After all, this system has worked for hundreds of years, so why fix what ain't broke – as the saying goes; there's nothing sinister about it.

The so-called secrets of Freemasonry are not the same as these proofs of membership. The secrets are contained within the teachings of Freemasonry themselves. And, whilst it is almost impossible to know what they are without actually being a Freemason, it is sadly true that many Freemasons do not know what the secrets are either. There is a saying used by some Freemasons: 'There are many more Freemasons in the world than those who have actually been initiated.'

Tracing Boards

As briefly discussed in Chapter 5, tracing boards are another important tool in Freemasonry and play a central part in the initiation of new candidates. They are essential tools in the ceremonies of the three degrees. Each tracing board represents a means by which all the symbols associated with a particular degree can be gathered together in one place. Freemasonry contains a wealth of symbols, with a number that are common throughout the Craft, but each degree has symbols that are exclusively relevant to it, and it is these that are given prominence on tracing boards.

The tracing board is used as a visual aid when a tracing-board lecture is given. These explain the symbols and, as the lectures can sometimes be quite lengthy, the use of the tracing board often helps to keep the lecturer on track. It is said that only twenty to thirty per cent of information communicated verbally is remembered, but that this

* I am aware that in a number of countries Masonic membership cards are now used.

percentage increases dramatically when supported by visual material in the form of a whiteboard, slides or film. The tracing board is therefore the Freemasons' PowerPoint presentation!

Tracing boards are typically stored in a box from which they can easily be slid out and put on display. I have also seen them individually hung up but covered by curtains, with the relevant one being revealed for the degree in question. Only one tracing board should be on view at any one time and it must always be the one that pertains to the degree being conferred. The display of the tracing board thereby shows everyone present which degree the Lodge will be conferring without the need for questions. This is one small example of how Lodges attempt to maintain the decorum of their meetings and reduce the need for small talk.

The First-Degree Tracing Board

The symbolism on tracing boards developed in tandem with Masonic ritual. One of the most striking aspects of a tracing board is its seeming jumble of symbols, which have no apparent connection with each other. But, unlike words in a sentence, there is no need for symbols to be linked obviously in order to convey meaning.

The First-degree tracing board is dominated by the pillars representing the Doric, Ionic and Corinthian orders of architecture, symbolizing wisdom, strength and beauty, the attributes associated with the three who 'rule' a Lodge, i.e. the master and his two wardens. The square, level and plumb rule are the badges of those three.

Also shown are the rough and smooth ashlars, an altar with a book and the square and compasses (Figure 12, page 91). A sword lies against the Doric column, indicating the watchfulness of the tyler. A twenty-four-inch gauge, a mallet and a chisel are also depicted: these are the working tools of the First degree. All of these items are placed on a chequered carpet.

The background shows a sun, a moon and seven stars, with a seven-pointed star beneath them. Between the seven-pointed star and the altar is a ladder on which there are three symbols representing faith, hope and charity.

It now becomes clear that this image is nothing more than a stylized representation of the inside of a Masonic Lodge room, together with some of the moral lessons taught during the First degree.

Figure 12 The First-degree or Entered Apprentice degree tracing board.

First-Degree Working Tools: the twenty-four-inch gauge, the mallet and the chisel

Before the moral Masonic interpretations of the working tools are given, the use that working stonemasons made of them is explained. This is historically interesting as those who claim that modern Freemasonry has no connection with the actual craft of stonemasonry are at a loss to explain why Masonic ritual discusses what stonemasons did with the working tools before Freemasons took them over: 'But as we are not Operative, but Free and Accepted or Speculative Masons, we apply these tools figuratively and in a moral sense.'

Masonic ritual tells us that the twenty-four-inch gauge was used by stonemasons to measure and lay out their work, enabling them to calculate how long it would take to complete and thereby to fix a price. The Freemason learns from the stonemason that the twenty-four-inch gauge represents accuracy and precision; qualities, which, when applied to the Freemason's own life, will help him to conduct himself properly.

The mallet is the first tool that a stonemason learns to use correctly as it is one of his most important instruments and little can be achieved without it. In the example of the mallet, the Freemason sees that brute strength is useless without skill and that therefore all good ideas are useless without the means to put them into practice.

The last working tool is the chisel, which the stonemason uses for a variety of purposes but essentially because it 'brings form and regularity to the shapeless mass of stone'. In order to achieve this, the stonemason must learn how to use it properly and then must use it repeatedly. Only in this way can one stone after another be properly prepared and added one to the other to create a building. The Masonic interpretation of this is that education and perseverance are necessary to obtain perfection; that nothing but 'indefatigable exertion can induce the habit of virtue, enlighten the mind and purify the soul'.

The combination of all these Masonic elements provides a grander lesson:

> . . . that knowledge, grounded on accuracy, aided by labour and prompted by education and perseverance, will finally overcome all difficulties, raise ignorance from its native darkness and establish happiness in the paths of life.

The Second-Degree Tracing Board

Unlike the First-degree tracing board, that of the Second degree is recognizably of a place, and the two large pillars tell us exactly where: the porch or entrance to King Solomon's Temple (Figure 13, page 94). This tracing board is accompanied by a lecture in which the 'Traditional History of the Craft' (the first three degrees) of Freemasonry is explained. The story of how King Solomon's Temple was built is given in detail, including the Masonic interpretations of events.

This is an appropriate juncture at which to explain what is meant by 'Traditional History'. Each degree and branch of Freemasonry has its own special history, which is designed to impart its particular moral lessons. The first three degrees are centred on King Solomon's Temple, how it was built, by whom and for what purpose. We have seen how the temple has always had a special resonance for stonemasons and that it takes pride of place in the Masonic 'system', having been included in the first and, for a considerable time, the only Masonic ceremonies in existence, and we have seen that, in them, the Lodge is equated with the temple (specifically with the entrance to it, although many forget this). The Traditional History is therefore allegorical, designed to convey particular messages, moral lessons and Masonic lore.

The Second-degree lecture explains how those who built the temple received their wages: by giving a word known to fellows of craft, but not entered apprentices. This meant that those not entitled to the wages of the higher degree could not receive something to which they were not entitled. The lesson here is 'do not try to be something that you are not' or, at a simpler level, don't be dishonest.

On the tracing board there is a considerable use of numbers that possess hidden meanings (in much the same way that symbols are used), with the staircase in the porch of the temple being divided into three groups of three, five and seven steps. Three 'rule' a Lodge because three ruled over the building of King Solomon's Temple (Hiram King of Tyre, Hiram Abiff and, of course, King Solomon himself). Five 'hold' a Lodge, which is an allusion to the five orders of architecture (Tuscan, Doric, Ionic, Corinthian and Composite), as well as the five senses. Seven or more make a perfect Lodge, referring to the seven and more years it took to build the temple. Seven also refers to the seven liberal arts and sciences that the Second degree encourages the new Mason to study in order to improve his mind for the betterment of all mankind. The references to the numbers needed to rule, hold and perfect a Lodge may have derived from the earliest known rituals (see questions 7 and 8 in the Edinburgh Register House MS in Chapter 4).

Figure 13 The Second-degree or Fellow Craft degree tracing board.

Second-Degree Working Tools: the square, the level and the plumb rule

We have seen how these symbols are used to designate the three senior officials of a Lodge, the master, senior and junior wardens. They are shown in the tracing board as a reminder that these are the working tools of this degree. Once again, the use that stonemasons made of them is explained.

The mason's square is used to check and re-check the accuracy of an angle of ninety degrees on a stone being dressed or on any other right angle, such as those of corners. The square teaches the Freemason to regulate his conduct in accordance with Masonic morality and virtue, constantly checking and re-checking, in much the same way that the square is applied.

The level is a tool used to check that a stone is level and horizontal, and matches the level of any other stones already in position. To the Freemason, the level demonstrates that human beings are essentially all the same, sharing the same hopes and aspirations and, sooner or later, the same fate.

The plumb rule is needed to check verticals, to prove that they are true and upright. The Freemasons' interpretation of the plumb rule is that it teaches us to be upright in our dealings in all walks of life.

The combination of all this imagery culminates in another Masonic lesson:

> Thus the square teaches morality, the level, equality, and the plumb rule, justness and uprightness of life and actions. Thus, by square conduct, level steps, and upright intentions we hope to ascend to a higher realisation of that Immortal Principal, whence all goodness emanates.

The Third-Degree Tracing Board

The Third degree is the concluding part in the trilogy of the three plays of Craft Freemasonry and, as we have seen, the central character in it is Hiram Abiff. As explained in Chapter 5, the central theme of the degree is that, just prior to the completion of King Solomon's Temple, some of the fellow crafts who had helped to build it were fearful that it would be finished before they could be promoted to the degree of master mason and be granted the access to secrets and privileges that they believed to be their due. On Hiram's refusal to impart the secrets, the fellow crafts decided that violence was the only means by which they could obtain them.

The candidate playing the part of Hiram Abiff is 'killed' and then raised from a temporary grave. This is dramatic and is intended to leave an indelible memory in the mind of the candidate. But this means he will never, it is hoped, forget the lessons being taught in this degree. These are principally the lessons of honour, trust and fidelity. Although the candidate is 'killed' and raised, it is subsequently explained to him that this was merely a figurative death in order to make him think. The dramatic nature of the experience is intended to suggest to him strongly that now would be a good time to reassess his life. To put it bluntly, it is designed to make him realize that he now has a second chance and that, with the guidance provided by the principles of Freemasonry, he will hopefully make good use of that second chance.

The tracing board of this degree appears to depict a jumble of unrelated symbols in much the same way that the First-degree tracing board does. But whereas the tracing board of the First degree has the effect of slight disorientation, that of the Third degree suggests a morbid or perhaps sinister message (see Figure 14, page 98). This is because this tracing board is dominated by a coffin and, as we all know, a coffin represents death. However, the *Masonic* symbol of the coffin does not represent death but is a reminder of it, a reminder that we all share the same inevitable fate. At the head of the coffin is a plant, actually a sprig of acacia such as that used to disguise the grave of Hiram Abiff (see Chapter 5, page 85). At the head of the coffin (on it) are the three working tools of this degree: the skirret, the compasses and the pencil. Below the working tools is a Masonic cipher.

A skull and two crossed bones are also prominent on the coffin. This is one of the most misunderstood, or misused, Masonic symbols. The combination of skull and bones was a common feature on gravestones in Britain after the Reformation(s).* As an emblem of mortality, it has long been used as a reminder of the inevitability of death and here too, within Freemasonry, it serves the same purpose in the same way as the coffin. It is also possible that it has some connection with the

* 1540 in England, 1559 in Scotland.

Edinburgh Register House MS ritual questions 12 and 13 (see Chapter 4), which refer to a grave and a 'bone box'. As a Masonic symbol it has nothing to do with pirates! Instead it is a very specific Masonic reminder of the untimely death of Hiram Abiff and a general reminder of the ultimate end for us all. The skull and crossed bones are often found in Masonic symbolism, together with the scythe and the hour glass. These too are reminders of the inevitability of death and are an implicit appeal (to the Freemason in this context) to take the opportunity to change for the better before it is too late.

Below this is a depiction of the porch of King Solomon's Temple and the chequered pavement. We have previously seen, in the Edinburgh Register House MS, that the first Lodge was said to have been in the porch of King Solomon's Temple and that connection between the Lodge and temple is again visually presented here as it is in the Second-degree tracing board. The chequered carpet, or pavement, is also mentioned in the Edinburgh Register House MS and is a prominent feature in many European Lodges. Its presence here in the porch of King Solomon's Temple is therefore quite consistent.

Through the porch it is just possible to see, indistinctly, into the temple, which is illuminated through a dormer window. For the first time, we are afforded a glimpse of the interior of the temple, but even then it is very obscure. This is because only the high priest could enter and have a clear view of the inner sanctuary. This imagery serves as an important reminder that Freemasonry is not a religion and can only view such matters at a distance. In order for the inner recesses of the temple to be seen, however poorly, one has to look through the Masonic Lodge, which is situated in the porch of the temple. The Lodge therefore allows for potentialities – possible futures – to be glimpsed, but only if the lessons of the degree are taken to heart and acted upon. The dormer, a window of the Lodge, casts some light – however dimly – on those potential futures and again suggests that the Masonic Lodge can, if used correctly, help the candidate see his way to a better future.

Below this image are a square, a level and a plumb rule, the working tools of the Second degree. Their presence here is because these were the tools used by the three fellows of craft to twice wound and then kill Hiram Abiff. These are a potent reminder to all Freemasons that even the most honourable decisions can result in the most unpleasant consequences.

This tracing board is the most enigmatic of the three because it is open to more personal interpretation than the others. The new member has been made to represent Hiram Abiff and, in that role, encouraged to consider moral choices made under extreme conditions, such as at the point of confronting death. The intention is that he will reflect upon his life before and after the experience, and hopefully will take the chance to improve himself in all respects.

Figure 14 The Third-degree or Master Mason's degree tracing board.

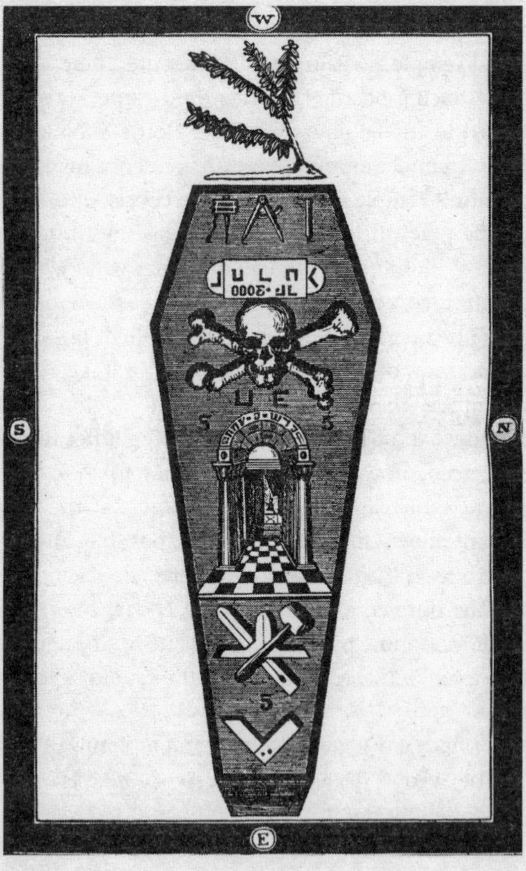

Third-Degree Working Tools: the skirret, the pencil and the compasses

The skirret is a tool that uses string coiled on a central pin. Coated with chalk, the string is used to provide a straight line for the foundations of a structure. In this, the Speculative Mason sees the moral lesson of the need to be straight in his dealings with everyone. This is one of the simplest and most important lessons for a Freemason.

The pencil is an essential tool for the stonemason to draft his plans and make calculations, but for the Freemason it is a reminder that TGAOTU (the Great Architect of the Universe, see page 229) already has a plan of which we are a part, and that all our decisions and actions ought to be made with this in mind.

The compasses are used by stonemasons to accurately draw a circle or parts thereof. For the Freemason, the compasses are one of the most important esoteric symbols available. However, despite the fact that they are a well-known symbol, their Masonic importance may not be common knowledge. They symbolize the need for the Freemason to raise himself above material considerations; inescapable though these considerations are, they must be placed in their proper context and not over-indulged. More specifically, the compasses direct the attention towards three great Masonic attributes of virtue, morality and brotherly love. This way of viewing the compasses might well have some connection with the manner in which stonemasons hundreds of years ago used them to make moral points, for example:

Sa gays ye compass evyn about
sa truth and laute do but doute
be hauld to ye hend q johne mordo

So goes the compasses evenly about
so truth and love you cannot doubt
remember your end quotes John Mordo

John Mordo (or Morrow) was a French stonemason from Paris who worked on several ecclesiastical buildings in Scotland during the late fourteenth and early fifteenth centuries. He was the master mason in Melrose Abbey, where this inscription is to be found together with the symbol of interlaced compasses. Whilst we must be careful not to

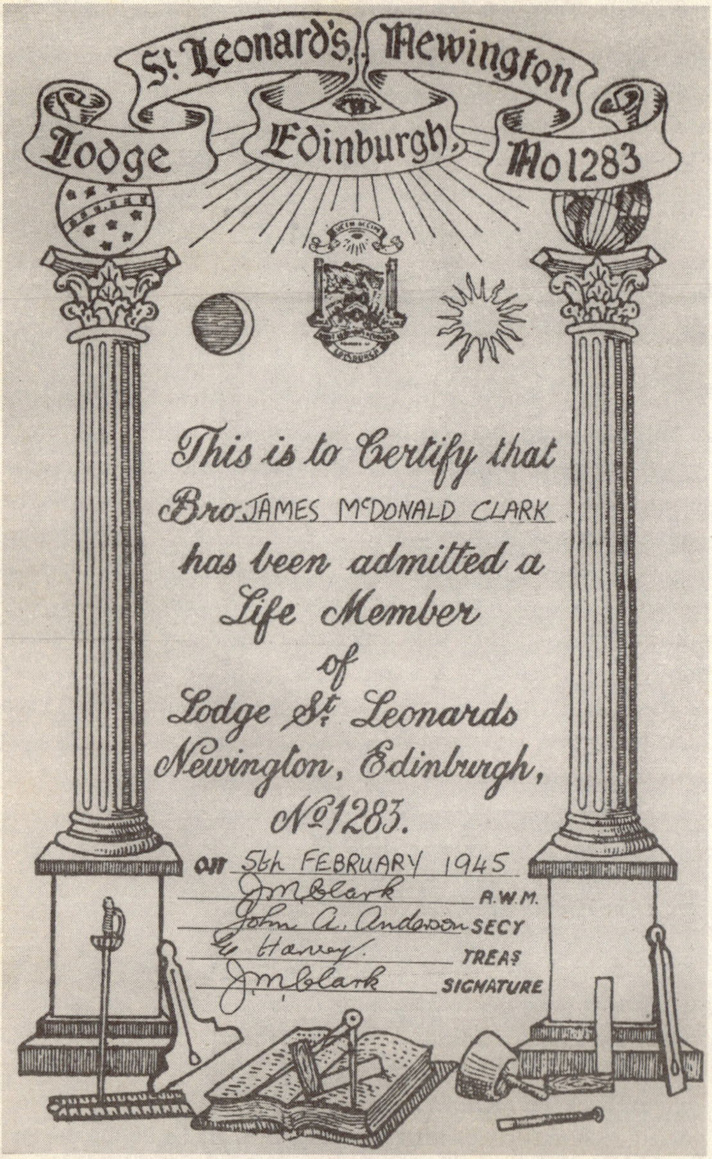

Figure 15 A Life Membership certificate issued by a Craft Lodge, which is loosely based on the imagery of the First-degree tracing board. Freemasons are given a number of certificates throughout their Masonic careers.

read too much into these few lines, it is clear that the compass (or 'compasses', as we more often describe them today) meant a lot more than just a working tool to this particular stonemason. In fact, whereas the lines contain no reference to their operative use, the last line charges the reader to contemplate 'your end', much in the same way as the other symbolism of the modern Third degree. When taken with the symbol (the above text is actually carved around it) it seems obvious that this symbol had a powerful esoteric content for this master mason.

7

SYMBOLS AND SIGNS

Freemasons truly love their symbols. As we have seen, Freemasonry itself has been described as 'a peculiar system of morality, veiled in allegory and illustrated with symbols'. There is an immense number of Masonic symbols, which has meant that some have fallen into disuse and the meaning of others has subtly changed over time. However, symbolism continues to play an important role in Freemasonry around the world.

The Origins of Masonic Symbolism

The most obvious symbol of an individual Freemason is his apron. A modern Masonic apron is rectangular and is obviously too small to be practical. Like many other things worn or used by Freemasons, the apron may therefore seem strange to non-Masons as it appears to serve no obvious practical purpose, but nevertheless it has an important symbolic function.

In order to understand the significance and development of Masonic symbolism such as aprons, we need to turn to the early days of Freemasonry. We know that early Freemasons wore the same kind of aprons as the stonemasons did. The stonemasons' were for protection during their working day, and the stonemasons took them and other familiar items such as their working tools with them when they attended their lodges in the evenings. But they did not use these items in their lodges in the same way as they used them on a building site. In the lodges these items became visual aids – symbols with which they could moralize.

For example, during the working day a square would have been used to check the accuracy of the angle of ninety degrees, i.e. whether a stone had been accurately 'squared'. At work, a stonemason would have received stone that had been roughly cut in the quarry, and perfected it by dressing it. The measurements of the square proved that something previously imperfect had been perfected. This process of perfecting a stone was achieved by perseverance, skill and hard work. In a lodge, which was obviously not a building site (although occasionally it may have been in one), the square was used for something quite different: it became a symbol. In his lodge the stonemason did not dress stone, but he used the square in an esoteric manner. He applied the square metaphorically to himself and to his fellow stonemasons, their lives and their actions. The example of the stonemasons' square continues to have different meanings at different times and in different situations.

In the days when the stonemasons were creating and developing their lodges and ceremonies, the great majority of the general population was illiterate. The medieval Church, for which the stonemasons built the great European cathedrals as well as other more humble structures, developed ways to explain the basic principles of the Christian faith to those who could not read. Stained glass, for example, was used to depict stories from the Bible. At one level stained glass could operate as a 'picture book', but simple representations of biblical stories would not have been adequate to transmit the more mystical or esoteric elements of Church teaching. An elaborate system of symbolism was therefore developed. There was, for instance, a range of symbols to represent Jesus Christ, the Holy Trinity and the Crown of Thorns, and other symbols were used to represent people, things and events as well as abstract concepts such as immortality, the resurrection and miracles.

Symbols and Signs

Unfortunately, few of us today can readily interpret symbols whose meaning would have been easily understood by most people in Europe during the medieval period. At the time of the Reformation (c. 1559 in Scotland) much Church ornamentation was condemned as idolatrous and destroyed or removed. The use of symbolism, and therefore knowledge of its meaning, has declined to the extent that some four hundred and fifty years later few understand medieval Catholic symbolism, its meaning or how it ought to be interpreted. The recent century has seen an accelerated secularization of society and this has contributed greatly to our inability to appreciate a true understanding of religious symbolism. Once symbols fall into disuse their meaning and purpose are lost to all but a few. They become part of a dead language.

In an increasingly secular, materialistic and empirical world we lack the ability to understand symbols that society once possessed. By symbols I mean something that is not a sign. There is an important difference to be explained here. Signs are designed for a specific purpose, e.g. to impart a particular piece of information such as 'roadworks ahead'. A sign does not have to impart any other layers of information, whereas a symbol is intended to transmit more than what can be seen at a superficial level, abstract concepts as well as facts. A symbol can therefore be a sign but a sign cannot be a symbol. No sign can say 'idea ahead' as if referring to roadworks.

Today there is a temptation to interpret most of what we see at the simple level of signs, signs with only a single, literal explanation or message. That is all well and good when it involves a straightforward roadworks sign. However, if it involves an unfamiliar Masonic symbol, confusion and suspicion may arise, as people try to second-guess the symbol's meaning and purpose, usually getting it wrong. Superficial interpretations may sometimes be offered and frequently accepted as correct, because the number of people with the knowledge necessary to understand the original interpretation is now very small.*

This modern perception of symbolism is one reason why many Freemasons find ritual and symbolism difficult to understand, if not meaningless; many of us have lost the ability to understand that the symbol of, say, the square and compasses is much more than simply an image of measuring instruments – that there is much more to it than meets the eye.

How, then, do symbols 'work'? One method to explain this is by the use of metaphor. Imagine you're in a room with a window through which open countryside can be viewed. At a literal level, the window

* This also implies that the original interpretation was, and remains, the correct interpretation.

is merely an object made of wood and glass, and if you focus on it, the landscape beyond is not seen. However, if you refocus and look through it, you do see the world beyond. A symbol works in much the same way, but in order to use it you must understand that there's more to it than its literal components, just as there is more to a window than its wood and glass. A symbol can be used to look beyond your present location in time and space, to the realm of abstract ideas.

Symbols generally work on at least four different levels:

1 *The Obvious or Literal Level*

At this level the symbol is generally understood by all; to use our metaphor, a window is a window.

2 *The Metaphorical Level*

Not only is it a window but it can also be considered to be 'a window on the world' etc.

3 *The Personal Level*

This way of understanding a symbol is specific to an individual or particular group who, in addition to the general understanding (above), actively uses the symbol: 'the window gives me the ability to glimpse another place and/or time'.

4 *The Mystical Level*

At this level the symbol becomes fully operational and allows the individual (or perhaps a very small group) to experience the numinous.

These four distinctions are useful, but they are also artificial in that it is quite possible to experience some, or all, of these levels of symbolism at the same time.

Symbols create a junction between two realms of reality: the conscious and unconscious. They are a meeting point between the microcosm and the macrocosm, man and God, etc. This way of appreciating symbols is not understood by many people today, including a fair number of Freemasons.

Freemasonry adopted much Christian symbolism and iconography.* However, it must be remembered that Christianity predates Freemasonry and so Masonic interpretations cannot be applied to

* Freemasonry doubtless used other sources and invented some but the majority were adopted from Christianity.

symbols that are used in a Christian context. It would, for example, be misguided to attempt to read the symbols in a Christian church according to the meanings that the Freemasons later accorded them. It would also be a grave error to believe that the symbols of Christian origin that are now used within Freemasonry can be given a Christian interpretation. This is another crucial point regarding symbols in general: it is often the case that symbols used in different places or by different groups may look similar or identical but have very different meanings. The use of the swastika in India and in Hitler's Germany is one example of this.*

Just to confuse matters even further, not all Masonic symbols have a fixed meaning and not all Masonic symbols mean the same thing to different groups of Freemasons! This is because Freemasonry has no dogma and so, unlike religion, it does not impose a fixed interpretation of its 'code' on its members. Let me try to explain by using an example. The symbol of the square, compasses and letter G is probably one of the best-known Masonic symbols. (It is actually a combination of three different symbols.) Many people believe that the letter 'G' in the symbol stands for God. However, the people of some faiths do not accept that God can be reduced to a mere symbol, especially a symbol created by such an imperfect creature as a human being, and the suggestion that this letter 'G' represents God is unacceptable. I know members of the Jewish faith who are Freemasons; they believe instead

Figure 16 The square, compasses and letter G.

* The swastika was used by many other cultures including the Chinese, Japanese and Native Americans.

that the letter G stands for 'Goodness' – the goodness, actual or potential, in everyone. Muslims apply a different understanding and take the letter G to mean 'Geometry' or 'Geometric', which is eminently suitable for a moral system deriving from stonemasons, whose work is based on that science.*

Masonic symbolism is quite complex and is not fixed in the ways that many other symbolic codes are. It is little wonder that non-Masons become confused when a multitude of different explanations and interpretations are offered to them by different members of the same organization! It is this lack of consistency that sometimes makes the organization appear suspicious – because apparently no one can give a straight answer to a straight question. But, as you can see, there is actually nothing sinister about it: unusual – yes, inconsistent – yes, out of step – yes (especially in this day and age of uniformity), but dubious – not at all. Masonic symbolism suffers a double disadvantage: not only is symbolism as a whole rarely understood in this modern age, but Masonic symbolism has always been fluid and open to interpretation by individual Freemasons. Taking into account the perceptions of non-Masons, it would seem that there are just about as many interpretations available for Masonic symbols as there are the people to make them!

Some Specific Masonic Symbols, their Meanings and Purposes

Masonic symbols are the visual manifestations of Masonic ceremonial. There are essentially two kinds of Masonic symbolism: those tailored to the individual Freemason and those that refer to Freemasonry in general.

Personal Symbols

The Apron

A modern Masonic apron measures 16 inches wide by 14 inches deep. It clearly serves no practical purpose, but within a Masonic Lodge it

* The square and compasses together with the letter G is used infrequently in England but is much more common in Scotland. This is another example of the differences within Freemasonry between the two countries.

plays a very important symbolic role – so important, indeed, that no Freemason can attend a Lodge meeting without wearing one.

As we have seen, Freemasons originally wore the same sorts of apron as their forebears, the stonemasons. These were long, heavy, leather aprons that covered the body from the neck to the ankles, and were designed to protect both the stonemason's body and his clothes.* However, in a Lodge where no actual work on stone took place, long heavy aprons were not required. The records of the Lodge of Aberdeen, dating from 1670, contain the following reference: 'Ane linen apron and a pair of good gloves to be presented by intrants [entrants – initiates] to each of the Brethren'.† A working stonemason would have had no use for a linen apron, as it would provide little protection and be of poor durability when working with stone. That a linen apron, together with gloves, was to be presented to every member of the Lodge of Aberdeen shows that by this time aprons worn in the Lodge had acquired a symbolic use, whether its members were stonemasons or not, and on 18 January 1724, the Lodge of Dunblane recorded in the Minute Book that aprons and gloves were to be presented to all non-stonemasons, also indicating a symbolic and/or ceremonial – as opposed to practical – use of aprons by members of Lodges.‡

The image of the Incorporated Trades of Edinburgh (Figure 2) shows ten tradesmen engaged in their various crafts.§ Published in 1893, the image originally dates from 1721, some fifteen years before the Grand Lodge of Scotland was founded. At that time there were eight lodges in Edinburgh and a further nine in the surrounding counties. The incorporated trades illustrated are (from left to right): a sievewright, a slater, a glazier, a cooper, a mason, a wright, a bowmaker, a painter

* That medieval stonemasons wore aprons as protection during their work is demonstrated by a number of medieval illustrations, particularly from England and France, such as *The Building of 12 Churches by Count de Roussilon and His Wife* (French MS 1448), Österreichische Nationalbibliothek. (This has been reproduced many times, for example in W. Kirk MacNulty, *Freemasonry: a Journey through Ritual and Symbol*, Thames & Hudson, 1991).

† A. L. Millar, *Notes on the Early History and Records of the Lodge, Aberdeen*, 1919.

‡ David M. Lyon, *History of the Lodge of Edinburgh (Mary's Chapel), No. 1*, 1900 (Tercentenary edn).

§ R. S. Mylne, *The Master Masons to the Crown of Scotland* (Scott & Ferguson and Burness, 1893).

(artist), a plumber and an upholsterer. Of the nine, only one – the painter – is not wearing an apron.

All the aprons have flaps (or falls), and four or perhaps five of these have buttonholes for affixing the flap to a jacket or waistcoat.* The flap, upturned and fixed to a jacket, would provide some protection to the upper body. All the aprons are large, and cover (with the flap down) from the waist to below the knee. Unfortunately, the stonemason's left arm obscures the flap of his apron, and any similarities between it and the other tradesmen's cannot be determined. However, given the common elements of all the aprons, it is not unreasonable to think that the design was the same for all the trades that used aprons for protective purposes.†

It is never likely to be established exactly when or where Scottish lodges began to use aprons for ceremonial purposes, by either stonemasons or non-stonemasons, but it appears to have been by at least c. 1670. When the Revd James Anderson (1680–1739) published *The Constitution of the Free-Masons* (1723), the work included a frontispiece engraved by John Pine (see Plate 3).‡ A figure on the left (described as the tyler) is depicted carrying a number of large aprons draped over his right arm, and he also carries a number of gloves in his left hand.§ The engraving depicts the ceremonial handing over of the constitutions to the Duke of Montague by the Duke of Wharton (installed as Grand Masters in 1721 and 1722 respectively). The individuals in the engraving are all Freemasons, and the figure holding the aprons therefore appears to be a symbolic reference to the fact that initiations were due to take place after the presentation of the constitutions. As the candidates were to be given aprons and gloves at their initiation, this again strongly suggests that they had a symbolic and possibly a ritual purpose.

Anderson was born in Aberdeen, Scotland. His father, also James,

* Of the remaining aprons, the place where there may be a buttonhole is obscured.

† There is a wright's (carpenter's) apron in the Grand Lodge of Scotland Museum which is obviously for ceremonial use. It is likely that this also developed from an apron worn by an operative wright. The elaborate aprons of the Order of Free Gardeners (Chapter 10) perhaps indicate a similar evolution.

‡ This engraving was also used in the 1738 and 1746 editions.

§ F. R. Worts, 'The Apron and Its Symbolism' in *AQC*, 74:133.

was several times Master (and Secretary) of the Lodge,* and it was he who created the Lodge's Mark Book, dated 1670, in which the entry regarding the presentation of aprons and gloves has been previously mentioned.† It can only be conjectured that Anderson was aware of his father's Lodge's 'regulation' regarding aprons and gloves, or that he was in communication with his father during his writing of the constitutions.

When the Grand Lodge of Scotland was founded in 1736, William St Clair of Rosslyn (1700–1778) was elected the first Grand Master. A painting, in oils, hangs in the Chapel of St John, which was the meeting place of Lodge Canongate Kilwinning No. 2 (founded 1677). This painting shows him wearing an apron very similar in size and shape of the lower portion to that worn by the tradesmen in Figure 2. The addition of a green trim around the body and flap of the apron differentiates it from those worn by stonemasons. It is to be noted also that St Clair is wearing the apron *under* his jacket. Was this an attempt not only to indicate the descent from stonemasons but also show that modern Scottish Freemasonry was not now 'operative' in nature?‡

The process of embellishing aprons was not confined to Scotland. It seems that it began in England, as suggested by the following resolution of the Grand Lodge in 1721: 'None but the Grand Master, his Deputy and Wardens shall wear their jewels in Gold or gilt pendant to Blue Ribbons about their Necks, and White Leather aprons with Blue Silk; which sort of Aprons may be worn by former Grand officers.' The shade of blue to be used was Garter (dark) blue, named for the colour adopted by the Order of the Garter.§ The Grand Lodge of Scotland followed this example and adopted Thistle green, the colour of the Order of the Thistle, the highest chivalric order in Scotland. The Grand Lodge of Ireland anticipated, accidentally or otherwise, the

* James Anderson Snr was not an operative mason. He describes himself as a 'glassier [glazier], Measson [Mason – of the lodge] and Clerk to our honourable Lodge'.

† The Mark Book most likely dates from later, but probably includes information from 1670. See David Stevenson, *The First Freemasons* (Grand Lodge of Scotland, 2001).

‡ This is almost certainly why Scottish Freemasons wear their aprons under their jackets.

§ Worts points out that the Rawlinson MS (c. 1740) states: 'Two Grand Masters aprons lined with Garter blue silk'.

establishment of the Most Illustrious Order of St Patrick by choosing light blue as its colour.*

During the eighteenth century the Grand Lodge of Scotland did not make or impose any rules regarding Lodge aprons. No doubt this accounts for the wide variation in the size, shape, decoration and material used for aprons owned by individuals until the late nineteenth century.† In the first of its 'own' constitutions and laws (1804 and 1836), the Grand Lodge of Scotland made no mention of aprons, only of 'clothing'. It was not until 1848 that sizes and decoration of aprons for entered apprentices, fellow crafts, master masons and masters and past masters were given.‡

It has been shown that, in Scotland at least, lodges of stonemasons during the seventeenth century began to admit men who were not working masons, and that they were provided with aprons and gloves. As they were not stonemasons, they did not own such items and, on becoming members of the Lodge, aprons and gloves had to be provided to them, most probably for symbolic use during the ceremonies.

There is one apron of particular interest, which suggests a transition from working stonemasons to non-stonemasons, and that aprons were part of that transitional process. It is made from an animal skin, probably a sheep; the remains of the forelegs and the fall (the animal's neck) are present. The apron has had a flap and trim added, both in green. It seems that a plain white stonemason's apron was not considered suitable for use in the owner's Masonic Lodge.§ Unfortunately, it is not possible to date the apron with any accuracy, but it is thought to be from before 1800.

Over a period of approximately a hundred to a hundred and fifty years the Masonic version of the stonemasons' apron became smaller

* F. J. W. Crowe, 'Colours in Freemasonry' in *AQC* 17:3 (1904).

† Scottish lodges have the right to choose the colour(s) of their regalia.

‡ Even at this late stage these are recommendations only. This is probably why wide variations existed until recently.

§ For example, all the members (including office-bearers) of the Operative Lodge of Aberdeen, No. 150, wear plain white aprons in acknowledgement of their operative origins. In other words the Lodge has rejected Masonic finery in favour of a demonstration of their stonemasons' origins.

and more stylized.* Particularly during the nineteenth century, many Freemasons took the opportunity to decorate their aprons with a multitude of symbols to such an extent that the aprons almost became tracing boards in their own right (see Plates 6 and 7). Today, most countries use aprons trimmed with sky blue. Of course Scotland is the odd one out, as each Scottish Lodge adopts its own colours. Therefore, as far as the Scots are concerned at least, there is no such thing as a 'Masonic colour'.

Like Masonic jewels (see below), aprons can be used to show a Freemason's position within the Lodge hierarchy (I dislike using the term 'rank' when describing the organization of the Lodge, because all Freemasons are on an equal footing not only with each other but with the whole of the human race). An entered apprentice is clothed with a plain white lambskin apron, which he wears until he takes the fellow craft degree. Then the plain apron is exchanged for another plain white lambskin apron that has the simple addition of rosettes in its bottom right and left corners. The two rosettes refer to the first two degrees that the candidate has attained. In the master mason's degree the apron is again exchanged and the replacement has a third rosette added to the flap. The three rosettes form an equilateral triangle, showing that the candidate has completed the three degrees and is a master mason.† However, it is quite acceptable, especially in Scotland, to attend a Lodge meeting wearing a plain white apron (sadly now often made from some artificial material because lambskin is expensive and difficult to obtain – but it is the symbolism that counts), with or without rosettes. There are in fact a number of Lodges in which everyone, from the master to the newest member, wears a plain white apron, as a reminder that all members are the same, on the level. But that is uncommon and, like other Masonic symbols, aprons have undergone considerable elaboration and alteration.

* Another, non-Masonic, example of this process is that of the gorget. Originally this was a piece of armour that protected the neck and the shoulder area below. Over time this became a small, entirely decorative, metal collar.

† The Third degree is traditionally known as the highest degree in Freemasonry, which arises from the fact that for a very long time it was indeed the 'highest' degree obtainable as no others existed. The addition of other Orders of Freemasonry and the creation of a large number of other Masonic ceremonies did not change this view of Craft Freemasonry.

Those who hold positions (master, wardens, secretary and so on) within a Lodge usually have a symbol displayed on their apron flap. The secretary will typically have two crossed quill pens, the master a square (with its point upwards), the senior warden a level and the junior warden a plumb rule. Past masters may add two decorative levels instead of the two rosettes in the right and left corners to show they have been Master of a Lodge.

Breast Jewels

Most people would probably describe Masonic jewels as medals and there is more than a passing similarity between the two. Figure 17 shows a typical Masonic breast jewel. However, unlike military medals, Masonic jewels are primarily designed to indicate 'membership' of a variety of things, such as a Lodge. When a Lodge is founded it is usual for a Founder's jewel to be struck and all the Founder members of the new Lodge are entitled to wear it. Many Lodges also have a member's jewel which indicates membership of that particular Lodge, albeit not as a Founder member.

Figure 17 Drawing of a breast jewel of the Master of a Scottish Lodge.

Another common jewel is used to show that a Freemason is a past master. Once a Freemason has been Master of a Lodge, typically for one year although occasionally for longer, he is entitled to wear a past master's jewel. There is no standard motif for these jewels and individual countries may use different designs.

Jewels may also be used to show that a Lodge has reached a significant anniversary such as a centenary or bicentenary, or to show that someone has made valuable contributions to charity. Needless to say, the opportunity is taken to decorate such jewels with a variety of Masonic symbols, which are there to remind the wearer of some of the lessons taught by Freemasonry. These symbolic 'reminders' include, for instance, the 'All-Seeing Eye' (see page 116), the square, the compasses and the 47th Problem of Euclid (see pages 95, 99 and 121).

Collar Jewels

Whereas breast jewels are usually owned by the individual, collar jewels are normally the property of the Lodge and are worn by a Lodge official. Similarly to the way that positions in the Lodge are often marked by the use of symbols, the Lodge official wears a collar jewel to indicate his office. In some Lodges, only those in senior positions wear such jewels, but it is more usual for all officials to wear them. As the

Figure 18 Drawing of a collar jewel of a past master of a Scottish Lodge.

term suggests, collar jewels are worn suspended from a collar. On them, the master's symbol is the square (in Scotland it is the square, compasses united with an arc of ninety degrees with a sun 'in his splendour'), the senior warden's is the level and the junior warden's is the plumb rule.

General Symbols

The Lamb

The lamb is by no means the most important Masonic symbol, but it serves as a good illustration of the way in which early Freemasonry adopted and then adapted Christian imagery to suit its own ends.

Religious persecution of the early Christians often caused them to disguise their activities and frequently led to the use of symbols, the meaning of which was only known to members. The symbol of the fish remains familiar today, as early Christians used it to indicate that they were followers of Jesus Christ the 'fisher of men'. The lamb was another a symbol of Jesus Christ, from John 1: 36: 'Behold the Lamb of God'. The symbol of the animal was often combined with a Passion Cross to signify Christ as the Agnus Dei (Lamb of God). The Agnus Dei was introduced into the Catholic Mass by Pope St Segius I (687–701) and the symbol was in general use by the Church by the ninth century.

The Poor Soldiers of Christ and Solomon's Temple (the Knights Templar) adopted the symbol, with its first appearance within the order dating to 1241. The Knights Templar therefore adopted an existing Christian symbol and retained its Christian meaning. It is far easier to use an existing symbol than to design a new one from scratch and so, in adopting the symbol of the lamb, the Templars were doing what many others had done before and since.

However, the symbol of the lamb as it is used within Freemasonry is very different. For a start, it does not refer to a lamb *per se* but to lambskin. Masonic aprons, the apparel of the Masonic brotherhood, are traditionally made from lambskin and the symbol of the lamb in Freemasonry therefore refers to the qualities of innocence *and* friendship. In the First degree the Freemason is taught:

this apron is made from lambskin and as the lamb has been from time immemorial the acknowledged emblem of Innocence and Purity, it will remind you of that purity of life and actions which should at all times distinguish a Freemason.

The All-Seeing Eye

Within Freemasonry, the terms 'the All-Seeing Eye', 'the Radiant Eye', 'the Eye of Providence' and 'Eye of Omnipresence' refer to the image of a single eye which, like the square and compasses (with or without the letter G), is a well-known Masonic symbol.

The Masonic 'All-Seeing Eye' (see Figure 19) has nothing to do with the Eye of Horus symbol. Confusion between the two may have arisen because of the possible influence on Freemasonry of Hermeticism, which was incorrectly believed to have originated in ancient Egypt. Originally, the Eye of Horus was a sign of royal power and the protection of the god Ra, but over time Horus became more important, transforming into a sun god and replacing Ra.

The Masonic All-Seeing Eye does not relate to Horus or Ra. The symbol of a single eye representing God was, and to a certain extent still is, common within the Western Christian tradition. It can be seen in a number of churches and cathedrals across Europe, including some in Rome, Aachen and Tours, and it appears in several religious works of art such as the painting *Sacred Allegory* by the Flemish artist Jan Provost (1465–1529). The Masonic version of the symbol relates to a part of Masonic ritual that states:

> Let us remember that wherever we are and whatever we do, He is always with us and his all-seeing eye observes us; and while we continue to act in conformity with the principles of the Craft, let us not fail to discharge our duty to Him with fervency and zeal.

Figure 19 The Masonic All-Seeing Eye.

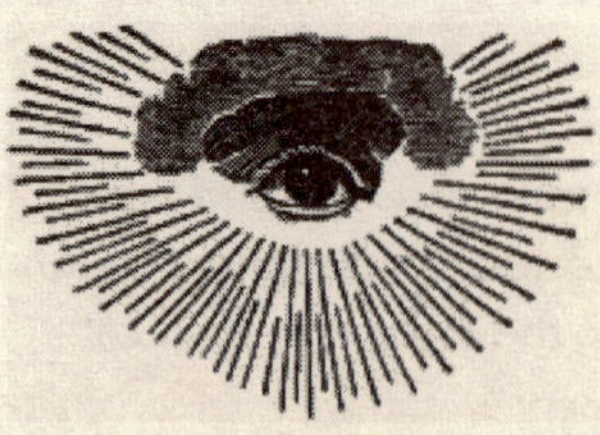

Figure 20 A detail from the title page of *The Spirit of Masonry* by William Hutchinson (1795). This shows one of the earliest uses of the All-Seeing Eye as a Masonic symbol.

'He' of the All-Seeing Eye is the Great Architect of the Universe (TGAOTU), a term which has the same meaning as Supreme Being. Freemasons try not to use the word 'God' because Freemasonry accepts men of all faiths, some of whom are – as we have seen in the discussion of the compasses above – uncomfortable with the explicit use of that word.

The symbol of the All-Seeing Eye in a pyramid is one that many people associate with Freemasonry. This appears to have arisen from the belief that on the reverse of the US one-dollar bill, the eye in the pyramid is a Masonic symbol that Freemasons were instrumental in having included in the bill's design. The one-dollar bill shows both parts of the Great Seal of the United States so this is the first flaw. The symbol would have had to have been incorporated into the Seal before it was reproduced on the banknote, as will become clear.

On Independence Day, 4 July 1776, a four-man committee was formed to design a seal for the new country. The men were John Adams, Thomas Jefferson, Benjamin Franklin and the artist Pierre du Simitière. The only Freemason on the committee was Benjamin Franklin and the records show that he proposed nothing of a Masonic nature to the designs considered. It was Simitière, a non-Mason, who contributed a variety of designs to the committee, which they accepted and which included the 'Eye of Providence' within a triangle. It is known that Simitière was knowledgeable regarding Renaissance art, from where he may have taken the image.

Congress rejected the first committee's proposal and that of the second committee. However, a consultant for it, John Hopkinson, did have some of his ideas used. In 1782, Congress accepted the design as it now appears on the one-dollar bill; it had been prepared by the artist William Barton under the supervision of the Secretary of Congress, Charles Thomson (1729–1824). He described the meaning of the design as follows: 'The Pyramid signifies Strength and Duration: The Eye over it and the Motto allude to the many signal interpositions of providence in favour of the American cause.'

Over the Eye are the words *Annuit Cœptis*. On the base of the pyramid there are the Roman numerals MDCCLXXVI (1776) and the motto *novus ordo seclorum*. The former means 'somebody [probably Providence, because of the Eye] has nodded at [our] beginnings'. The latter re-translates into 'a new order of the ages', although this is frequently incorrectly rendered as 'New World Order' (which fits neatly into the mind set of some conspiracy theorists).*

As can be seen, the eye is placed in an equilateral triangle. However, whilst the All-Seeing Eye and the Equilateral Triangle existed as separate Masonic symbols, they were never originally shown in combination as on the one-dollar bill. In fact, although first referred to in writing by Masonic writers in 1772 in Britain and in America in 1797, the All-Seeing Eye was not used as a symbol until 1819.† When it was adopted by Freemasons, a surrounding triangle was not included with it and its meaning was given as:

> And although our thoughts, words and actions, may be hidden from the eyes of man yet that All-Seeing Eye, whom the Sun Moon and Stars obey, and under whose watchful care even comets perform their stupendous revolutions, pervades the inmost recesses of the human heart, and will reward us according to our merits.

* I am grateful to my friend and colleague Dr S. Brent Morris for permission to quote from his article 'The Eye in the Pyramid'. See *The Grand Lodge of Scotland Year Book* (2003), p. 98.

† In William Preston's *Illustrations of Masonry* and Thomas S. Webb's *The Freemasons Monitor.*

Sun, Moon and Stars

In Chapter 3, we discovered that the Masonic symbols of the sun, moon and stars may have Hermetic connections, but that today these potential connections have been largely forgotten or have at least become obscured (and not only in relation to these particular symbols). This is probably owing to the multiple meanings ascribed to Masonic symbols, with the most recently applied interpretation having become the one that is best known and therefore dominant.

The symbols of the sun, moon and stars provide an example of how a later meaning may have obscured an earlier one. In Freemasonry, the three who rule a Lodge are the master, the senior warden and the junior warden. Almost inevitably, over the years some Freemasons came to associate the three symbols of the sun, moon and stars with these three office-bearers.

That simple and rather attractive interpretation has also now changed, with the new focus being on the sun. Modern Masonic ritual places the junior warden in the south, where he is to mark the sun at its meridian (that is, when it reaches its highest point) and 'to call the Brethren from labour to refreshment'. Traditionally then stonemasons would cease work for a midday meal, and the sun at its meridian was a rough and ready measure of when they should cease work. The senior warden is placed in the west to mark the setting sun and at the direction in which the master is to close the Lodge. Again, this is a reference to the working practices of stonemasons in that they could not work at night and so the lodge was closed at sunset. The final part of this trilogy of symbols is related to the Master of the Lodge, who is placed in the east; for 'as the sun rises in the east and opens and enlivens the day so the Master is placed in the east to open the Lodge and employ and instruct the Brethren in Freemasonry'. Again we can draw a parallel with working periods. Just as daylight was required for people to work, so Freemasonry too can only 'work' in the light and not in the dark. The connotation of sun = light = work = good + Freemasonry is intended to reinforce the notion that Freemasonry works for the good of all. There were probably once interconnections with other Masonic symbols, such as the beehive (meaning industry, meaning the Lodge), but these have been forgotten with the disuse of the symbol.

Apart from the possible Hermetic connotations of the symbols, the sun, moon and stars were probably added to the ritual during the pre-industrial age, when particular note was taken of the seasons, the time of day and night and the need to work while the sun shone.

The Five-Pointed Star

The five-pointed star alludes to the 'Five Points of Fellowship', which is a lesson about Masonic relationships – how to treat each other and therefore all of humanity – which is explained visually in Masonic ritual. The five points are first referred to in stonemasons' rituals from the late sixteenth century and were contained within the fellow craft or Second degree. The fact that they are used in the master mason or Third degree today is a crucial piece of evidence that demonstrates the evolution and elaboration of modern ritual from older and simpler stonemasons' ritual, such as detailed in the Edinburgh Register House MS. The five-pointed star appears frequently on old aprons and in some Masonic books and charts, but it is no longer a prominent symbol in modern Freemasonry. Although important, the Five Points of Fellowship are not central to modern Masonic ritual practice and so use of the five-pointed star has declined.

However, the first use of a five-pointed star by, or with reference to, Freemasonry occurs in 1641, by Sir Robert Moray (1608–1673). As this is the earliest known use of a Masonic symbol by someone who was not a stonemason, it has particular significance.

Although Sir Robert's early life is not well documented we know he was born in Perthshire and that a military career took him to London, where he pursued his interests in mineralogy and natural history. He associated with many people of influence and he became friendly with Charles II. From these contacts he was able to convince the king to establish the Royal Society in 1660, and in honour of its Scottish founder, the society still holds its AGM on St Andrew's Day. He is buried in Westminster Abbey.

Moray was the first non-stonemason to be initiated in a Lodge in England, in 1641. Moray was quarter-master general of the Scottish Covenanting army, besieging Newcastle-on-Tyne. Part of the army contained a 'logistics corps' in which there were members of the Lodge of Edinburgh, and it was these stonemasons who initiated Moray and also Alexander Hamilton, who was general of the Scots' artillery.

Figure 21 Sir Robert Moray's Mason's mark.

As discussed earlier, the apron is the item that is nowadays most usually associated with the Freemason. Yet Moray never mentions an apron in his writings. The implication is that he did not have one or, if he did, he did not think it as important as his Mason's mark. I think that we might guess why. The apron, the 'uniform' of the Mason, was common to all members of a Lodge, whereas a Mason's mark was particular to an individual (see the discussion of Schaw's monument in Chapter 2, pages 26, 27). This means that the apron was not so intensely personal.

Moray used his mark as an intricate personal device with which to examine the world around him. He certainly believed that there were many dimensions to symbols. His Mason's mark, which he describes as a star, could be interpreted at face value, but Moray believed that there was more – just as there is more to the stars themselves than mere pinpoints of light in the sky, so there was more to his symbol than its design alone. This is typical Hermetic thinking, whereby a symbol becomes a means to explore and understand hidden matters, and so has the potential to control the invisible forces that influence all life. Unfortunately, Moray never explained whether he used it as a focus for the exploration of major questions or simple yet ever-present questions such as 'What is important to me?', 'Why do I do what I do?' and 'How can I improve myself?'. But, however he used it, it was clearly in the knowledge that it was a (Free)Mason's mark.

47th Problem of Euclid

Freemasonry is closely associated with architecture, from which it has derived a great amount of inspiration and symbolism. It is therefore not surprising that 'The 47th Problem' has been adopted as a Masonic symbol.* It first appears in a Masonic setting in the frontispiece of Anderson's *Constitutions* of 1723. (This is the engraving that shows Freemasons preparing to don long leather aprons in the same fashion as those worn by stonemasons.) The problem that is symbolized is familiar to many: 'In right-angled triangles the square of the hypotenuse is equal to the sum of the squares of the other two sides.' That means: $A^2 + B^2 = C^2$.

As well as providing the symbol Anderson makes written reference to the 47th Problem: 'The Greater Pythagoras provided the Author of the 47th Proposition of Euclid's first Book, which, if duly observed, is the Foundation of all Masonry, sacred, civil, and military . . . '

This suggests that in the early days of Freemasonry, at least in the days of Freemasonry of the English Grand Lodge type, the 47th Problem was important. Today the references within Masonic ritual are brief:

> This wise philosopher (Pythagoras) enriched his mind abundantly in a general knowledge of things, and more especially in Geometry, or Masonry. On this subject he drew out many problems and theorems, and, among the most distinguished, he erected this, when, in the joy of his heart, he exclaimed Eureka, in the Greek language signifying, 'I have found it' and upon the discovery of which he is said to have sacrificed a hecatomb. It teaches Masons to be general lovers of the arts and sciences.

The importance of the symbol in some strands of Freemasonry is reflected in the fact that it is the recognized symbol for the past master of a Lodge and is incorporated into the breast jewel worn by past masters.

However, whilst many people assume Freemasonry to be a homogeneous fraternity across the globe, the use of the symbol is one example that this is not strictly the case. The part of ritual quoted above does not exist in some countries nor is the symbol used in their Lodges or past masters' jewels. It is not used in Scotland, for example.†

* It is also known as the Pythagorean Problem because Pythagoras discovered it – Euclid published it.

† That does not mean that no Scottish Freemasons of Lodges make use of it, but this is not common.

Figure 22 A traditional beehive, once an important symbol in Freemasonry.

The Beehive

The beehive is an old Masonic symbol that was originally borrowed from elsewhere. It is normally depicted as a hive with bees buzzing around outside it, and it is generally accepted to represent industry – of being 'as busy as a bee'. Whilst this holds true, in Freemasonry the beehive has a number of possible meanings, the most common being that it represents the Lodge and its members: everyone can see the Lodge (the beehive) and everyone can see the bees (Freemasons), but one who is not a 'bee' can never see what goes on inside the Lodge. It is another excellent example of how a standard symbol, whose meaning is commonly known, has a different twist for the Freemason.

The Future of Masonic Symbolism

As Freemasonry has developed around the world, different countries and different cultures have influenced the Craft in various ways and this is particularly apparent in the way that Masonic symbols are used. In Europe, it is not common for Masonic symbols to be put on public display, as the tendency has been to treat Masonic symbolism as the private language of the Craft. The Freemasons' Halls in London, in Edinburgh and in Dublin (the homes of the Grand Lodge of England, Scotland and Ireland respectively), for example, do not display the square and compasses (with or without the letter G). This is in complete contrast to, for example, the Grand Lodge of New York, which boasts what must be the biggest square and compasses in the world! Neither is right and neither is wrong. This is another example of how diverse Freemasonry can be across the world.

8

CONSTITUTIONS AND ORATIONS

With the founding of Grand Lodges in England (1717), Ireland (1725) and Scotland (1736), and the level of centralization and organization that this brought, the Craft experienced an explosion in popularity, spreading from Britain to Europe. And as Freemasonry spread, it captured the attention of various influential individuals who determined the ways in which it came to be viewed and understood by the world at large. Following in William Schaw's footsteps, Anderson, Prichard and Ramsay are among the most prominent of those who helped to shape modern Freemasonry.

Anderson's *Constitutions of the Free-Masons*

In Chapter 4, we touched briefly upon the contribution of James Anderson (c. 1678–1739) to the codification of Masonic ritual. Born in Aberdeen, Anderson helped to establish many of the ground rules and regulations of modern Freemasonry. Significantly, his father, also named James, was the Master and Secretary of the Lodge in Aberdeen. The Lodge had a 'mixed' membership but stonemasons were in the minority, being considerably outnumbered by lawyers, aristocrats, merchants and 'men of the cloth'. (Records show that the Lodge dates from at least 1670; it still exists, although it is now called the Lodge of Aberdeen, No. 1[3].) Anderson senior held each of the most prominent positions within the Lodge several times and Anderson junior therefore grew up with a father who was an extremely active Freemason in a Scottish Lodge before the existence of the Grand Lodges.

He qualified as a minister and took the degree of MA at Marischal College. He went to London about 1710, where he took up duties as a Dissenting preacher in the French Protestant chapel in Swallow Street. Unfortunately, there is no way of knowing whether he became a Freemason in his father's Lodge (a common Scottish practice) before he left for London, because the Lodge's records for that period are missing. However, he certainly became involved in Freemasonry in London and was invited in 1721 by the new Grand Lodge to 'digest the old Gothic Constitutions in a new and better method': in effect, to write rules and regulations for the new organization.

In 1723 Anderson's *The Constitutions of the Free-Masons* was published. It contains a short but fantastic history of Freemasonry intended to be used by all Lodges, begining with the biblical figure of Adam and progressing to 1723, listing the most significant patriarchs along the way. Important civilizations, such as ancient Egypt, Greece and the Roman Empire, are also mentioned. According to Anderson's history, after the fall of the Roman Empire at the hands of the Goths and Vandals, the Royal Art ('Masonry') passed through France to Britain. The French King Charles Martell (686–741) was particularly instrumental in its spread. During the reign of Edward IV (1442–83) it was reported that, although the records had been destroyed, Athelstan (*fl.* 924–39) had been a central figure in bringing Masonry to England and that his son, Edwin, had convened a Grand Lodge at York, over which he presided as Grand Master. Anderson sprinkles his history with numerous other historical personages such as Pythagoras, Euclid, Archimedes, Vitruvius and Augustus (claimed to be a Grand Master), as well as a host of significant buildings and architectural styles. Unsurprisingly, he devotes considerable space to a discussion of King Solomon's Temple.

Anderson, a Scot, could not resist mentioning his own country, but he did so briefly, which is not surprising given that his work had been commissioned by the Grand Lodge of England. But there is more than a hint of pride when he states that Scotland preserved 'true Masonry' until it could be revived in England by James VI of Scotland, who became James I of England. Anderson states:

> Yet the great Care that the Scots took of true Masonry prov'd afterwards very useful to England; for the learned and magnanimous Queen Elizabeth [of England 1558–1603; b. 1533], who encourag'd other Arts, discourag'd this; because, being a Woman, she could not be made a Mason, tho', as other great Women, she might have much employ'd Masons, like Semiramis and Artemisia.
>
> Upon her Demise, King James VI of Scotland, succeeding to the Crown of England, being a Mason King, reviv'd the English Lodges; and as he was the First King of Great Britain, he was also the First Prince in the World that recover'd the Roman Architecture . . .

Anderson's history of Freemasonry is clearly not accurate but we cannot be too harsh with him because the means of historical research available to him would not come close to modern methods for another two hundred years. A fellow Freemason writing in the first half of the nineteenth century was one of the first – in Scotland at least – to point out the shortcomings of the existing scholarly methods of studying the past. Charles Mackie (1688–1770) was the first history professor at the University of Edinburgh, and his attacks on what he described as 'historical error' provide an indication as to the way that the past was then considered. He defined the historical error as being owing to fondness for high antiquity, the marvellous and travellers' tales, prejudice for one's country or religion, ignorance, laziness and negligence, writing in verse and family and funeral oration.

Mackie was a Freemason and a Free Gardener (a related society that is discussed in Chapter 10), and whilst we do not know for sure what opinion he had of Anderson's work, it's not unreasonable to suppose that in his definition of historical error, he was reacting to Anderson's fantastic history: it certainly contains many of the errors that he describes. In his history, Anderson confuses 'masonry' (stonemasonry) with 'Masonry' (Freemasonry), perhaps because he wanted to create a long pedigree for the Grand Lodge, and references to specific buildings, architects and 'masons' are most likely made in order to allow him to push back the origins of Freemasonry as far as, well, Adam in the Garden of Eden!

Anderson created a precedent that can be traced in the writing of many modern authors on the subject. However, at least his approach to history is pardonable in that it was shared by many of his contemporaries: modern authors who perpetuate many of his flaws, such as confusing 'Freemasonry' with 'masonry', and who repeat a large number of his factual errors, cannot be excused in the same way. Anderson also assumes a 'flow of knowledge' about 'Masonry' (stonemasonry and Freemasonry) without explaining in any detail anything substantial about that knowledge. Some modern authors follow in his footsteps in this respect with their discussions of an 'underground stream of knowledge' whose nature they never define or explain. It almost appears as though, through his history, Anderson effectively obscured rather than illuminated the true origins of Freemasonry.

Masonry Dissected by Samuel Prichard

In 1730 the writer Samuel Prichard decided to capitalize on the secrecy surrounding Freemasonry with a work that he introduced as follows:

> Masonry Dissected; being a Universal and genuine Description Of all its Branches from the Original to the Present Time. As it is deliver'd in the Constituted, Regular Lodges, Both in City and Country, According to the Several Degrees of Admission; Giving an Impartial Account of their Regular Proceedings in Initiating their New Members in the whole Three Degrees of Masonry, viz. I. Entered 'Prentice; II. Fellow Craft; III. Master. To which is added, The Author's Vindication of himself. The Third Edition. By Samuel Prichard, late member of a Constituted Lodge. London; Printed for J. Wilfords, at the Three Flower-de-Luces behind the Chapter-house near St. Paul's. 1730 (Price 6 d).

It is not known if Prichard truly was a Freemason; given his inclusion of a lengthy vindication of his decision to publish the rituals and secrets of Freemasonry, he clearly felt somewhat guilty about what he had written. Such publications of the ceremonial degrees are known in Freemasonry as 'exposures', and Prichard was the first to publish the details of the Third, or master mason's, degree. As he says, his work contains a 'Genuine Description Of all its Branches', and this milestone in the history of Freemasonry affords some insight into how Freemasonry developed. In Chapter 4, we discovered that the stonemasons' lodges in Scotland had but two ceremonies. These were relatively short, and although the content differed, the form of the ceremony (the procedures and movements) was much the same for both parts. Prichard's exposure shows in detail that within the space of a few years a third ceremony had been developed, which contained new material and some elements taken from the stonemasons' fellow craft degree.

As the first two ceremonies existed in Scotland and the new Third degree came into being in England this tends to support the view that Freemasonry (as practised in Scotland) was taken to England, where it was refined into the three degrees. This may have happened because the early Scottish ceremonies were too rough and ready for some. A possible philosophical explanation is that, as the entered apprentice degree was equated with birth (Masonic 'birth', i.e. initiation) and the fellow craft with life (Masonic 'life', i.e. education), there was obviously a part missing in the proceedings, i.e. death. As we discovered in Chapter 5, this final aspect of human life is the focus of the Third degree. Here then, in Prichard's account, we have a possible description of what Freemasonry may be about: the esoteric mysteries of birth, life and death.

Ramsay's *Oration*

Chevalier Andrew Ramsay, the son of a baker, was born in Ayr, Scotland, not far from Kilwinning, the Lodge that William Schaw had dealings with in 1599, and which is intimately connected with the arcane lore of Scottish Freemasonry. Ramsay was initiated in the Horn Lodge (London) in March 1730 and therefore his Masonic experience was not Scottish but English. James Anderson was also a member of the Horn Lodge, being recorded as such in 1723, but it is not known whether he met Ramsay there.*

Ramsay was a convert to Roman Catholicism (although a Quietist), and in 1737 he obtained the position of orator at the Grand Lodge of France, in Paris. His duties were to deliver lectures on Masonic subjects in the Grand Lodge and in local Lodges. In the year that he obtained

* Arnold Whitaker Oxford, *An Introduction to the History of the Royal Somerset and Inverness Lodge* (Bernard Quaritch, 1928), p. 16.

his post he was due to deliver an oration in the Grand Lodge, but by law it had to be given to the French censors first. He gave the written form to the censor, Cardinal Flurey, who refused to grant permission for him to deliver it publicly. (It has been argued that the oration was subsequently given at a meeting of the Grand Lodge of France in 1737, but many now consider this to be unlikely.)* Following Cardinal Flurey's censorship, his Masonic career was effectively over and there is no record of him ever taking part in Masonic activity thereafter.

However, Ramsay's undelivered lecture, known as his *Oration*, still existed in written form (two versions of which still exist). The fact that it was to have been delivered before the Grand Lodge of France has ensured its importance in Masonic history and it was subsequently distributed within French Masonic circles.† At that time, the members of the Grand Lodge of France and the majority of French Freemasons were drawn from the ranks of the aristocracy. It appears that Ramsay simply could not countenance the thought of telling them that Freemasonry originated with humble Scottish stonemasons; and, in his view, Anderson's claim that 'masonry' originated in the Old Testament was equally unpalatable. Ramsay therefore adopted an entirely different tack. In his *Oration* he claimed that Freemasonry was refined by Crusaders in the Holy Land who had revived a very corrupt form of the Craft and restored it to its present glory. He states: 'The word Freemason must therefore not be taken in a literal, gross and material sense, as if our founders had been simple workers in stone, or merely curious geniuses who wished to perfect the arts',‡ and the suggestion that Freemasonry was ultimately chivalric and Christian in origin and nature made it much more acceptable to his aristocratic readers. But in allowing that Freemasonry predated the Crusades he was in agreement with Anderson:

* Lisa Kahler, 'Andrew Michael Ramsay and his Masonic Oration' *Heredom* (Scottish Rite Research Society, Washington DC), vol. 1, pp. 19–47.

† Robert Freke Gould, *The history of Freemasonry, its antiquities, symbols, constitutions, customs etc. Embracing an investigation of the records of the organisations of the fraternity in England, Scotland, Ireland, British colonies, France, Germany, and the United States*, revised by Dudley Wright (6 vols: C. Scribner's sons, 1936), vol. 5. p.79.

‡ Cyril N. Batham, 'Ramsay's Oration: the Épernay and Grand Lodge Versions', *Heredom* (Scottish Rite Research Society, Washington DC), vol. 1, pp. 49–59. This article allows the two known versions of the *Oration* to be compared.

> Our ancestors, the crusaders, gathered together from all parts of Christendom in the Holy Land, desired thus to reunite into one sole Fraternity the individuals of all nations.*

> Our order, therefore, must not be considered a revival of the Bacchanals, but as an Order founded in remote antiquity, renewed in the Holy Land by our ancestors . . . †

Although he speaks of the Crusaders and the Order of St John, he does not mention the French Knights Templar as being the originators of Freemasonry:

> Our Order formed an intimate union with the Knights of St. John of Jerusalem. From that time our lodge took the name of Lodges of St. John. This union was made after the example set by the Israelites when they erected the second Temple who, whilst they handled the trowel and mortar with one hand, in the other held the sword and buckler.‡

Some have suggested that Ramsay was mistaken and did indeed mean to refer to the Knights Templar and not to the Crusaders and Hospitallers. This suggestion seems to stem from the facts that within a relatively few years of the publication of the *Oration*, the Masonic Order of Knights Templar (and some other high grades) was created in France and that the Order's romantic ideas with respect to their deeds, wealth (which they claimed had been 'lost') and unfair abolition made them the natural targets for the new Masonic ceremonial suggested by Ramsay's arguments (see below). However, assertions such as 'Ramsay made a point of stressing to the brotherhood that they were descended from the Crusader knights, which was a thinly veiled reference to the Templars' can be no more than guesswork.§ If Ramsay was referring to any particular group of Crusaders, it was most likely to have been the Order of St Lazarus, because he was a knight of that order, but, in the absence of any evidence, even this must be mere speculation.

* Ibid., p. 50.
† Ibid., p. 57.
‡ Ibid.
§ Lynn Picknett and Clive Prince, *The Templar Revelation*,. p. 131.

What is inescapable is that the only direct connection he made was between Freemasonry and the Knights of St John of Jerusalem, and he did not mention the Knights Templar.

However, he did provide a Franco-Scottish connection that continues to be used

> in Scotland, because of the close alliance between the French and the Scotch. James, Lord Stewart of Scotland [? –1309], was Grand Master of a lodge established at Kilwinning, in the West of Scotland, MCCLXXXVI [1286] shortly after the death of Alexander III, King of Scotland [1249–1286; b. 1241], and one year before John Balliol mounted the throne. This Lord received as Freemasons into his Lodge the Earls of Gloucester and Ulster, the one English, the other Irish.*

In this passage Ramsay introduces a claim that has been adopted by those who suggest a connection between Freemasonry and the Knights Templar: that in the thirteenth century Kilwinning was a centre of Freemasonry. However, it is important to note here that although he allows that Freemasonry existed in Kilwinning in the thirteenth century, he makes no mention of the Knights Templar. He does, however, state that Scottish, Irish and English members of the nobility were involved in Freemasonry from the outset.

The flaws in Ramsay's theory are numerous and many have been perpetuated to this day. For example, in spite of his claims, the alliance with France did not exist until 1296 and up until 1286 Scotland was at relative peace, Alexander III having married the daughter of Henry III (1216–1272; b. 1207) of England. The facts, however, were irrelevant. Ramsay was intent on creating a venerable history of Freemasonry that, although it was not based in factual evidence (he produced no proof whatsoever in support of his theories), appealed greatly to the aristocracy of France, who were attracted to the idea that Freemasonry had been moulded by chivalric ideals. Ramsay's sales pitch to the nobility worked: French Freemasonry, although disapproved of by

* Batham, op. cit., pp. 57–8. The James referred to is the 5th High Steward of Scotland, who died 1309. His son, Walter, was knighted on the field of Bannockburn by Robert I.

the Church there, continued to grow and attracted more members during subsequent years.

However, the impact of the *Oration* went far further than simply making the Craft attractive to the upper strata of French society. When the chivalric Crusader ideals promoted by Ramsay were compared with the three degrees of entered apprentice, fellow craft and master mason, there was clearly some disparity between existing Masonic ceremonial and the knightly influences described in the *Oration.* To many, this meant that the three degrees must merely be a basic element of Freemasonry and that other aspects must have existed to articulate the chivalric ideals that Ramsay spoke of, but that these aspects had been either lost or destroyed.

This conjecture gave rise to an explosion of ceremonies, especially in France. Some of the ceremonies attempted to reconcile Ramsay's claims about the origins of Freemasonry with existing practice, whilst others seemed to bear little relation to Freemasonry at all. It has been conservatively estimated that more than a thousand different ceremonies were created in the hundred years or so following the circulation of Ramsay's *Oration.* Many of the ceremonies have since disappeared without a trace whilst others are now part of the Masonic system.

Anderson's *New Constitutions*

For all his impact, Ramsay did not have a monopoly on Masonic history. In 1738, Anderson published another set of constitutions, the *New Constitutions.* Whether he had any knowledge of Ramsay's *Oration* of the previous year is unknown. The *New Constitutions* contains a belated response to Prichard's exposure of Masonic ritual under the title 'Defence of Masonry, published A.D. 1730. occasioned by a Pamphlet call'd Masonry Dissected' (eight years having elapsed since the publication of that work), and it may also have been influenced by the establishment of the Grand Lodge of Scotland in 1736. The work elaborates greatly on the fantastic history provided in the *Constitutions* of 1723. It certainly does not adopt any of the ideas contained within Ramsay's *Oration.*

Although the *Constitutions* of 1723 and 1738 both contain large amounts of fiction, the differences are very striking between the two editions in the treatment of the history of Scottish 'Masonry'. The 1723 edition offers a vague, generalized account, e.g. 'The Kings of Scotland very much encouraged the Royal Art . . .' and does not name one king. Anderson does, however, state that the 'Masons' of Scotland had a 'fix'd Grand Master and Grand Warden who had a Salary from the Crown'. This is the earliest suggestion that there was a Grand Master of Scottish Masons (Freemasons) and that he was an 'employee' of the monarch.

In Chapter 6 of the *New Constitutions*, Anderson details 'Masonry in Scotland till the Union of the Crowns' (which occurred in 1603) and provides a great deal more information relating to the history of Freemasonry in Scotland than had been included in the 1723 *Constitutions*.* He begins by making passing reference to the Picts and Scots before beginning a specific history that commences with Fergus II in AD 403.† He then lists the monarchs of Scotland and takes the opportunity to mention individuals who were noted for their building activities, the first being Malcolm III (c. 1031–1093), who is mentioned thus:

> He built the old Church of Dunfermline, a Royal Sepulchre, and levell'd the Footstone of the old cathedral of Durham, which he richly endow'd. He fortified his Borders, Castles and seaports, as the Royal Grand Master and Patron of Arts and Sciences, till he died, A. D. 1093.

Anderson claims that Malcolm III was the first Grand Master of Scotland, stating that at least one other monarch 'patronised' the Craft. Anderson's use of this word is perhaps indicative of knowledge of the content of the St Clair 'Charters'. Below is a list of historical figures claimed by Anderson to have held Masonic positions:

* This suggests that he may have received details from a source in Scotland. The Grand Lodge of Scotland was founded in 1736 and it also began from the outset to create its own traditional history.

† It is now generally accepted that Fergus II died *c.*501.

Name	Birth – Death	Masonic Position
Malcolm III	1031 – 1093	Grand Master
Alexander I	c. 1078 – 1124	Patron
David I	1084 – 1153	Grand Master
William the Lion	1143 – 1214	Grand Master
Henry Wardlaw, Bishop of St Andrews	? – 1440	Grand Master
James I	1394 – 1437	Grand Master
William St Clair, Earl of Orkney	c. 1404 – 1480	Grand Master
William Turnbull, Bishop of Glasgow	? – 1454	Grand Master
Sir Robert Cockeran	? – 1482	Grand Master
Alexander, Lord Forbes	? – 1491	Grand Master
William Elphinston, Bishop of Aberdeen	1431 – 1514	Grand Master
Gavin Dunbar, Bishop of Aberdeen	? 1455 – 1532	Grand Master
Gavin Douglas, Bishop of Dunkeld	? 1474 – 1522	Grand Master
George Creighton, Abbot of Holyrood House	?	Grand Master
Patrick, Earl of Lindsay (?)	? – 1526	Grand Master
Sir David Lindsay	? 1551–1610	Grand Master
Andrew Stewart, Lord Ochitree	fl. 1548–1593	Grand Master
Sir James Sandilands, Knight of Malta	? – 1579	Grand Master
Claud Hamilton, Lord Paisley	? 1543–1622	Grand Master
King James VI & I	1566 – 1625	Freemason

According to Anderson, the first Grand Master of Scottish 'masons' lived in the early eleventh century, almost a hundred years before the Order of the Knights Templar, and his detailed chronological account of 'Masonry' in Scotland shows that it was considered, by those at the very centre of Freemasonry, to have existed long before the Knights Templar. As we saw in Chapter I, Robert the Bruce has long been regarded as a key player in the theory that Freemasonry is connected to the Knights Templar. This is what Anderson has to say about him:

> Robert I. Bruce fled to Scotland. And was crown'd 1306 And after many sore Conflicts, he totally routed King Edward II. [1307–1327; b. 1284] of England at Bannockburn, A.D. 1314. obtain'd a honourable Peace, and died illustrious, A.D. 1329.*
>
> During the Competition [for the crown], Masonry was neglected; but after the Wars, King Robert I. Bruce, having settled his Kingdom, forthwith employ'd the Craft in repairing the castles, Palaces and Houses; and the Nobility and Clergy follow'd his Example till he died, A.D. 1329.†

Many popular books about the Knights Templar today include mention of Rosslyn Chapel and the St Clair family that built it. Anderson too makes mention of William St Clair (c. 1404–1480), Earl of Orkney:

> In this reign [of] James II [1430–1460] William Sinclair the great earl of Orkney and Caithness was Grand Master, and built Roslin Chapel near Edinburgh, a Master Piece of the best Gothic, A.D. 1441. next Bishop Turnbull of Glasgow, who founded the University there, A.D. 1454.‡

However, it should be noted that Anderson only refers to St Clair as one in a succession of Grand Masters, seventh in a list of twenty. This was potentially controversial, given that in 1736 the Grand Lodge of Scotland listed William St Clair of Rosslyn as its first Grand Master, of which he would have been aware.

After Anderson

By the middle of the nineteenth century the central tenets of Freemasonry were fairly stable, with Anderson's views dominant in

* Anderson, op. cit., p. 84.
† Ibid., p. 86.
‡ Ibid., p. 7.

Britain and Ramsay's in Europe. However, that is not to say that it was not complex. We have seen how the creation of the Grand Lodges was greeted with enthusiasm in England and France, but met with a mixed response in Scotland, with some Lodges refusing to acknowledge their supremacy. The Grand Lodges themselves also saw some ups and downs in the process of becoming established.

The Royal Order of Scotland

The Royal Order of Scotland possesses one of the two earliest known Traditional Histories of other 'branches' of Freemasonry that survive today. Created at some point between 1741 and 1767, the Royal Order's origins are obscure, but along with the influences of Anderson and Ramsay, this branch of modern Freemasonry had a considerable influence on shaping the persisting theory of a Knights Templar–Masonic connection.

It is appropriate here to mention briefly the Order's traditional history, as it is from this that part of the theory is drawn. In his history *The Royal Order of Scotland*, the late Brother Robert S. Lindsay points out that for the first twenty-six years of its life, the order made no reference to Robert I or the Battle of Bannockburn; it claimed the 'King of Scots' to be the hereditary Grand Master of the Order, but no particular monarch was named.* However, the rules and regulations published on the 5 January 1767 completely changed this position:

> The Election of these Officers shall be annually upon the fourth day of July being the Anniversary of the Battle of Bannockburn, fought anno 1314, after which King Robert Bruce held a Grand Lodge of this Order and created several Knights upon or near the Field of Battle as he did afterwards many more at Kilwinning. This was the beginning of the Bruce tradition . . .†

The Royal Order was the first branch of Freemasonry to claim a connection with Robert the Bruce, Bannockburn, Kilwinning and 'knights' all at the same time.† However, even this Masonic Order

* See, for example, Robert S. Lindsay, *The Royal Order of Scotland*, 2nd edn (Edinburgh, 1972).

† This traditional history *may* have been influenced by Ramsay's *Oration*.

couldn't quite get the facts right: the battle of Bannockburn was fought over 23 to 24 June, not 4 July! This suggests that, rather than one based on fact, the order had adopted their own traditional history much as Anderson created his for the Grand Lodge of England.

At the time that the Royal Order of Scotland came into being, the Jacobite Rising of 1745 to 1746 would have been very fresh in the memory of many. Therefore, this new Masonic Order's connection with Bruce – a figure fiercely associated with Scottish independence (seen by many as having been lost at the Union of Parliaments in 1707) – might be considered to be 'cocking a snook' at the authorities. These same authorities vigorously enforced laws that tried to eliminate some of Scotland's more obvious cultural differences (e.g. wearing tartan and playing the bagpipes).* But perhaps the authorities were simply unconcerned about events of more than four hundred years previously, as the Order appears to have led a fairly healthy and active life until c. 1788, when it began to exhibit the first signs of decline, and it was virtually moribund between 1794 and 1839.†

The Ancient and Moderns

Founded in 1717, the Grand Lodge of England had begun to experience some problems by 1750 as the Grand Master, William Byron (1722–1798), the fifth Lord Byron and great-uncle of the poet, simply did not attend to his Masonic duties and the Lodge's administration became very poor. Freemasonry had become increasingly socially exclusive and a number of old traditions were changed or dropped altogether. In addition to this unhappy state of affairs, changes in the use of certain Masonic words in the 1730s caused the creation of a new, rival Grand Lodge in 1751, 'the Grand Lodge of England According to the Old Institutions'. It was also known as the 'Ancient' or 'Atholl' Grand Lodge – titles that clearly demonstrate its adherence to earlier Masonic practice and which confirm that its creation was a reaction to the changes afoot.‡ Inevitably the other Grand Lodge, which was of

* The 1747 *Act of Proscription* was repealed in 1782.

† There were sporadic and poorly attended meetings between those two dates. *See*: Lindsay, op. cit., pp. 101–4.

‡ The title Atholl Grand Lodge is due to the fact that two Dukes of Atholl presided over the Grand Lodge for more than half of its existence.

course older than the Ancient Grand Lodge, came to be described as the 'Moderns' because of the innovations it had permitted to be introduced.

The Ancient Grand Lodge was composed almost entirely of Irish Freemasons resident in London who had apparently been denied access to existing Masonic Lodges – perhaps this was why they wished to have a Grand Lodge of their own. By 1754 the Ancient Grand Lodge, under the energetic direction of Lawrence Dermott, the Grand Lodge Secretary, had matured enough to publish its first Book of Constitutions under the title *Ahiman Rezon*, indicating that it was attracting members and funds.

Unlike the Moderns and the Grand Lodge of Scotland, the Ancient Grand Lodge embraced the Royal Arch Ceremonies, with Laurence Dermott claiming to have been a Royal Arch Masonic Mason in Dublin in 1746. The earliest reference to this ceremony was made in Dublin in 1743, 'the Royal Arch carried by excellent Masons' during the St John's Day parade of Youghall Lodge, No. 21,* and in 1744 there is another, 'I am informed in that city is held an assembly of Master Masons under the title of Royal Arch Masons', but there is no way of knowing the nature of the ceremony itself.†

The Ancient Grand Lodge makes the first reference to the ceremony in minutes of 4 March 1752, when it considers a complaint made by Thomas Phelan and John Mackey who alleged that 'leg of mutton Masons' had made 'Royal Archmen' for the sake of a meal. The implication is that these 'Royal Archmen' were not even Freemasons. The first record of the ceremony of the Holy Royal Arch being conferred in a Masonic Lodge occurs in the Lodge at Fredericksburg, Virginia, on 22 December 1753. It was in this Lodge that George Washington (1732–1799), later the first President of the United States, had been made a Freemason the previous year. It is therefore ironic that the first record of the conferral of the Royal Arch ceremony in a Masonic Lodge took place, not in an Ancient Lodge or an Irish Lodge

* Faulkner's *Dunbin Journal*. January 1744. This must refer to St. John the Evangelist's Day, 27 December 1743.

† Fifield Dassigny, *A Serious and Impartial Enquiry into the Cause of the Present State of Decay of Freemasonry in the Kingdom of Ireland* (Dublin, 1744).

(which embraced the ceremony as being a normal part of Freemasonry), but in a Scottish Lodge which did not!

The traditional history of the Royal Arch is concerned with the release of the Jews by Cyrus, King of Persia, who allowed them to return to Jerusalem to build the second Temple under the guidance of Zerubabbel. This ceremony, which is now part of mainstream Freemasonry, appeared soon after Chevalier Andrew Ramsay's *Oration* of 1736 (see Chapter 8). It is now conceded (and is the subject of ongoing research) that although Ramsay's *Oration* made no reference to the Knights Templar or the Royal Arch, it was the inspiration for the creation of the so-called higher degrees of Freemasonry, which include the Knights Templar and Royal Arch.* In any event it is significant that none of these *hauts grades* existed prior to the *Oration*. Those who claim that they must have existed base that claim on the fact that there is no evidence that they did not, but this is using a negative to 'prove' a positive.

Surprisingly the Moderns Grand Lodge did not react at all to the creation of this new Grand Lodge. Its existence was simply ignored – at least initially: the Ancient was a relatively small body whose members were not part of the existing Masonic 'establishment' in London. The first official reaction came in 1777, when it was decided that the Grand Lodge of 'Ancient' Masons should not be recognized. This may mean that until that point both Grand Lodges had at least tolerated each other and perhaps had permitted visiting between their respective Lodges.

The Grand Lodge of Scotland maintained cordial relations with the Ancient and officially recognized that body in 1772, no doubt as a consequence of the third Duke of Atholl, who was Grand Master of the Ancient Grand Lodge from 1771 to 1774, becoming Grand Master Mason (of Scotland) in that year. In 1782, the Grand Lodge of Scotland also officially recognized the Moderns Grand Lodge.

In May 1813 the Duke of Sussex (1773–1843) was elected Grand Master of the Moderns and shortly thereafter his brother, the Duke of

* It is unlikely that a comprehensive list of Masonic and pseudo-Masonic degrees and ceremonies will ever be compiled because of the sheer number that were invented during the eighteenth century.

Kent (1767–1820), was elected Grand Master of the Ancients. It was through the influence of these two brothers that the union of the Ancient and Moderns was brought about in December 1813.*

* The Ancient and Moderns Grand Lodges have been discussed in a number of places. See, for example: Cyril N. Batham, *The Grand Lodge of England according to the Old Institutions*, AQC Vol. 98; A. R. Hewitt, *The Grand Lodge of England – History of the first 100 years*, AQC Vol. 80; Robert F. Gould, *The Grand Lodge of the 'Schismatics' or 'Ancients'*, AQC Vol. 6 and John Hamill, *The History of English Freemasonry* (Lewis Masonic, 1994).

9

POCKET COMPANIONS AND THE REWORKING OF HISTORY

The official histories produced by Anderson for the Grand Lodge of England and by Ramsay for the Grand Lodge of France were works that would have been well known to the 'Mason in the Lodge', or at least to those Freemasons in Anderson's and Ramsay's respective countries. However, in addition to these official publications there were pirated editions whose sales and popularity inform us what the Freemasons of the time commonly understood the facts of Masonic history to be (works that were at variance with what these Freemasons believed they *knew* to be their history simply would not have sold).

Pocket Companions

Pirated copies of Anderson's 1723 *Constitutions* were in circulation from at least 1735, beginning with Smith's *Pocket Companion* (London, 1735). At the formation of the Grand Lodge of Scotland, office-bearers were supplied with copies of the *Pocket Companion* for their guidance, implying that the Lodge, which was the only national Masonic body then in existence in Scotland, recognized the validity of the contents. The work was also published in Dublin in 1735, and reissued by Torbuck in London in 1736, with a second edition in 1738. The fact that these editions were published throughout Britain and Ireland shows that the *Pocket Companion* referred to a body of material that was common to all Freemasons. (The pirated copies may have been one of the motivating factors behind Anderson's publication of his *New Constitutions* of 1738: he wished to recapture the market for his authorized history.) Pirated copies were common during the eighteenth century: it was obviously a lucrative market and in total forms an identifiable pool of Masonic knowledge against which the various theories can be assessed.

In 1752 the first 'Scottish' *Pocket Companion* was published by W. Cheyne (Edinburgh).* This is nothing other than a blatant copy of Anderson's *Constitutions,* but at least the printer is unashamed and up front about his source material, for in the Preface he states: 'At the Desire of a great many of the Brethren this History was comprised, (which, for the most Part, is extracted from Dr. Anderson's Constitution-Book).' What is immediately striking is that Cheyne's edition makes no mention of Scottish Masonic history and omits even Anderson's limited references. The only concession to Scotland is the inclusion of 'An alphabetical list of the Lodges that are in the Roll of the Grand Lodge of Scotland',† which suggests that Anderson's established view of the history of Freemasonry was accepted in Britain and Ireland and that Cheyne felt no need to create a distinctively Scottish version.

As late as 1759 a *Pocket Companion* published in England by J. Scott (a third edition) still made no reference to Scotland, which, together with Cheyne's similar omission, suggests that a Scottish Masonic history had not yet been established although was probably in the process of being created by this time.

It is not until 1761 that we find the first reference, in Scotland, to that country and its Masonic history. A *Pocket Companion* by Ruddiman, Auld and Company of Edinburgh initially follows Anderson's 1738 version of Scottish history, beginning with the Picts, but quickly moves on to a more detailed history. The author states: 'The Fraternity of Free-Masons in Scotland always owned their King and Sovereign as their Grand Master.'‡ The writer then claims that prior to 1441 Kings of Scotland were Grand Masters of the Craft and that, when a king was not, he appointed one of the Brethren as his

* James Reid of Edinburgh copied Cheyne's edition in 1754, also citing Anderson as the source.

† pp. 111–14.

‡ p. 111.

deputy. He states that James I (1406–1437; b. 1394) was a 'Royal Grand Master', and the narrative then proceeds:

> 1441. William St Clair Earl of Orkney and Caithness, Baron of Roslin, etc, etc, got a grant of this office [Grand Master] from King James II. [1437–1460; b. 1430].
>
> *By another deed of the said King James II this office was made hereditary to the said William St Clair, and his heirs and successors in the Barony of Roslin; in which noble family, it has continued without any interruption till of late years.*
>
> They [the St Clair family] held their head court (or in Mason style) assembled their Grand Lodge at Kilwinning in the West Country [Ayrshire] where it is presumed Masons first began in Scotland to hold regular and stated Lodges.*

Ramsay's *Oration* was the first to mention Kilwinning, by stating that 'James, Lord Steward of Scotland, was Grand Master of a Lodge established there' and giving the date as 1286, but the Ruddiman and Auld edition elevates the status of the St Clair family by describing them as presiding over the Grand Lodge there as Grand Masters and claiming that they had presided in this way since c. 1286. Here we can see the seeds that were to grow into the theory of a connection between Freemasonry and the Knights Templar, but even at this very early stage contradictions are evident. For example, how could St Clairs have been Grand Masters in 1286 if, as claimed in Anderson's original *New Constitutions*, they were first appointed to that position in 1441?

In 1763, Ruddiman and Auld published a second edition of their *Pocket Companion*, and a similar work was printed by Alexander Donaldson of Edinburgh. Neither added anything new to the history. (Interestingly, Donaldson's book states that it was sold in his shops in London and Edinburgh.) In 1765, a further edition was published by Auld and Smellie of Edinburgh. This too had nothing new to say. In 1765, an almost exact replica of this edition was published by Galbraith of Glasgow, and in 1771, Peter Tait of Glasgow published a very similar *Pocket Companion*, which repeated, with some minor variations, the same chapter on the 'history' of Scottish Freemasonry. It is clear that there was a considerable demand for such works at this

* Ibid., p. 112.

time, and given the repetition of the same 'history' in each, it might be argued that this version of the past had gained a wide circulation and acceptance. More importantly, there were no alternative histories on offer.

In 1769 Wellins Calcott published *A Candid Disquisition of the Principals and Practices of the Ancient and Honourable Society of Free and Accepted Masons*; . . . (London). It contained a verbatim reproduction of the chapter called 'An Account of the Establishment of the Present Grand Lodge of Scotland from Ruddiman and Auld', and demonstrates that by 1769, this version of Scottish Masonic history was circulating in England as well as in Scotland. Although Donaldson's *Pocket Companion* was being sold in London, Calcott may have been the first entirely English source to give a Scottish version of Masonic history.

Rosslyn

In 1774 a small booklet entitled *An Account of the Chapel of Roslin* was published in Edinburgh by James Murray. Written by the Episcopalian bishop Dr Robert Forbes (1708–1775), it provides an early description and history of the chapel. However, despite the connection between the chapel and the St Clair family, Bishop Forbes does not refer to Anderson's *Constitutions* or to any of the numerous *Pocket Companions*, nor does he mention Freemasonry or the Knights Templar, demonstrating that at this time the chapel had no overt Masonic connotations. Indeed, the only Masonic connection is in a pirated edition of the work printed in 1778. Following the death of the first Grand Master, William St Clair, in February of that year, the printer's dedication was:

> Humbly inscribed to the Ancient Fraternity of FREE AND ACCEPTED MASONS.

The dedication may have been intended to capitalize on a market created by the death, but this pirated edition contained no other references to Freemasonry.* Given the large amount of material relating to

* Reprinted by the Grand Lodge of Scotland, 2000 and again in 2002.

the history of Scottish Freemasonry in circulation in Scotland at this time, it seems that a connection between Scottish Freemasonry, the Knights Templar and Rosslyn Chapel had yet to be invented.

The Creation of a Traditional History for Scotland

With the establishment of the Grand Lodge of Scotland came the need for a Scottish traditional history to rival Anderson's *Constitutions* for the Grand Lodge of England. Key stages in the elaboration of a distinctly Scottish traditional history can be traced in the writings of a number of individuals and in what these writers do, and do not, include in their own works.

William Preston (1742–1818)

Preston was born in Edinburgh and is best remembered for his *Illustrations of Masonry* (1772), a work so popular that seventeen editions were published (not including modern reproductions). Although Preston was a Scot and although the first edition of *Illustrations* was published eleven years after the first Scottish 'history' of Scottish Freemasonry had appeared, he made no reference to a Scottish history in it. His account of the origins of Freemasonry are similar to Anderson's (whom he quotes), although he differs in that he begins with the Druids, rather than Adam, and charts the Grand Masters (of England) from St Alban (c. 264–304) to the then Grand Master (of the Grand Lodge of England), Robert Edward, ninth Lord Petre (1742–1801). However, of interest to us here is the following passage from a later edition:

> During the reign of Henry II the grand master of the Knights Templars superintended the masons, and employed them in building their Temple in Fleet Street, AD 1155. Masonry continued under the patronage of this Order till the year 1199.*†

Preston describes the relationship between the Knights Templar and 'the masons' as that of employer and employee, and nothing more. He,

* The Temple Church was consecrated in honour of the Blessed Virgin Mary on 10 February 1185 by Heraclius, Patriarch of Jerusalem.

† *Preston's Illustrations of Masonry*, ed. Andrew Prescott (Academy Electronic Publications Ltd, 2001), 2nd edn (1775), p. 205. This CD-ROM contains the nine editions published during Preston's lifetime.

like many writers before and after him to this day, confuses 'masons' (stonemasons) with 'Masons' (Freemasons), but importantly we can see from this reference that he places Masonry (Freemasonry) before the formation of the Knights Templar (c. 1118). In this instance, the Knights Templars' only connection with 'Masonry' was for a period of forty-four years, presumably the period it took to build the church. According to Preston's account, the employer–employee relationship was a contractual one only and ceased a long time before the medieval Knights Templar were suppressed. But even this brief reference is not included in Preston's very first edition of the *Illustrations* in 1772.

William Hutchinson, FSA (1732–1814)

Another influential author of the period who should be mentioned is William Hutchinson. His book, *Spirit of Masonry,* was first published in London in 1775 and, like Preston's and Anderson's work, it was officially sanctioned by the Grand Lodge of England. Hutchinson was therefore regarded as an accepted expert on Freemasonry, and there are a number of references in his work that are of significance to the present discussion:

> . . . all Europe was influenced with the cry and madness of an enthusiastic monk, who prompted the zealots in religion to the holy war; in which for the purpose of recovering the holy city and Judea out of the hands of the hands of the infidels, armed legions . . . in tens of thousands [they] poured forth from every state of Europe, to waste their blood . . .
>
> It was deemed necessary that those who took up the ensign of the cross in this enterprise, should form themselves into such societies as might secure them from spies and treacheries: and that each might know his companion . . . as well in dark as by day.
>
> . . . the priests projecting the Crusades, being possessed of the mysteries of masonry, the knowledge of the ancients, and of the universal language which survived the confusion of Shinar [Babel], revived the orders and regulations of Solomon and initiated the legions therein who followed them to the Holy Land:- hence that secrecy which attended the crusaders . . .
>
> Amongst other evidence which authorizes me to in the conjecture that masons went to the holy wars, is the doctrine of that order of masons, called the HIGHER ORDER. I am induced to believe that order was of Scottish extraction; separate nations might be distinguished by some separate order: but be that as it may, it fully proves to me that masons were crusaders . . .

> We may conjecture that these religious campaigns [i.e. the Crusades] being over, that men initiated in the mysteries of masonry, and engaged and inrolled under those rules and orders, which were established for the conduct of the nations in the holy war, would form themselves into Lodges, and keep up their social meetings when returned home, in commemoration of their adventures and mutual good offices in Palestine and for the propagation of that knowledge into which they had been initiated.*

Hutchinson's main points are:

- Participants in the Crusades were formed into 'societies', which protected them from spies and allowed them to identify each other by night as well as by day.
- These 'secret societies' were condoned and encouraged by the Roman Church.
- Priests were 'masons' and they possessed the mysteries of masonry and the knowledge of the ancients, and knew the universal language; that is, the pure language which existed prior to God's introduction of multiple languages.
- It was these priests who initiated and organized those going to the Crusades into secret societies.
- Some Scottish masons were part of a Higher Order of 'masons'.
- Freemasons, especially Scottish 'masons', were Crusaders.
- Once these Initiates returned home they wished to maintain contact with each other for the propagation of '*initiated knowledge*' as well as for social, and personal reasons. The most obvious method was to perpetuate their Lodges.

Although Hutchinson was not a Scot (he hailed from Barnard Castle, Co. Durham), he clearly had some thoughts as to how, and where, the Scots fitted into the origin and development of Freemasonry, particularly in relation to the Crusades. He suggested that a 'Higher Order' of 'mason' was of Scottish origin and that 'masons' were Crusaders. He clearly believed that Freemasonry predated the Crusades, so the Knights Templar, which he never mentioned, must have come into being after Freemasonry.

Hutchinson's book became very popular in Scotland and after its

* pp. 180, 180, 184, 184, 213.

publication Alexander Deuchar (1777–1844) established the modern Scottish Masonic Order of the Knights Templar (the Edinburgh Encampment of Knights Templar, later the Royal Grand Conclave) in 1808.

The first Scottish edition of *Spirit of Masonry* was published by McEwan of Edinburgh in 1813; a second edition was published in the same year, and a third edition, by Dick (Edinburgh), appeared in 1815. Three editions in two years indicates a very strong interest in this publication and therefore in Hutchinson's ideas regarding early Freemasonry. All these editions were produced soon after Alexander Deuchar had began to take charge of 'foreign' ceremonials as practised earlier by some Scottish Craft Lodges but which had been declared by the Grand Lodge of Scotland not to be Masonic, and it is not unreasonable to suggest that those Scottish Freemasons interested in the ceremonials eagerly purchased Hutchinson's work. The material from which to create the Knights Templar myth was readily available and widely read.

An Elaborate Scottish Masonic History

In Chapter 2, we discovered how Father Hay's work on the St Clair muniments brought to the attention of Freemasons the existence of documents (principally two letters) that might suggest a long lineage for Scottish 'masonry'. Those involved in the formation of the Grand Lodge of Scotland interpreted these documents as being evidence of the existence of even earlier Royal Charters, which granted the St Clair family unspecified hereditary rights and privileges over the stonemasons of Scotland. All the flaws, errors and ambiguities in the 'Charters' were ignored. By having William St Clair, a direct descendant of the St Clair to whom the 'Charters' had originally been addressed, resign these alleged hereditary rights and electing him the first Grand Master of the new Grand Lodge, the first steps were taken in the creation of a traditional history for the new Grand Lodge of Scotland.

In 1723 Anderson issued, under the authority of the Grand Lodge of England, his brief and fantastic history of Freemasonry in which he claimed that kings of Scotland had been Grand Masters and that one, at least, had 'Patronised' the Craft. By 1738 he had compiled a list of the Grand Masters of the Scottish Craft, beginning with Fergus II. Included in the list was William St Clair, Earl of Orkney, who was said to be a Grand Master during the reign of James II. From then until the Union of the Crowns (1603) Anderson lists twelve Grand Masters of Scotland.

Ramsay's *Oration* introduced the concept of a connection between Freemasonry and the Holy Land, and mentioned Crusaders. He specifically linked Freemasonry with the Knights of St John of Jerusalem. In common with all histories of Freemasonry at this time, he made no mention of the medieval Order of Knights Templar.

In 1761, Ruddiman & Auld's *Pocket Companion* elaborated on Anderson's unsubstantiated claim that William St Clair was a Grand Master by stating:

> By another deed of the said King James II. this office was made hereditary to the said William St Clair, and his heirs and successors in the Barony of Roslin: in which noble family, it has continued without interruption till of late years.*

This is a major advance in the development of a theory of a Knights Templar/Masonic connection. Until now St Clair had been but one fictional Grand Master out of a total of nineteen Scottish Grand Masters.† The list, together with the rest of Anderson's 'history', was (and is) obviously, from a modern perspective, fantasy and no one sought to disprove St Clair's (or anyone else's) alleged position as 'Grand Master'.

The elevation of St Clair to the position of hereditary Grand Master resulted in all twelve of the Grand Masters listed by Anderson in 1738 as succeeding him being erased from Scottish Masonic history as if they had never existed. This doesn't appear to have caused a problem for the Freemasons of the time, but it raises an important question: if all twelve Grand Masters following St Clair were not, in fact, Grand Masters of Scottish masons (stonemasons or otherwise) what credence can be placed in Anderson's assertion that the five preceding St Clairs were Grand Masters (six if we include the 'Patron' Alexander I)? As a

* *Pocket Companion* (Ruddiman, Auld & Co.), op. cit., p. 112.

† Anderson, op. cit.

consequence the suggestion that St Clair was a Grand Master is also doubtful. Indeed, Ruddiman and Auld eliminate five of the six pre-St Clair Royal Grand Masters – the exception being James I.

The embryonic theory had already begun to develop, and 'facts' previously accepted as being accurate were suddenly ignored, or changed, in favour of new ones that enhanced a particular view of the history of Scottish Freemasonry. The description of St Clair as a hereditary Grand Master in a published history was almost inevitable as, at the formation of the Grand Lodge of Scotland in 1736, William St Clair of Roslin (1700–1778) signed a 'Deed of Resignation of the Office of Hereditary Grand Master'. The Knights Templar, however, were still not mentioned.

Ruddiman and Auld appear to have realized that the establishment of a new traditional history of the Grand Lodge of Scotland was in the offing. They also appear to have been aware of the current Scottish Masonic climate and to have understood the implications of the revisions in Anderson's *New Constitutions*, for in their *Pocket Companion* they created a blend of various elements to embellish their version of Masonic history. They left intact Anderson's assertion that the Romans introduced 'Masonry' into Scotland but subtly changed his claim that six kings before St Clair had been Grand Masters to the assertion that it was the Freemasons themselves who recognized the King to be their Grand Master (e.g. 'The Fraternity of Free-Masons in Scotland always owned their King and Sovereign as their Grand Master').

They were also aware of St Clair's 'Deed of Resignation' and gave an explanation as to why it had been required:

> William Sinclair of Roslin Esq: (a real Mason, and a gentleman of the greatest candour and benevolence, inheriting his predecessors virtues without their fortune) was obliged to dispose the estate: and, having no children of his own, was loth that the office of Grand Master, now vested in his person, should become vacant at his death: more especially, as there was but small prospect of the Brethren of the country receiving any countenance or protection from the crown (to whom the office naturally reverted, at the failure of the Roslin family), as in ancient days, our Kings and Princes continually residing in England.*

* *Pocket Companion*, op. cit., pp. 113–14.

It is argued in the deed itself that it was necessary because if St Clair died childless the office of hereditary Grand Master would revert to the crown (and, presumably, the soon-to-be created Grand Lodge of Scotland could not countenance the monarch imposing a hereditary Grand Master upon them). However, the deed, and the need for it, was no more than one influence in the creation of a traditional history for the new body, comparable with that created by James Anderson for the Grand Lodge of England. This can be demonstrated by an examination of the deed and the circumstances surrounding its creation. In the first place it is a myth that St Clair died childless. He had several children:

> The male representation of the family of Rosslyn terminated in William Saintclair, who married Cordellia, daughter of Sir George Wishart of Cliftonhall, by whom he had three sons and five daughters, who all died young, except his daughter Sarah.*

St Clair signed the 'Deed of Resignation' on 24 November 1736, when he was thirty-six years of age, and it is almost inconceivable that he willingly signed away rights that could, by hereditary right, be passed to his daughter, Sarah, or any of her children. It would be unnatural that he would sign away such rights at the early age of thirty-six when it was not impossible for him to marry again and have more children. This, and the fact that he lived for another forty-two years, suggests that the 'Deed' was created for the benefit of one party only: the Grand Lodge of Scotland.

The sole beneficiary of the alleged and unspecified 'rights' – the Grand Lodge – enhanced its antiquity, and therefore its legitimacy, especially in comparison to the fantastic and mythological 'history' of the Grand Lodge of England created by Anderson. Ruddiman and Auld, who reproduced the 'Deed of Resignation' in full, made complimentary remarks about St Clair of Rosslyn, who was still alive in 1761 when their *Pocket Companion* was published. This, then, is a contemporary source that reveals the perceptions of the history of Scottish Freemasonry at that time.

Although it can now be seen that this view of the past is seriously

* Maidment in *The Genealogie of the Saintclaires of Rosslyn* (Edinburgh, 1835), p. ii, quoting *The Baronage of Scotland*, p. 249 by Sir Robert Douglas of Glenbervie Bt. (Edinburgh, 1798).

flawed, this 'history', or at least parts of it, is often repeated uncritically today. The claim that 'Masons' 'always owned their King and Sovereign as their Grand Master' neatly sidesteps the problems created by stating that certain kings of Scotland were Grand Masters. In 1761 Freemasons themselves claimed them all to be Grand Masters (according to Ruddiman and Auld). This was a meaningless claim but it still managed to convey the impression that over many centuries monarchs were involved with 'Masons'.

In this way, the 'historical' emphasis of Scottish 'Masonry' began to become focused on the St Clairs of Rosslyn and the two monarchs, James I and James II. In modifying the myth, Ruddiman and Auld had James I establish a system of governance for the Freemasons of Scotland, which was then adapted by his son, James II:

> Accordingly we find James I. That patron of learning, countenancing the Lodges with his presence, as the Royal Grand Master; till he settled an yearly revenue of four pounds Scots, to be paid by every Master-Mason in Scotland, to a Grand-Master chosen by the Brethren, and approved of by the crown, one nobly born . . .*

This crucial element of the myth is still repeated today, e.g.:

> By the time of James II Stewart, the St Clairs had changed their name to Sinclair and William Sinclair, Earl of Caithness, Grand Admiral of Scotland, was appointed Hereditary Patron and Protector of the Scottish Masons by King James II in 1441. The document of appointment, is held by the Grand Masonic Order, of Scotland, and is Lodged [sic] at Freemasons' Hall in Edinburgh.†

The theory goes that, with James I having created this system for the benefit of 'masons', it was James II who, in 1441, made William St Clair, the builder of Rosslyn Chapel, the Grand Master of masons and thereafter by another, separate 'Deed' created him and his heirs and successors hereditary Grand Masters.‡ However, there is no evidence

* *Pocket Companion*, op. cit., p. 111.

† Michael J. A. Stewart, HRH Prince Michael of Albany, *The Forgotten Monarchy of Scotland*, pp. 101–102. Despite the author's assertion that the 'document of appointment, signed by James' is in Freemasons' Hall, I can confirm that it is not.

‡ *Pocket Companion*, op. cit., p. 112.

connecting James I to Masonic Lodges, that he ever visited such Lodges or that he was Grand Master of 'masons' of Scotland. The earliest possible reference to a lodge in Scotland is in 1491 and that is to a stonemasons' lodge. It is alleged that his son, James II, appointed St Clair the Grand Master (of masons) in 1441 and also made that position hereditary, but James was born in 1430 and would therefore have been eleven years of age when he allegedly made St Clair a Grand Master. It is known that James II took no part in government until 1449 when he was nineteen and so could not have conferred that title on anyone.[*]

More to the point, however, is that the position of Grand Master simply did not originally exist. The offices of the Scottish crown (for example, the Chancellor, Chamberlain, Comptroller, Justiciar of Scotland, Custodian of the King's Person, etc.) are well documented, but the post of Grand Master is never one of them. The term first appears in the eighteenth century and is used in a Masonic context by James Anderson in 1723, when he claims that the Patriarch Moses was the first Grand Master![†] The title was applied, retrospectively, by subsequent writers on Freemasonry.

Father Hay found no trace of deeds from James I or James II when he examined the Sinclair muniments in c. 1700. In the absence of such proof, later authors accepted the claim in the second St Clair 'Charter' (c. 1628) that there had previously been such deeds and that they had been lost in a fire. This means that the charters allegedly issued by James II were lost by fire sometime after 1441 but before 1601.

There is a report in Hay's *Genealogie of the Sinclairs of Rosslyn* that such a fire took place in 1447 but that St Clair's chaplain rescued all the documents: '*. . . declared how his charters and writts were all saved.*'[‡] This being so, the charters allegedly granted by James II must have been destroyed in another fire sometime after 1447 but before 1601. Another fire at Rosslyn Castle occurred in 1722.[§] There appear,

[*] Christine McGladdery, *James II* (John Donald, 1990), p. 49, makes it clear that James II did not take up royal authority until 1449.

[†] Revd Dr James Anderson, *Constitutions* (London, 1723), p. 8.

[‡] Father Richard A. Hay, *The Genealogie of the Sainteclaires of Rosslyn*, ed. James Maidment (Thomas G. Stevenson, 1835), p. 28.

[§] *The Temple and the Lodge*, Michael Baigent and Richard Leigh (Corgi, 1997), p. 164.

therefore, to have been a total of three major fires at Rosslyn Castle but fortunately the two St Clair 'Charters' survived on each occasion. Unfortunately, the deeds allegedly issued by James I and/or II, one appointing St Clair Grand Master and the other making that position hereditary, did not survive – assuming, of course, that they ever actually existed.

This, with all its flaws, was the generally accepted version of Scottish Masonic history that prevailed until the end of the nineteenth century, albeit with minor variations and occasional elaborations.

A Revised History

In 1804 Alexander Lawrie (1768–1831) published a book that changed the view of Scottish Masonic history. It had a wordy title: *History of Freemasonry drawn from authentic sources of information with An Account of the Grand Lodge of Scotland, from its institution in 1736, to the present time, compiled from the records; and An Appendix of original papers.*

Lawrie was Bookseller and Stationer to the Grand Lodge of Scotland. The dedication suggests that he had an eye on his future, as it was dedicated to George, ninth Earl of Dalhousie (1770–1838), who was Depute Grand Master at the time the book was published. Described by Lawrie as Grand Master Elect, Dalhousie did indeed become Grand Master Mason on 30 November 1804 and served in that capacity for two years.

The minutes of a meeting of the Grand Lodge on 3 August 1801 reveal that Lawrie was appointed Bookseller and Stationer to the Grand Lodge in recognition of years of service to that body. The minutes of the next meeting, on 2 November 1801, include the following:

> The Substitute Grand Master [John Clark] stated that he had received a letter from Brother Lawrie bookseller and Stationer to the Grand Lodge inclosing a prospectus of a History of Freemasonry that Brother Lawrie proposed to publish which letter being read it is as follows
>
> Parliament Square No. 24–2nd November 1801
>
> Right Worshipful Sir,

> I take the liberty of sending you a prospectus of a work which I intend to publish, I shall esteem it a particular favour if you will communicate the same to the Grand Lodge of Scotland for the honour which the Grand Lodge conferred on me last Quarterly communication to be their Bookseller and Stationer I shall always be grateful and if I should be fortunate enough to obtain their sanction to the above work it will add another favour which will be highly gratifying to your most obedient and humble servant . . . Alex Lawrie.
>
> The above mentioned prospectus having been read the Substitute Grand Master proposed that the above work should be sanctioned by the Grand Lodge which was unanimously agreed to and the Grand Lodge further authorised the Grand Secretary and Grand Clerk to furnish Brother Lawrie with the records and other writings belonging to the Grand Lodge and with every material within their power which may in any degree lend to the advancement of the work.

Here, then, it would seem that Lawrie's motive in creating such a history is that of a devoted servant seeking to promote the body that had recently recognized his services. However, if he hoped for promotion within the Grand Lodge as a consequence then he must have been disappointed, for he had to wait until 1810. And even then his promotion was to Joint Grand Secretary with William Guthrie (? –1812), who had served as Grand Secretary since 1797. In 1812, Lawrie became Grand Secretary in his own right, probably on Guthrie's death. He remained Grand Secretary until 1826, when he again became Joint Grand Secretary, this time with his son William Alexander (1799–1870), and continued in that joint position until 1831 when his son became sole Grand Secretary – a position he held until 1870.

While Grand Secretary, William A. Lawrie reproduced the book bearing his father's name, in 1859. He introduced no fundamental changes, but reworked each chapter, making them fuller and using more factual information. He also included considerable new additions, which principally described the activities of the Grand Lodge until 1859 (which had been listed until 1804 in his father's edition), together with an account of the Mark, the Royal Arch and Ark Masonry and other orders including the modern Masonic Knights

Templar. His 'history' of the Knights Templar follows that created by the Grand Conclave during 1842/3.* Utilizing more historical evidence than appeared in his father's book, William Lawrie took the opportunity to mount a vigorous attack on Abbé Barruel's opinion of the Knights Templar as expressed in *Mémoires pour servir a l'histoire du Jacobinisme*. Abbé Barruel is one of the first – and certainly the first non-Freemason – to claim that there was a link between the medieval Knights Templar and Freemasonry.†

However, the preface to William Lawrie's work suggests additional motives. The author alludes to the events in Europe and to Freemasonry's possible part in them, specifically mentioning the French Revolution. The allegations that Freemasonry played a part in the original revolutionary 'conspiracy' probably puzzled Scottish Freemasons, especially as the British government had exempted Lodges from the strictures of the Unlawful Oaths Act (1797) and the Unlawful Societies Act (1799), which were designed to eliminate, or at least control, organizations thought to be potentially subversive or revolutionary. In that sense the difference between Freemasonry in Scotland and Europe is demonstrated.

But Lawrie's avowed motive for publishing the *History* was stated to be that:

> The best way of refuting those calumnies which have been brought against the fraternity of Free Masons, is to lay before the public a correct and rational account of the nature, origin, and progress of the institution; that they may be enabled to determine, whether or not its principles are in any shape, connected with the principles of revolutionary anarchy.‡

This laudable aim, reinforced by the view that previous histories of Freemasonry were 'of such a repulsive nature . . . that a new and accurate work was necessary', suggests that the book was highly

* The Grand Conclave is the equivalent of a Grand Lodge but it has jurisdiction over the Masonic ceremonies of the Knights of Malta and the Knights Templar. These bodies are now known as the Great Priories in the UK and as Grand Commanderies in some other parts of the world such as the USA.

† Barruel was a member of the Jesuit society. The first two volumes of his *Mémoires* were published in 1797, followed by volumes three and four in the following year.

‡ Alexander Lawrie, *History of Freemasonry* . . . etc. (Edinburgh, 1804), p. vii.

anticipated.* It is divided into two parts, the first being a fantastic 'history' of Freemasonry from prehistoric times and the second part an annual summary of the activities of the Grand Lodge of Scotland, from its foundation in 1736 to the date of the book's publication. Interestingly, the two manuscripts transcribed by Father Richard A. Hay, and known as the 'St Clair Charters', are reproduced as Appendices, where they are again described as 'charters'. This demonstrates once more the importance placed on these documents, even if their original purpose was not understood. In the book they are described as Charters granted by James II, and the Appendix describes them as being Charters granted by the 'Masons' of Scotland.†

It is ironic that this book, which Alex Lawrie apparently put so much effort into producing, was not even written by him, but by a ghostwriter who received no credit. However, having received the official sanction of the Grand Lodge to produce it, he appears never to have denied being the author. The contrary appears to be the case, as the Minutes of Grand Lodge dated 6 February 1804 contain the following:

> Br. Carphin stated that he had read with great satisfaction a late publication upon Masonry under authority of the Grand Lodge. He considered that the book in question would prove of good utility to Masonry in general and most useful to the Grand Lodge and the Lodges holding under her when this was considered, he was satisfied that every member present would heartily join him in moving the thanks of the Grand Lodge to Brother Alex. Lawrie author of the publication alluded to – this motion having being seconded the thanks of the Grand Lodge was unanimously voted to Br. Lawrie.‡

Who, then, was the unnamed author? Most authorities agree that Sir David Brewster (1781–1868) penned the material and this view is confirmed by the following undated entry in a copy of the book that belonged to Dr David Irving (1778–1860), Librarian to the Faculty of Advocates:

* Ibid., p. viii.
† Ibid., p. 100 and Appendix I & II, pp. 297–304.
‡ Grand Lodge of Scotland, *Minute Book No. 1*, p. 227.

> The history of this book is somewhat curious, and perhaps there are only two individuals now living by whom it could be divulged. The late Alexander Lawrie, Grand Stationer, wished to recommend himself to the Fraternity by the publication of such a work. Through Doctor Anderson, he requested me to undertake its compilation, and offered a suitable remuneration. As I did not relish the task, he made a similar offer to my old acquaintance David Brewster, by whom it was readily undertaken, and I can say was executed to the entire satisfaction of his employers. The title-page does not exhibit the name of the author, but the dedication bears the signature of Alexander Lawrie, and the volume is commonly described as Lawrie's History of Freemasonry.*

While Sir David Brewster made an immense, albeit anonymous, contribution to the history of Scottish Freemasonry, he was also an important figure in Scottish society and academia. At the time of publication he was a young man and had not yet determined a course in life. No doubt he found the monetary reward most useful. His involvement in Scottish Freemasonry appears to have been limited to the production of the book for Lawrie.

After this time the Masonic Order of the Knights Templar, founded by Deuchar in 1808, experienced indifferent fortune and was on the verge of extinction. The individual who revived the order was James Burnes (1801–62), whose great-grandfather was the brother of William Burnes, father of Scotland's national bard, Robert Burnes (later Burns, 1759–96). The life and Masonic career of Burnes has been described elsewhere.† Of relevance here is his publication in 1837 of *A Sketch of the History of the Knights Templars*, a year after he and many others became members of the order.‡ The book was dedicated to 'His Royal Highness, Prince Augustus Frederic, Duke of Sussex, K.G. &c., P.R.S., Grand Prior of England.'

The significance of this book cannot be overestimated for it contains the modern theory of a connection between the Knights Templar and Freemasonry in full. Small omissions are later embellishments,

* That it was common knowledge that it was the work of Brewster is affirmed by Maidment's reference to *Brewster's Encyclopædia* in *The Genealogie of the Sainteclaires of Rosslyn*, op. cit., p. v.

† Robert F. Gould, 'Masonic Celebrities: No. VIII – The Chevalier Burnes', AQC, Vol. XX, pp. 44–53.

‡ Printed by William Blackwood and Sons, Edinburgh.

such as the details of a few fugitive knights fleeing to Argyll from France. The creation of the theory can be explained simply. With the formation of the Scottish Masonic Knights Templar as a semi-formal body in c. 1808, in common with all branches of Freemasonry, its members sought a traditional history as a basis for their ritual, lectures and moral lessons. However, until 1837 they did not have such a history, which may well be one reason why they had fallen on hard times, for without it they would have been hard put to explain what their purpose was. In that year their saviour appeared in the form of James Burnes, who had read extensively about the original Knights Templar, and was familiar with the new versions of the Knights Templars' stories that were by then in existence in Europe, particularly in France. As the French traditional history was not suitable for the Scots who were intent on creating a new Scottish Order, Burnes supplied them with exactly what was required, in the form of a history that blended historical fact with considerable fiction. He gave this a Scottish setting. As long as that position remained fixed then matters were quite clear.

The traditional history of the earliest Craft Lodges was based on King Solomon's Temple. The history of the Holy Royal Arch took as its basis the story of the Jews returning to Jerusalem to rebuild the temple. The Royal Order of Scotland made use of one of the most Romantic periods of Scotland's history. The Knights Templar also made use of Bannockburn but was but one part of a much larger story.

These histories were separate and distinct: if, in the eighteenth or nineteenth centuries, you visited a Royal Arch Chapter, the ritual you would have watched or perhaps participated in would not have been based on the building of King Solomon's Temple. Similarly, if you had attended a Craft Lodge working a First degree, you would have heard nothing about Robert the Bruce and the Battle of Bannockburn, as would have been the case with the Royal Order of Scotland. That was true more than two hundred years ago and it is still true today. Each of these traditional histories was invented specifically for the branch of Freemasonry concerned; and, what is more, they were invented for allegorical purposes. In other words, they were not intended to be taken as literally true nor was it ever intended that they be lumped together. However, in recent years a variety of writers have taken the separate and distinct histories, made them out to be factually correct and then rolled them all together to make one grandiose story – a story which our forebears would simply not have recognized and would probably have laughed at!*

Freemasonry today remains much in the same position as it was about a hundred and fifty years ago. There have been changes, of course, including fluctuations in membership, with high intake following the world wars in particular, and also some declines in membership. Freemasonry continues to exist in many parts of the world, especially where there are tolerant political and religious regimes. Men continue to be attracted to such an unusual organization, unusual in that it has no one 'head office', no dogma and no single leader, but boasts a membership of millions, has some of the most beautiful buildings around and has the mystique of Solomon's Key.

* There is one significant addition to the Masonic 'family' which I have not mentioned, the Scottish Rite, and that is because it arrived only lately on the Masonic scene, in Scotland at least. It was established there in 1846 and does not therefore have a large part to play in the story being related here. I am aware that the Scottish Rite appeared in North America earlier but again it does not significantly impact on the principal content of this work. That is not to say that this part of Freemasonry is not of interest, it is simply beyond the scope of this book.

10

THE ORDER OF THE FREE GARDENERS

Any mention of Lodges, fraternities or secret societies will nearly always bring to mind the Freemasons; it would seem that Freemasonry is the only organization of its kind in the world.[*] Frankly, it sticks out like a sore thumb because it seems to be unique.[†] Yet this was not always so. At one time there were a number of other secret – or at least semi-secret – organizations, of which Freemasonry was but one.

Some of these organizations may be familiar: for example, the Oddfellows, the Antedeluvian Order of Buffaloes, the Rechabites, the Order of Good Templars, the Druids, the Foresters, the Shepherds – to name but a few. There also existed other more obscure groups, such as the Horsemen, the Free Potters, the Free Fishermen, the Free Carpenters, the Free Colliers and Free Carters. These groups shared many similarities with Freemasonry, whilst also differing from it in various respects. The similarities principally lay in the existence of esoteric and ritual elements within the organizations (to a greater or lesser extent), whilst some of the many differences were, for example, of a religious nature.[‡] One of the most obvious differences between

[*] Always bearing in mind the reservations about it being an 'organization' in the normal sense of the term.

[†] I am aware of the existence of quite a number of fraternities but I am speaking here of common perceptions.

[‡] Or they espoused a cause promoted by a church, or churches, such as the temperance movement which manifested itself in the Good Templars and the Rechabites.

Freemasonry and other fraternities is the way in which most, if not all, of these other organizations had financial concerns that were not present in Freemasonry. Occasionally, the financial element sometimes became such a preoccupation that some of the organizations developed into 'Friendly Societies' – a sort of insurance company.

Unlike the majority of these other societies, Freemasonry has flourished and survived. Nevertheless, the organizations have much to teach us with respect to Freemasonry – one in particular, the Free Gardeners, which is probably the oldest equivalent organization after Freemasonry and also the only other one to claim a connection with King Solomon's Temple.

The Origins of the Order of the Free Gardeners

During the seventeenth century the lesser nobility began to copy the designs and Renaissance architecture of the formal gardens of the crown and higher nobility. The formation of the Order of Free Gardeners roughly coincides with wealthy landowners' new-found interest in landscape design and their subsequent employment of a large number of working gardeners. Although there are indications that the Free Gardeners were operating informally without records from as early as 1602, the earliest written evidence is contained in a minute book from Haddington, East Lothian and is dated 16 August 1676. It begins 'Interjunctions for ye Fraternitie of the Gairdners of East Lothian' and consists of fifteen regulations. The early minutes are mainly concerned with maintaining 'the Box' (a money box), the attendance of members and the need to improve the behaviour, pride and honour of local Free Gardeners. There is also discussion about how best to implement the rules they have drawn up.

When the Constitution of the Free Gardeners was written in 1676, many other trades, such as the baxters (bakers), masons, wrights and hammermen, were already recognized public institutions, having been granted the status of incorporations by the burghs. However, the Gardeners never obtained incorporation status for the simple reason that the majority of practical gardeners lived and worked outside the burgh and so theirs could not be considered a burgh trade. Without this official stamp of recognition, the Gardeners nevertheless organized themselves as best they could, with their 'Constitution' detailing the organization of labour, the strict control of the trade, payment of 'trade dues' for benevolence and the supply and sale of plants. The Constitution shows that they were prepared to cooperate, control their members, educate them and strive to improve their morals. Records of their Interjunctions of 1676 suggest that, even though they did not enjoy incorporation status, they modelled their organization along lines similar to other trades. Especially in view of their ceremonial activities, it seems reasonable to believe that they specifically emulated the Masons who, as we have seen, had an additional level of organization beyond that afforded by the incorporation, i.e. the Lodge.*

The Free Gardeners' Lodges

According to the scholar John Hamilton, writing in c. 1873, 'in 1715 Lodges of Ancient Free Gardeners were known to exist in: Linlithgow, Falkirk, Haddington, Arbroath, and many other places'.† Hamilton states that 'the Ancient Fraternity of Free Gardeners at Haddington existed prior to 1716 and were for a long period in communication with Lodges in Germany, importing seeds and roots from them and distributing them amongst their members at prime cost'. However, although Hamilton was aware of the antiquity of the Free Gardeners' lodge at Haddington in East Lothian, he accepts the precedence of the Dunfermline Lodge in Fife within the order, basing this on the existence of their Bond of Union of c. 1715. The existence of a Bond of Union dated 1 May 1677, prepared by a writer (lawyer) by the name of John Smyth and included in the Haddington Lodge minute book, was apparently either unknown to or ignored by Hamilton. This is perhaps because it was not a 'public' document and there was only one

* The Gardeners of Glasgow did achieve incorporation status. Their original Seal of Cause (1625) was burnt by the authorities along with the household effects of their deacon after he died of the plague in 1649. A new Seal of Cause was granted in 1690. This suggests that where the order obtained incorporation status it felt no need to copy the Masonic Lodge type of organization. A Free Gardeners' Lodge was not, as far as can be ascertained, formed in Glasgow city, until the nineteenth century.
† John Hamilton was Master of the Glasgow Olive Lodge.

signature on it belonging to an important person, Sir Thomas Luntoune (Linton).

Three more Gardeners' Lodges came into existence towards the end of the eighteenth century, Bothwell, Cumbnathan (Cambusnethan) and Arbroath.* By 1849, twenty Lodges were known to exist, and on 6 November 1849 a meeting was held at Lasswade, Midlothian, to which all known Lodges were invited, with the intention of establishing a Grand Lodge. Following that meeting, many Lodges previously unknown to each other came into contact for the first time and through the diligence of the first Grand Lodge office-bearers even more Lodges were identified throughout Scotland and brought into the fold.

Following the creation of the first Free Gardeners' Grand Lodge in 1849, mid-nineteenth-century records show an explosion of new Lodges in a manner reminiscent of that which took place with the founding of the first Masonic Grand Lodge more than a century earlier. Sixty-nine new Gardeners' Lodges were formed, including three in the United States of America and one in the Edinburgh militia.

By 1859 the need for better organization had become apparent and a meeting of Lodges was called in Edinburgh, at which upwards of one hundred Lodges were represented.† The principal subject of debate was the future form that the Scottish Grand Lodge should take: whether it should be a single permanent body, have a provincial structure or be a nomadic Grand Lodge in the manner of the Free Gardeners' Grand Lodge of England.‡ In Scotland, a compromise appears to have been reached, with the formation of an Eastern Grand Lodge and a Western Grand Lodge. After the final stage of Grand Lodge development in the Order of Free Gardeners in 1859, only two independent Lodges were

* Hamilton states that the Lodge at Arbroath existed long before this but there is nothing to substantiate this claim.

† John Hamilton.

‡ Further information regarding this Grand Lodge has not been found although it may refer to the schismatic body known as the 'Order of Ancient Free Gardeners' Lancashire Union' founded in 1842. The formation of this body was due, apparently, to the refusal to reduce the 'tramping allowance' of two shillings per day paid to Free Gardeners whilst seeking work and the refusal to commit the ritual to print. This implies that there was some other form of central authority in existence in England prior to 1842 but if so there appears to be little known of it.

formed, in 1863 and 1864, with all others recognizing the precedence of the Grand Lodge.

Without access to the records of a wide range of Lodges it is difficult to know the precise breadth and nature of the order's normal activities and practice; it may be that Lodges organized under Grand Lodges were entirely 'speculative' (certainly in the nineteenth century), and that the independent Lodges continued some association with practical gardening.

Lodge Regulations

Perhaps unsurprisingly, the Lodge of Haddington provides the most complete and detailed information regarding the order's early activities and existence. According to its written constitution, the purpose and aims of the organization can be divided into three main areas: administration, control of the craft and mutual benevolence.

The order in which the regulations are recorded reflects the concerns of the person who transcribed them. The Lodge's clerk, likely to be more literate than his brothers and probably a writer (lawyer), wrote down the rules in order of their importance *to him* as an administrator. An example is the rule that no members can be admitted (initiated) 'without the presence of the President or Chairman or one of the Joint Masters' and, significantly, 'ye Clerk always being present'. Here, then, is a man who knows his central position in the running of the Lodge and who has laid down his principal duties: the recording of names, the keeping of minutes etc.

The first twelve rules all mention money: the collection of sums by way of fines for the breaking of those rules, sums due for admission and annual fees. It is not until we reach regulation 13 that there is any reference to paying out money, to 'distressed widows, orphans and the poor of the Fraternity', naming those authorized to disburse such charity.

Of particular note is the third rule, which allows for the entry of gentlemen, but only on payment of a higher fee than that of a gardener! In other words non-gardeners could be admitted to this Gardeners' Lodge but they had to pay for the privilege. From the outset, then, the order (at least in its first formalized form) arranged for the admission of non-gardeners, but at a premium.

In essence the lairds had nothing to do with the 'craft of gardenery' but, as suggested by the constitution, the mutual benefits of a closer association between the two social groups must have been recognized by the Lodge, with the admission of 'Noblemen, Gentlemen' (i.e. non-gardeners) clearly being of financial benefit. It is likely that having important local men as members helped to legitimize the Lodge, which of course had no official incorporation status. In return, the minutes of the Lodge show that it provided practical assistance to landowners, particularly in supplying produce. In 1693, for example, it is recorded that the Laird of Athelstoune (Athelstaneford) bought two dozen 'colliflowers' and the Laird of Nunland bought one pound of leek seed. By 1704, the supply and sale of plants and seeds had ceased, or at least this activity was no longer recorded in the minutes.

The remainder of the Haddington regulations are concerned with the control of the gardening craft for the mutual improvement of all the members. For example, no Brother shall 'intyse [entice] or seduce his Brother's Prentice or Servant or procure ane service for him without his libertie [permission] first had and obtained', and 'Brethren admitted shall give his best counsell to his Brother for Levelling, Contryving, Planting and Dressing of Ground'. The regulations were designed to improve the conditions of the gardeners financially and also to improve the morals of the members, with one regulation stating for example that 'none of the said Fraternity shall presume to curse and swear' and 'none . . . shall presume to back byte, or speak evill'. Any violation of these regulations was liable to incur fines.

Lodge Activities

Having rules and regulations was all very well but what did the members of this order actually do? The early minutes of the Haddington Lodge record the collecting of funds for the support of distressed members and their dependants, the dissemination of horticultural knowledge and advice, the supply and selling of plants and seeds, the recording of the admission of new members and the regulation of those members engaged in the craft of gardening.

It is not until the eighteenth century that the minutes begin to reveal more information. Specifically, new members are recorded in more detail: 'Wm. Low in Ballincreiff was received among ye fraternity and paid what was usual to others' (20 October 1719). An entry dated 6 August 1776 gives some indication of the social mores of the time:

> Then the Master made a complaint to the Fraternity that reflections had been made against him for excluding the wives of members out of the Gardeners' seat in the church and desired that the Fraternity to put it to the vote of the members present whether the members' wives should sit in the seat or not and the vote being put it was voted unanimously by the members present accept one that no members' wives or any woman had the right to sit in the Fraternity's seat and ordered the door keeper to exclude the women accordingly.

Later the Lodge became more public by increasing its social activities and holding biannual flower shows. As John Hamilton states, 'the Gardeners' Lodges in Scotland were the first to introduce and establish those exhibitions and competitions of flowers, which were so popular'. These flower shows were open to anyone, but, according to Hamilton, 'many of the best prizes remained in the hands of the members [of the order] although the judges were not connected with them'.

The Haddington Lodge was by no means insular with respect to other Lodges and organizations. The minutes reveal, for example, that on '3 July 1855, The Oddfellows request the use of the Free Gardeners' forms (benches) and tables for their annual dinner Tuesday next – agreed'; and on '1 November 1859, proposed invitations be sent to the Free Gardeners' Lodges of St Cuthbert's, Barony of Broughton and St James', Lasswade, for AGM (and competition) on 2 August 1860'. St Cuthbert's Lodge was one recognized by the Eastern Grand Lodge of Free Gardeners. St James' Lodge has not been found in the records consulted, suggesting that, like the Haddington Lodge, it was independent of any higher authority.

An entry in the Haddington Lodge minutes dated 14 December 1880 states: 'Two complimentary tickets for the Order of Foresters' Soiree, Concert and Ball, received and two Bros. appt. to attend. Resolved to invite [to what is not stated] two members from Oddfellows, Foresters and two Bros. from Dunbar, two complimentary tickets to Edinburgh Horticultural Society.' From these – admittedly randomly selected – entries from the minutes of the Free Gardeners' Lodge at Haddington, it can been seen that the Lodge was an accepted part of the local community, on good terms with what might in other circumstances be considered to be rival organizations.

Records of the Lodge in Dunfermline, Fife show that from the outset this Lodge also admitted non-gardeners, with a merchant, a writer and a smith being recorded as members in 1716.* As the Lodge attracted more and more men of high social status, it became increasingly ambitious. Whereas in 1719 all the proceeds of the box (the Lodge 'bank') had been spent on importing rare seeds for the use of its members, between 1734 and 1766 it purchased twenty acres of land (to the north-east of Dunfermline), which were divided into three parks and feued (a form of rent) to various individuals. It even sponsored an annual horse race and horticultural exhibition.† By 1809 it was realized that the original aims of the Lodge were not being fulfilled and an attempt was made to resurrect the annual flower show. However, interest continued to wane in these activities, as did the Lodge's financial position. In 1832 all existing regulations were rescinded and the Lodge reorganized on more stringent financial lines. All widows (who had traditionally been supported by the Lodge) had their right to any future financial assistance cancelled by a one-off payment of £2.

The Friendly Society Acts of 1829 and 1850 had a great impact on the Lodge's benevolent activities, which is one explanation for the increase in the number of Lodges at that time. The Free Gardeners' Friendly Society made it a precondition that those wishing to join it first had to be initiated in a Lodge. The 1896 Friendly Society Act finally forced all voluntary benefit societies over a certain membership to register as a friendly society. The Ancient Society of Gardeners in

* 'Laws of the Ancient Society of Gardeners in and about Dunfermline', printed 1918. Dunfermline Public Library.

† The race took place along a public highway – Carnock Road, Dunfermline. This required the permission of the local authorities. The annual race had been instituted as early as 1723 as the following entry, of 30 April, from the burgh records, shows: 'The said day the counsell, for incouraging of the Gardener's race to be keept up here they agreed that the town shall next year Contribute thirty shillings sterling for buying and putting a plete [a plate? – as a prize?] for next year'.

and about Dunfermline fell into this category and by 1918, at the latest, the Lodge at Dunfermline had so registered. By this time all of that Lodge's gardening activities had apparently ceased.

Ritual

The earliest known records of the Free Gardeners at Haddington, such as the regulations, bond of union and early minutes, contain no absolute proof that the Lodge taught 'initiates' any secret knowledge. Such evidence as there is suggests a purely businesslike approach to trade and to charity. It may, however, be deduced that there was something more to the early Order of the Free Gardeners than simply a benefit society, for the members of a higher social status who became attracted to it did not need the financial protection offered by the order. What then was that 'something extra' that appealed to them?

Later entries in the minute books of the Haddington Lodge show that the order *did* indeed impart esoteric knowledge to its initiates. Early minutes are evasive regarding that knowledge, stating only that men were 'received among the fraternity', and it is not until the minute of 28 January 1726 that the existence of esoteric knowledge is disclosed:

> which day ye Fraternitie considered a complaint against George Wood, one of their number, for vilifying ye by saying that they [the Deacons] worst not capable to give either word or sign of ye Craft. . .

George Wood was fined £5 (Scots) for this offence.

A later, more specific reference to secrecy was recorded on 6 October 1772:

> The which day Hew Dalrymple Esq. of Nunraw and Robt. Howdon Baker in Haddington were duly admitted and received members of this Fraternity. Having received the word and Secret, heard the articles read and they Bind and oblige themselves to Implement the articles made or to be made in the fraternity

And on 24 May 1799:

> The above members [eight names] being duly met and the Hall constituted, John Affleck, Shop Keeper to Messers Dickson and Co. was admitted a member and received all the signs and Secrets of the Fraternity and paid the sum of Five shillings and all dues.

By 1848 this knowledge is recorded in the minutes as 'Signs, Secrets and Grips'.

Early minutes of the Haddington Lodge reveal that a man was proposed at one meeting and initiated at the next, with no further ceremony taking place in relation to that initiate thereafter. However, the more detailed minutes of later years reveal the gradual development of ritual from a basic ceremony – to impart the 'word' – into something much more elaborate, culminating in a three-degree system by the late nineteenth century. Thus, new members were initially recorded simply as being admitted as members; later they were given the 'word'; later still 'the word and secret'; then they were entrusted with 'the words and secrets', and later on with 'words, secrets and grips'. (Not surprisingly, surviving rituals do not provide information regarding the words, signs and grips.)*

A booklet dated 1930 entitled 'Lectures on Craft: As sanctioned by Grand Lodge' was printed in Edinburgh under the auspices of the Scottish Grand Lodge and was therefore used by all the Lodges under its authority. It shows that there were three degrees in existence by the time of publication. These were the First (or apprentice) degree, the Second (or journeyman) degree and the Third (or master) degree. The degrees took the form of catechisms, or series of lengthy questions and answers, possibly 'test questions'. Additionally, there were installation and funeral rituals.†

* Although occasionally these may be implied from the ritual, e.g., 'What does that sign signify? To having my heart plucked out . . . ' 'The Ancient Order of Free Gardeners' by W. Bro. T. W. R. Proctor, PPSGW, published in the *Transactions of the Somerset Masters Lodge, No. 3746*, Vol. 9 (1948).

† However, it appears that independent Lodges did not practise any of these later ceremonies and may have kept to the simple rituals suggested in the early Haddington minutes. Likewise, the fragmented nature of the Order of the Free Gardeners suggests that its rituals may have developed differently depending on whether or not a particular Lodge was under the authority of the Eastern or Western Grand Lodge, or remained independent.

The Origins of the Teachings

With respect to the origins of their teachings, the Free Gardeners provided the following definitions of 'Gardenery' and 'Free Gardenery':

> Gardenery may be defined as the art of disposing the earth in such a manner as to produce whatever vegetables and fruits we desire, in large quantities and the greatest perfection of which their natures are capable.
>
> Free Gardenery is the applying of the cultivation of the ground and its productions as symbols expressive of the necessity of cultivating the mind in intelligence and virtue.*

These basic definitions directly link 'Free Gardenery' – that is, non-operative (speculative) 'gardenery' – to the operative craft of gardening. The moral teachings of the order are clearly based on the operative craft, and go on to use the earliest references in the Old Testament to any 'craft'.

Genesis II:8 states 'and the Lord God planted a garden eastward in Eden: and there he put the man whom he had formed', with Genesis II:15 continuing, 'and the Lord God took the man and put him into the garden [of Eden] to dress it and keep it'. The first man in the first garden was none other than Adam in Eden, a place whose perfection reflected his own. All that he had to do was to tend the garden, a task which would have been negligible in a perfect place and as such was a ceremonial role only.

Adam was permitted to eat freely of all the fruits in the garden but was cautioned never to eat of the Tree of Knowledge. Indeed, he was warned of dire consequences if he did so: he would surely die (spiritually), thorns and thistles would grow and he would 'eat bread, till thou return unto the ground: for out of it wast thou taken: for dust [soil] thou art and unto dust shalt thou return'. However, the Lord God sensed the loneliness of Adam and so created a companion for him, Eve, from one of his creation's ribs. But the Serpent tempted Eve, who in turn tempted Adam, with the consequence that both of them ate the fruit of the Tree of Knowledge. When Adam ate the forbidden fruit and lost his innocence the Garden of Eden could no longer reflect his

* Partial lecture printed in 1908 but delivered in 1873 by John Hamilton.

previous perfection. Reflecting the Fall of Adam, the Garden of Eden sprouted thorns and briars – the worst enemies of a gardener. For this original sin, God ejected Adam from the garden into the profane world whence he had come. With Adam removed, the garden returned to its perfect state.

The ritual of the order of the Free Gardeners begins with Adam and Eve in the perfect garden, in perfect harmony and in perfect peace. Adam is the first Free Gardener (or first 'non-practising' gardener), until Eve tempts him with forbidden fruit – the apple of the Tree of Knowledge. This first sin, despoiling as it did the perfect garden of TGGOTU (the Great Gardener of the Universe), meant that Adam became the first true journeyman or working gardener, as he travelled the world in a vain attempt to restore horticulture to the perfect state that it had been in at the creation. The thorns, briars, weeds and pests had arisen in the world as manifestations of his sin and so he spent the rest of his life trying to destroy them.

The Three Degrees

The First Degree

The ritual of the First, or apprentice, degree is based closely on the story of the Garden of Eden and Adam's fall from grace. The ritual tells of words, signs, grips and steps and is, in many ways, similar to the Masonic rituals that exist today. For instance, the candidate is prepared and divested of 'all means, minerals, metals and parts of his clothing'. He is blindfolded and his obligation is taken kneeling on a bare left knee. Words are 'lettered or divided' and there is an explanation of 'working tools'. The candidate is invested finally with an apron (following the Fall of Adam and Eve, Genesis III:7 explains, 'And the eyes of them both were opened, and they knew they were naked: and they sewed fig leaves together and made themselves aprons').

The first question asked of the candidate is: 'What did you come here upon?' His answer is, 'My mother earth.' Whilst this is a possible allusion to the Garden of Eden, it also contains connotations of pre-Christian and pagan suggestions of an Earth Mother goddess.

The second and third questions are more revealing:

'What are you?'

'A man.'

'How do you know yourself to be a man?'

'By having that revealed to me which was never revealed to woman.'

This secret, only revealed to Adam, not Eve, is the secret of Free Gardenery. This demonstrates the basis for a male-only membership as only a man, Adam, had possession of the original secret.

There then follows an examination of the candidate's willingness to give the words, which he deflects by agreeing to letter or divide them. The first 'Word' is 'DAK' and is stated to be the Gardeners' motto. Unfortunately, it has not been possible to determine what this 'word' (or the letters) actually means, although it has been suggested that it is an abbreviation of 'Delving And Knowledge'.* The 'Pass' word is also lettered, or divided, and is: 'AND'. The letter A means 'All things', for God made all things; N means 'Nothing', for God made all things out of nothing; the third letter, D, is for 'Dust', for 'Dust thou art and unto dust shalt thou return' (Genesis III:19). The test word is ADAM, the name of the first head or apprentice gardener. All three words require a sign, but only the sign for the last can be conjectured with any degree of certainty, for, when the candidate is asked, 'Why that Sign?' he answers: 'A. . . [Adam] when he knew he was naked, he was ashamed and hid his face' (Genesis III:10). The second and third words also demand a Grip, but the ritual provides no indication as to what these were or how they were given.

The candidate is then asked questions relating to how he applied to become a Free Gardener (by approaching someone he thought to be a member); how he was first prepared (in his heart); divested of all means, minerals and metals, parts of his clothing; blindfolded and led up to a door. He was divested of all means to show that he had nothing offensive or defensive to take into the Lodge; divested of clothing to prove that he was not a woman; blindfolded to demonstrate that he was in darkness and taken to a door to seek a new life. He explains that he knows that he is at a door for he hears a number of knocks from without and a number from within.

On admittance he is asked in whom he puts his trust and he replies, 'In God.' Thereafter, he is led a specific number of times around the

* I am grateful to A. Trevor Stewart for offering this possible interpretation.

Lodge to show that he is duly prepared. He then takes two steps backward and three steps forward 'in order to show that I would rather take three steps forward than two backward to the assistance of a brother in distress'.

The candidate then takes his obligation: 'I was taught to kneel on my bare bended left knee, within three circles, on three squares of a Gardener's apron: my left hand on the Holy Bible, Square, Compass and Knife: my right hand extended towards heaven, holding the most useful, yet most dangerous implement of Gardenery, and my face due East. It was there I took that most solemn vow an obligation as an apprentice Free Gardener.'

The explanation of the working tools is revealing. The square is said to signify 'squaring moral actions'; the compasses were 'To encompass me with due submission to the rules, not only of my Lodge, but of every other well regulated Lodge of Free Gardeners'. The knife is intended to signify: '. . . the most useful implement of Gardenery for pruning and engrafting, teaches me to cultivate my mind by casting off these vices which are inherent in our nature, and engrafting these virtues of brotherly love and kindly affection which ought to characterise every true gardener.' (Again we can draw comparisons with Masonic ritual, although there are interesting differences.)

With respect to the three circles mentioned by the candidate, the first circle represents the world that he (Adam) has to walk around and earn his bread in by the sweat of his brow. The second circle represents the Free Gardeners' Lodge to which he is now bound. The third, central or inner, circle is said to be a direct reference to scripture: 'When the Angel of the Lord stood with one foot on the dry land and the other on the sea, he called with a loud voice: "As long as earth remains, day and night, summer and winter, seed time and harvest shall never cease."' (Genesis VIII:22).* The candidate's right hand is directed towards Heaven in order to call on God to witness the sincerity of his obligation. He takes his obligation on his bare left knee 'To show that unto God every knee should bow and every tongue confess'. Three Great Lights are mentioned: the Light of the Law, the Light of the Gospel and the Light of Free Gardenery.

* This may refer to Revelation, X:1–6, which is mentioned in the ritual from the mid-nineteenth century.

The Second Degree

The Second degree links the Garden of Eden with Noah. This degree is known as the journeyman's degree and centres round the newly admitted apprentice's symbolic journey as a Free Gardener. He travels as far as the Garden of Eden, where he finds a river that flows out of the garden and divides into four great rivers (Genesis, II:10ff. and 13ff.). These rivers are Pison, representing 'changing extension of mouth', Gihon, being 'the valley of Grace', Hiddekel (Tigris), meaning 'a sharp voice or sound' and Euphrates, denoting 'fruitful and plenteous'. The 'Word' PGHE, resulting from their names, is said to be whence the Free Gardeners' alphabet derives, but no further details of this are given. This word is accompanied by a grip and another word, the latter signifying 'four heads' (of the rivers).

The journey continues to the Garden of Nuts (Song of Solomon, VI:11) where the apprentice observes pomegranates, vines and grapes. Thence it is to Bethlehem in Judea, where the bright and glorious star is seen and 'who [the star – Jesus Christ] sayth: "I am the vine, ye are the branches" ' (John XV:5). Only the first line of this verse is used in the ritual.

The journey ends in the Garden of Gethsemene, where the apprentice finds the plant of renown and, when asked who was the plant of renown, replies, 'Christ,' He being 'our mediator and elder brother'. He also finds the passion flower, which 'bleeds and the rays of innocence arise out of its bloody blossom'. This appears to be allegorical of the Passion (death) of Christ and his Resurrection. When asked to describe Gethsemene, the apprentice states: 'a small village in Judea, before which lay the garden of Gethsemene, planted by Kings David and Solomon, enlarged and improved by their succeeding Princes . . . ' Although there is no explanation of the sudden transition from Old Testament to New Testament stories, here is an attempt to link the Old and New Testaments within the ritual. The attempt is flawed as there is no reference in the Bible to Gethsemene's being planted by King David or King Solomon; indeed there is no reference to Gethsemene at all in the Old Testament. (There is a reference to a garden belonging to King David in the Book of Ezdra, in the Apocrypha, but this has no bearing on the Free Gardeners' ritual.)

The ritual then turns to the word of that degree, referring once more to Genesis and focusing on the son of Lamech: 'and he called his name Noah, saying, This same shall comfort us concerning our work and toil of our hands, because of the ground which the Lord hath cursed' (Genesis VI:29). As Noah is regarded as the second head gardener, or journeyman gardener, for he was the 'first head of all mankind after the flood', the word of this degree is NOAH, lettered or divided. It is explained how Noah planted a vineyard but became drunk on its produce and so was ridiculed by his sons (Genesis IX:20). The apprentice is thereby taught that he can partake of drink but not to excess lest he too becomes dishonoured in the eyes of the Lord.

The sign is of 'having my heart plucked out, being the second penalty of my obligation'. Four 'Jewels' are described: the altar, which teaches gratitude to God; the ark, demonstrating God's preserving care of the righteous; the rainbow, being representative of faith in the promises of God; and a dove with an olive branch in its beak, which teaches that we should live at peace with all men. There are four lights in the Lodge, during this degree, each representing one of the four jewels.

The Third Degree

The word in the Third or master's degree is SOLOMON, which, as before, is only imparted by lettering or dividing. The sign is suggestive of knowledge and there is also a grip. According to the ritual, Solomon is the third head gardener or master gardener, for he planted a garden in Balhama and had knowledge of all the trees, shrubs and other plants from the lofty Cedars of Lebanon to the lowly ivy and hyssop.* The cedars were used to strengthen and beautify the temple, ivy for garnishing its walls and hyssop for sprinkling and purification. The 'Watchword' is OLIVE and is also given by lettering or dividing. The sign associated with this word signifies two olive leaves put together, which contain 'the whole secrets of Free Gardenery . . . and was chosen because it was an emblem of peace'. This emblem is explained fully: 'In the first instance when Noah sent the dove out of the Ark, lo in the evening it returned with an olive branch in its mouth as an emblem of peace, signifying that God was again reconciled with man.'

* This 'word', Balhama, has not been identified, by the author, as originating from biblical texts. It may be a secret 'constructed' word the meaning of which is known only to Free Gardeners.

In the second instance, 'when the High Priest went into the Holy of Holies once a year to make intercession for the sins of the people, he took in his hand an olive branch as an emblem of peace, showing unto us the peaceful means by which we may be again admitted into the favour of God.' In the third instance, 'when our blessed Lord and Saviour went up to the Mount of Olives to pray, He said: "Tarry ye here until I pray yonder." For these reasons the olive leaves are selected above all others to contain the whole secrets of Free Gardenery.'

There are five jewels in this degree: the olive, meaning peace; a crown with five points ('as Solomon ruled the Children of Israel with knowledge so may you rule your passions and tempers with the aid of the five senses'); cedar and hyssop, which indicate study ('although we may gain knowledge from the study of great objects [Cedar], still there is nothing so insignificant [Hyssop] but from which we may derive much useful information'); the vine, which teaches the lesson 'I am the Vine, ye are the branches' (John, XV:5); and the garden door, which teaches the need to protect the watchword.

When the journeyman gardener is asked if he has travelled any further he replies: 'In ideas, but not in realities.' He explains that in ideas he has travelled as far as New Jerusalem and that he saw there 'a pure river of water, clear as crystal, proceeding out of the throne of God and the Lamb, on either side of its banks grew the tree of life, bearing twelve manners of fruits. Yielding its fruits every month, and whose leaves are used for the healing of nations, and under whose ample boughs, every true and lawful brother will at last find rest.' Finally, he is asked to name the twelve manner of fruits, which are: 'Righteousness, Peace, Pardon, Acceptance, Adoption, Sanctification, Wisdom, Power, Holiness, Comfort, Grace, and Glory.' He continues with a passage from Psalm LI:

> Behold now the inward parts
> With truth delight art
> And Wisdom thou shall make me know,
> Within the hidden part,
> Do thou with hyssop sprinkle me,
> I shall be cleansed so
> Yea wash thou me and then I shall
> Be whiter than the snow.

Although it gives a clear insight into the sources upon which it is based, the ritual of the three degrees gives no indication as to the actual ceremonial, duties or positions of the office-bearers, nor to Lodge procedure.

As the records of the Lodge at Haddington suggest a simple form of initiation which, over time, developed into a much fuller ceremony, the ritual described above should be considered a much more modern refinement of the original mode of initiation. Here again we can see parallels with Freemasonry.

The Installation Ritual

The installation ritual of the 'Western Grand Lodge of Free Gardeners' is dated 1896. Although it is entitled 'Ceremony to be observed at the Installation of Office-Bearers', it contains no details of the actual ceremony itself and is more a collection of addresses to the various office-bearers. This does, however, reveal some of the esoteric teachings of the order, such as those implied in the address of the retiring Right Worshipful Master (originally the term Chancellor was used) to the office-bearers, below:

> *Retiring R.W.M.* [Right Worshipful Master] – Worthy Office-Bearers, it gives me great pleasure to address you at this time. You have been elected from amongst the Brethren as men worthy of the honour to which they have called you. Let it, therefore, be your pride and your glory to fulfil with zeal and love the duties you are about to take upon you. Show unto the Brethren, and to all men, by your prudence and deportment in life that you are worthy of the honour. Show that while you take the stately and majestic Cedars of Lebanon for your Emblem, you do not forget the humility and modesty of the Hyssop, nor the unassuming beauty of the Rose of Sharon and the Lily of the Valley. In the Garden you will find Flowers of various hue: learn their nature and their fragrance, that you may be enabled to transplant them into a harmonious whole, so that Love and Truth may dwell together. In the Garden you will find also straight and crooked paths. Let it be your pride and ambition to plant along the borders of the straight walk, in order to beautify it, Shrubs of renown and Trees of righteousness, so as to entice the Brethren from the crooked path which leads down into the Valley where groweth rank the Poppy, the Hemlock, and the deadly

> Nightshade, whose exhalations produce vice, misery, and death, into the straight walk of Faith, Hope, and Charity, where blooms in luxuriance the Tree of Life. I humbly trust and pray that it will be the aspiration of each and all of you to taste of the delicious Fruits, and enjoy the glory and beauty of Eden restored.

The obligation states that an office-bearer will abide by the Lodge by-laws, obey the Master and office-bearers and be 'affectionate to all the Brethren'. When the retiring RWM addresses the RWM-elect he charges him to care for the Lodge, and direct the office-bearers in their duties because if he does not do so, 'the prosperity of the Lodge might be blasted, and it wither away like the leaves of autumn, whereas by your directing influence, the Lodge may flourish like the green Bay Tree, beneath whose branches many find shelter, happiness and repose'. Immediately thereafter the outgoing RWM is invested with his jewel of office as Immediate Past Master and then places the RWM in 'the Chair'.

The Funeral Ritual

The funeral ritual, dated 1894, is also likely to be a modern rendition of a practice that existed at least eighty years previously. A minute dated 5 March 1814, for example, reads: 'The death of Brother James Samuel was intimated. The meeting unanimously agree that Four Gardner Lads should precede the Funeral of the Deceased (if agreeable to the relations) from his House to the Church Yard with their spades inverted, and in mourning, on the day of interment.'

Regalia

Many of the signs and symbols of the Order of the Free Gardeners are very similar to those of the Freemasons and it is not surprising that the trappings of the two orders are occasionally mistaken for each other.

The Apron

At first glance any one looking at a Free Gardeners' apron is very likely to assume that it is Masonic. Indeed it is quite possible that, as with other symbols and regalia, the Gardeners copied their apron from that of Scottish Freemasonry. However, just as the Scottish Masonic apron appears to have derived from aprons originally used by stonemasons, the 'modern' Gardeners' apron could also have been based on the apron worn by practising gardeners.

In any event, the Free Gardeners' aprons have a semicircular flap that is similar to those of modern Scottish Masonic aprons (a triangular flap is common to most other parts of the Masonic world). In an example of a Free Gardener's apron owned by the Grand Lodge of Scotland, the symbols of the square and compasses are embroidered on the flap, along with a pruning knife at a similar angle to that of the square. As early records appear to make no mention of the square and compasses as symbols used by the Free Gardeners, the inclusion of them here may be a more modern innovation 'borrowed' from Freemasonry, with the pruning knife added to distinguish the order from Freemasonry.* The apron measures sixteen inches by sixteen, whereas (modern) Scottish Masonic aprons measure sixteen inches wide by fourteen deep.

Jewels

Like those belonging to Freemasons, 'jewels' were possessed by the Past Masters of the Free Gardeners. Examples of these indicate that some members were quite prepared to spend considerable sums for quality regalia during the inter-war years when the Order was experiencing a revival. A depiction of a Free Gardener's Past Master's jewel, decorated with a square and compass and pruning knife, was reproduced in an advertisement within the Year Book of Lodge Union, No. 332, in 1924. It is interesting to note that this was the year book of a Masonic Lodge. The prominent use of these symbols, together with details of Masonic regalia available, suggests that at that time Freemasonry and Free Gardeners may have had members who belonged to both Orders (even though dual membership appears to have ceased in the year that the

* Exactly when the order began to 'borrow' Masonic symbolism (assuming that it did) will probably never now be established but there was considerable overlap in the working tools of both orders. For instance, a stone marking the 'plot' of the Greenock Gardeners' Society, dated 12 July 1754, shows the Tree of Knowledge in the centre, crossed rake and spade to the left and on the right a level and a skirret. The latter working tools would have been used extensively by operative gardeners. This stone also suggests that the organization was more widely spread than the existing written records suggest.

Masonic Grand Lodge of Scotland was created). Or perhaps the regalia manufacturer simply confused the orders.

Banners

Two banners of the Order exist in the museum of the Grand Lodge of Scotland. Both are specific to Free Gardeners' Lodges. The first belonged to Lodge Ballieston, No. 21 (on the outskirts of Glasgow), and displays all the symbols of the Order. The other belonged to Lodge Cambuslang Philanthropic and again shows the full range of the symbols of the Order. Both are hand-embroidered. Although they may be considered amateurish by some standards, there can be no doubt that a considerable amount of time and effort went into their production. The brethren of the Order were clearly devoted to their own Lodges (although one has to say that it is unlikely that these banners were executed by men).

Parallels with Freemasonry

In terms of their early organization and development, the similarities between the Order of the Free Gardeners and Freemasonry are striking. Both formed gatherings of members into Lodges, with those Lodges remaining outside the jurisdiction of the burgh. Both sprang from operative origins dedicated to providing mutual support in times of individual financial difficulty, the dissemination of knowledge of their trade and practice, and the transmission of esoteric knowledge. Both soon admitted (and recorded) the membership of non-operatives, charging higher admission fees for those non-operatives, until such a time that the operatives – the stonemasons and the gardeners – were in a substantial minority within their respective organizations.

In much the same way that 'speculative' Freemasonry developed, it appears that the Order of Free Gardeners increasingly came to be a speculative organization over the years, with records suggesting that the Free Gardeners' Lodge in Haddington was essentially an operative Lodge equivalent to the Masonic Lodge in Edinburgh (even though Haddington came to include non-gardeners early on), whereas the Free Gardeners' Lodge at Dunfermline was roughly equivalent to the speculative Masonic Lodge at Haughfoot or Lodge Canongate Kilwinning, No. 2. Similarly, both Freemasonry and the Order of the Free Gardeners appear to have spread from Scotland to England, with the evidence suggesting that after 1603 a large number of gardeners moved to England, where their presence was often resented.*

Another parallel between the two organizations lies in the fact that both Masonic Lodges and Free Gardeners' Lodges existed long before the formation of their Grand Lodges. Yet even before the creation of the Grand Lodges, the Lodges within both organizations shared a strong desire to be seen as 'legitimate'. In Chapter 4, we saw how the Masonic Lodge of Canongate Kilwinning, No. 2, received its authority in 1677 from Lodge Mother Kilwinning, No. 0, some forty years before the first Grand Lodge was formed. Similarly, the new Gardeners' Lodges sought authority from existing Lodges before a Grand Lodge of Free Gardeners was established. Thus the Free Gardeners' Lodge formed in the Edinburgh Militia Regiment during the Peninsular War received its authority from a Lodge in Berwick-upon-Tweed.

This early haphazard method of founding Lodges in both orders is likely to have given additional impetus to the formation of Grand Lodges. Even the time frame involved is not that dissimilar, give or take a decade or so. A period of 138 years separates the first known Masonic records in 1598 from the formation of the Masonic Grand Lodge of Scotland in 1736. Similarly, 173 years elapsed between the creation of the first records of the order of Free Gardeners in 1676 and the founding of their first Grand Lodge in 1849. There is little evidence of dual membership of both orders except for a few men of high social station, with dual membership virtually ceasing from 1736, the year of the foundation of the Grand Lodge of Scotland.

The early organization of Masonic Grand Lodges meant that there was an opportunity for members to progress beyond local Lodge level: Freemasons of high social standing could be honoured at a higher level and accorded more responsibility, ensuring that they became more

* 'In our [Scotland's] history there were at least three occasions between 1603 and 1707 when emigration was possible. . . The first was the accession of James VI to the Throne of England, the second the Restoration [1660], and the third, the Union of the two countries. That a great many Scotsmen held high positions in gardens in England during the eighteenth century is abundantly proved . . . Ill feeling which must have simmered for years came to a head when Scotsmen began, about 1760, to make a success of nursery gardening near London. Then the English in retaliation rushed into print and attacked Scottish gardeners tooth and nail'. E. H. M. Cox, *A History of Gardening in Scotland* (Chatto and Windus, 1935).

involved in the Grand Lodge's activities. In contrast, the highest position one could hold in the order of Free Gardeners was that of Chancellor, or Master, of the Lodge and they had no equivalent of the higher Masonic positions until the creation of their Grand Lodge, by which time the most prominent members of society appear to have lost active interest in the Order.

The Decline of the Order of Free Gardeners

The Order of Free Gardeners survived until the middle of the twentieth century and the friendly society later still, but its eventual decline can be traced to a range of factors. Amongst a variety of considerations, religious influences and age restrictions (and perhaps a combination of both) may have played a part. As we have seen, Freemasonry became substantially 'de-Christianized' over the years and it is now possible for people of all faiths to become members, as long as they respect some form of benevolent higher power. This has certainly had the effect of making Freemasonry universally acceptable and enlarged the 'pool' of potential members. However, with the Free Gardeners the opposite appears to have been the case, with the order becoming increasingly steeped in religious considerations.

With respect to the age of its members, as early as 1773 the 'Charter' granted to Free Gardeners in Dunbar states that 'none shall be admitted into the Fraternity but such as are of a fair and unexceptional character and not under sixteen nor above forty years of age'. This age qualification later became common for 'benefit societies' as dictated by the various Friendly Society Acts of the nineteenth century, with the age restrictions being necessary in order to ensure that the finances of the organizations remained viable. Although the 'Laws of the Ancient Society of Gardeners in and about Dunfermline', printed in 1918, make no reference to the applicants' religion, the 'Articles of the Cambuslang Free Gardeners' Philanthropic Society', printed in 1929, state at article 1: 'He must be between 16 and 40 years of age, of good moral Character, and of the Protestant faith, for which extracts and certificates must be produced within twelve months if required'. Exactly why the religious qualification was added as a requirement for admission to some Lodges, at least, is not known, nor is the impact on their recruitment, but it can be safely said that it is likely to have had a limiting effect.

In the early twentieth century, the order of the Free Gardeners was struggling to maintain its traditional activities in the face of changing social conditions. The lack of a truly central organization meant that considerable competition, if not friction, existed between its various parts, and the obligation to register as a friendly society placed an additional administrative burden. The retention of 'operative' aspects and 'bureaucratic' benevolence from as early as 1829, owing to the Friendly Societies Acts, divided the time of the voluntary members between the esoteric, benevolent and operative functions, and – if the records of Haddington are anything to go by – it appears that the esoteric function was the one to suffer the most, at least in the independent Lodges.

Even then the order might have survived had the recruitment of members been maintained. Finance does not seem to have been an immediate problem but as the need to join a Lodge prior to becoming a member of the friendly society was removed, especially after the institution of the welfare state, Lodge membership declined dramatically. The order could not survive, as the destinies of the Lodges of Dunfermline and Haddington, legally terminated in 1953, prove.

The Truth about King Solomon's Key?

The Free Gardeners were, and are, more secretive than Freemasons. However, it appears that they offered esoteric knowledge on a par with that offered by Freemasonry. Some may even consider their knowledge to be of more interest because of its relative obscurity as the ritual contains Cabbalistic elements as well as other idiosyncratic features.

As we have seen, the first three degrees of the Free Gardeners contained references to King Solomon's Temple. There may well be a hidden dig at Freemasonry here, for although the ancestors of the Freemasons – the stonemasons – built the temple, the inference is that it was the Free Gardeners who completed it by supplying cedars to strengthen and beautify its structure, ivy to garnish its walls and hyssop for sprinkling and purification. Similarly, long after the 'Masons' had finished the temple the Free Gardeners continued to be involved in it: it was they who supplied the high priest with the olive branch that he took in his hand into the Holy of Holies. It is also worth noting: 'the olive leaves are selected above all others to contain the whole secrets of Free Gardenery'.

Does the Key of Solomon lie with the Free Gardeners after all, and not the Freemasons?

11

FREEMASONRY AND A NEW WORLD

It is said that wherever Scots settled in times past, the first thing they did was to build a kirk, then a bank and then a pub. I don't know about the exact sequence, but I do know that in the top four would have been a Lodge!

North America

The first known Freemason in North America was John Skene, who was originally from the Lodge of Aberdeen. It is not recorded when he arrived in New Jersey, but he may have been the John Skene who landed at Burlington in 1678. He was, however, in Pennsylvania in 1681 and in 1682 bought the estate of Peachfield in Burlington County.

He was a Quaker and probably went to America to escape religious persecution. He was followed in 1684 by another member of his Lodge – John Forbes, also a Quaker. He landed at Perth-Amboy and, although he purchased land, he did not stay in the area long but is known to have returned to Scotland after 1686.

The Lodge at Aberdeen seems to have been in existence since at least 1670 and its significance lies in the fact that it was a 'mixed' Lodge, i.e. it was not just a lodge of stonemasons. Its members included merchants, ministers, members of the aristocracy, craftsmen and stonemasons, with stonemasons appearing to have comprised at most twenty per cent of all fellows of craft (that is, the Lodge's full members). Skene and Forbes may have had knowledge of the opportunities in New Jersey from contacts in the Quaker community there; certainly other Quaker members of the Lodge of Aberdeen bought land in New Jersey although they never went there.

John Cockburn is recorded in the minutes of the Lodge at Melrose (now the Lodge of Melrose St John, No. 1[2]) of 1675. He emigrated to New Jersey in 1684, where he wrote a letter to his uncle, George Faa (or Fall), a shoemaker in Kelso, wherein, notwithstanding his uncle's opposition, he encouraged others to emigrate in the following terms: 'I am at the building of a great Stone house in New Perth, Amboy, with another Scotsman.' This is fascinating: who was the other Scotsman? Could it have been Skene or Forbes from the Lodge of Aberdeen? I say fascinating because Cockburn was a member of a stonemasons' lodge and he was almost certainly a stonemason. If his building project with 'another Scotsman' involved Skene or Forbes, here is the first example in North America of a Freemason working with a stonemason/freemason to build in stone – the ultimate synthesis of creating a 'temple of the mind' with the erection of a physical building. In this collaboration, the art of memory meets the art of stonemasonry. Note the emphasis that Cockburn uses: 'a great Stone house'. The intimate connection between Freemasonry and stonemasonry is an almost entirely Scottish phenomenon. The overlap between the two exists nowhere else.* This intimate link was to have further repercussions.

It is speculation whether Skene, Forbes and Cockburn ever formed a Lodge or initiated anyone into such a Lodge. There are no records to suggest that they did. However, they were a long way from home and there was no Grand Lodge in existence in their new country from which they could obtain 'authority' to form a Lodge. Nor were there any other Lodges on the continent that could legitimize their Masonic existence.

The first known legitimate Lodge in North America was the Lodge of St John, located in Boston, Massachusetts. Founded in 1733, it received a warrant from the Grand Lodge of England. Thereafter Lodges slowly spread across the continent, with the first Lodges in Canada being formed in 1755.

* There were a couple of Lodges in the north-east of England with characteristics of stonemasons' lodges but they have been dismissed as being Scottish in everything but name and place.

The first 'official' Scottish Lodge was the Lodge of St Andrews, Boston, founded in 1756. Paul Revere (1735–1818) and Joseph Warren (1741–1775) were both members; in fact, both were more than just members. Revere became the Lodge's Secretary and later Master, and Warren was appointed by the Grand Lodge of Scotland to be the Provincial Grand Master of Scottish Freemasonry in the colonies. There is some indication that it was to this Lodge that those of a Republican outlook gravitated; indeed many Freemasons came to view Freemasonry, as an institution, to be Republican.

The colonies were greatly influenced by the 'country' Whig party within British politics, one of its principal complaints being the corruption surrounding the 'court' Whigs, who were hardly distinguishable from Tories. This divide developed into a political ideology called 'Republicanism' and became widespread in America by 1775. Many loyal to Britain recognized the force of the argument. Republicanism emphasized the duty of the citizen to be moral and virtuous, and to fight for his country when required. Corruption came to be associated with the British aristocracy and was increasingly condemned by the colonies. All fifty-six of the American 'Founding Fathers' were strong advocates of Republicanism, especially the nine Freemasons among them.

Whilst Republicanism stressed the duties of the citizen, another stream of thought was liberalism as advocated by the philosopher John Locke (1632–1704). This ideology argued that government, any government, could exist only with the consent of those governed. In other words, the government must guarantee the rights of citizens to 'life, liberty and estate', which Jefferson amended to 'life, liberty and the pursuit of happiness'. Significantly, Locke said that any government that did not guarantee these things would not have the consent of the governed, i.e. the people. Without that guarantee and consent, the people had the right to rebel. These ideas had an enormous influence on the development of the 'science' of political philosophy. Locke is considered to be one of the most important and influential Enlightenment philosophers and thinkers. Together with the writings of many Scottish Enlightenment thinkers, he influenced the American revolutionaries, a fact that is reflected in the American Declaration of Independence.

An analysis of political thought and philosophy of the time and its impact before, during and immediately after American independence is far beyond the scope of this book, but the idea that Freemasonry had some resonance, some effect on the founding of the United States is most interesting.* The influence of Scottish Freemasonry, as opposed to Freemasonry in general, in North America has not yet been researched in specific detail, which is something of a pity as its distinctive nature ought to make it relatively easy to examine.

Indeed, Washington, the capital city of the United States of America, is named after someone who had strong links with Scottish Freemasonry.

George Washington and Forbes

The life of George Washington (1732–1799), the first life President of the United States, is very well documented. So too is his Masonic career, which is celebrated and commemorated by the George Washington National Memorial in Alexandria, Virginia.† He was born in Westmoreland County on 22 February 1732. His father died when he was only twelve years old and the family farm on the Rappahannock River was the total estate. His education was short and rudimentary, ending when he was sixteen. At the death of his elder brother, Lawrence, in 1752, George succeeded to his position as major and adjutant general in charge of one of the military divisions of the state.

The Seven Years War, known as the French and Indian War in the USA, broke out in 1756 (ending in 1763).‡ The French claimed a vast area west of the Appalachian Mountains and the Mississippi River, from the Great Lakes down to the Gulf of Mexico, and had begun to build a series of forts. In 1754, Colonel Fry, accompanied by Washington, who was by now a lieutenant colonel, was ordered to negotiate boundaries with the French as well as to gather intelligence

* An examination of the different democratic methods employed in a Scottish Lodge might be revealing.

† See: http://www.gwmemorial.org.

‡ The dates for the Seven Years War are the declaration of war and the treaties (Treaty of Hubertusburg and the Treaty of Paris) which ended it – fighting had been taking place for some time prior to 1756.

as to their strength and intentions. Meanwhile, fresh forces were awaited from Britain. On Fry's death, Washington assumed command of the Virginia Regiment and marched towards Fort Duquesne (now Pittsburgh, as renamed by General John Forbes – see below), which was strategically located where the Allegheny and Monongahela rivers meet to form the Ohio. Washington stumbled into some French at Jumonville Glen and in a skirmish a French officer was killed. He and his men moved a few miles further and established Fort Necessity (Farmington, PA), but French pressure forced him to surrender the fort and he and his men were allowed to leave without their weapons.

On 4 November 1752 George Washington was initiated into Freemasonry in Fredericksburg Lodge. He was passed on 3 March and raised on 4 August 1753. As was briefly mentioned in Chapter 4, that Lodge was what is known as a 'self starter' – a Lodge formed by Freemasons without a Charter from a Grand Lodge. Bearing in mind how much slower communications were some two hundred and fifty years ago, it is commendable that Freemasons decided to form a Lodge that would, today, be considered illegal and clandestine; for had they not done so then the First American President might never have become a Freemason. As has been suggested earlier, another factor in the decision to create a Lodge without a charter may have been the number of Scots involved, who may have baulked at the thought of paying for one before the Lodge was well and truly established.* The Charter was duly granted by the Grand Lodge of Scotland on 25 July 1758. George Washington is therefore considered by many to be a Scottish Freemason.

Born in Perthshire, Scotland, General Edward Braddock (c. 1695–1755) was sent to North America in 1754. Arriving from Britain at the head of two regiments of Redcoats, he was ordered to capture the French stronghold of Fort Duquesne. The British troops were supported by many elements from the colonies. When Braddock advanced across the Monongahela River, the French and their Indian allies launched a surprise attack. The distinctive uniform of the Redcoats provided excellent targets (a fact still not fully appreciated

* The Lodge also had a number of Scottish visitors (one Simon Fraser visited in 1753). Washington therefore had some contact with Scottish Freemasonry from the start of his Masonic career.

until some twenty years later), and on 9 July 1755 Braddock was shot through the lungs. George Washington, Braddock's aide, and another officer carried him from the battlefield; he died four days later. Sir Peter Halket of Pitrrane (Dunfermline, Fife), a Free Gardener, and his youngest son, James, were also killed. More than a thousand British and colonial soldiers were killed and the massacre would have been much worse had George Washington not organized a 'fighting retreat'. Again Washington was in contact with Scots.

The French continued to occupy parts of North America and the British to fight against them. John Forbes (1707–1759) from Dunfermline, Fife, was promoted to Colonel of the 17th Regiment of Foot on 25 January 1757, in which year he was sent to America as Adjutant General and was promoted to Brigadier of the Regiment that December. In 1758, he was ordered to capture Fort Duquesne, which had been built by the French on the banks of the Monongahela River. This would also have the effect of avenging Braddock's defeat. Forbes had under his command 1,200 Montgomerie Highlanders, 2,700 Pennsylvanians, 1,600 Virginians, elements from Delaware, Maryland and North Carolina and assorted wagoners, labourers etc. (about 1,000) and 400 Royal American Troops. Colonel George Washington was in command of the Virginians.

Forbes arrived in Philadelphia at the end of April 1758 and in November captured Fort Duquesne. He suffered greatly and despite being afflicted with dysentery oversaw the whole operation, until he was forced to retire to Philadelphia, where he died on 11 March 1759. He was laid to rest in the nave of Christ Church with full Masonic and military honours three days later.

Brigadier General John Forbes was described as being a just man, without prejudices; brave with ostentation; uncommonly warm in friendship, yet capable of flattery; well bred, but absolutely impatient of formality and affection; steady in measure, but open to information and counsel (true attributes required by a leader and a Mason).

The Grand Lodge of Ireland had granted a charter to a Lodge in the 17th Foot in 1748. Therefore Forbes took command of a regiment that had within it a Masonic Lodge. He was a Freemason before he took command, having been initiated in 'the Ludge of Dunfermling' (founded before 1598), now Lodge St John, No. 26. He was also a member of Lodge Kilwinning Scots Arms (founded in 1729 and dormant by 1754). As the Lodge within the regiment had a 'travelling warrant' (or charter) it's likely that George Washington participated in its meetings whilst on active service. He was therefore once more in contact with men who were Freemasons from Scotland. As we have seen, Washington continued to have contact with Freemasonry for the rest of his life.

After the American Revolution (1774–1783), he settled down to establish the institutions necessary to run a new country. It is said that existing examples of government did not meet the aspirations of the Founding Fathers and that they may have looked to Freemasonry for inspiration. It would, however, be going too far to say that the American system of government replicated the Masonic 'system'. Be that as it may, of fifty-six signatories to the Declaration of Independence (1776) and of the forty-eight of the Articles of Confederation and Perpetual Union (1781), nine were Freemasons. Thirteen of the thirty-nine signatories to the Constitution (1789) were known to be Freemasons.

Washington and the White House

In the earliest days of the United States of America, buildings were almost entirely constructed from the most readily available material, wood, but imposing and long-lasting buildings cannot be built and easily maintained if they are built of timber. Brother Washington realized that the new country, of which he had been the midwife, required all the permanent trappings of a nation state. Independence secure, his thoughts turned to founding and building a capital city for the new nation. The new city was named after him but he modestly never referred to it as such, always calling it the Federal City.

Pierre Charles L'Enfant (1754–1825), a French-born architect and a major in the United States Army, designed the initial layout for the 'Federal City', which was in the shape of a diamond. Each side measured ten miles, totalling a hundred square miles. Washington laid the foundation stone of the Capitol Building on 18 September 1793 in a Masonic ceremony.

Before 1790 his thoughts had turned to the need for a house fit for a president: the President's House or, as it is now known, the White House. In 1791 he personally selected the site of the new building and James Hoban (1761–1831), an architect from Ireland, was appointed to draw up the working plans. The foundation, or corner, stone was laid in a Masonic ceremony in 1792.

Such an edifice had to be built from stone, but the sheer scale of the new city meant that there was a severe shortage of qualified stonemasons. That fact must have occupied the minds of those in charge even before any decision about the design or site had been made. It can therefore be no coincidence that one James Traquair, a member of the Lodge of Journeymen Masons, No. 8, was in America by 1790. Traquair is recorded as being in the Lodge as early as 1783. The Lodge records show that in 1784 he paid his sixpence every quarter, as was required by all members. From 1785 to 1788 his name is recorded on the roll of members, but no payments are recorded. This is unusual, for other members who failed to pay their quarterly dues were removed from the Lodge roll after two years. The entry for 1790 shows him still on the roll, but on this occasion, beside his name, is the word 'america'. This continues until 1795 (with the word 'abroad' used instead from 1794), until 1795 when his name (and 'abroad') are written but have been scored out.

It is clear that those planning to build the White House and indeed, the entire city of Washington DC, realized that there was shortage of skilled stonemasons. Collen Williamson (c. 1728 – c. 1799) had arrived in New York in 1792 and was a cousin of John Suter, proprietor of the Fountain Inn.* He was a native of Dyke, Morayshire, Scotland and that was where he was apprenticed as stonemason. He worked on numerous buildings in the area, the most important being Moy House, which he designed and built during the 1760s. He was also a Freemason, having being initiated in the Lodge of Dyke, which received a charter from the Grand Lodge of Scotland in 1753. He appears to have been well aware of the shortage of stonemasons and he may well have been the one who put his cousin in touch with the Commissioners (three men who had been appointed to oversee all arrangements for the building of the city). Williamson was immediately

* The exact relationship is not clear and was perhaps through a marriage rather than blood.

engaged and was first put in charge of the work at Aquia Quarry, Stafford County, Virginia, which was to supply large amounts of stone for the buildings of Washington DC – including the President's House.

On 17 July 1792, Hoban was notified that he had won the competition for a design. Thomas Jefferson (1743–1826), the first Secretary of State (1789–1793), had suggested that foreign stonemasons be invited to immigrate; the Commissioners rejected the idea but very quickly realized their mistake. Jefferson knew that work had commenced on another Presidential House in Philadelphia and that the Master Mason in charge was James Traquair, who had come to the USA in about 1785. He therefore arranged a meeting with him. Traquair revealed to Jefferson that he had a contact who could arrange for some of his fellow countrymen to come to the USA. His contact was Alexander Crawford – a member of the Lodge of Journeymen Masons, No. 8 (Edinburgh, Scotland).* Traquair seems to have communicated with Crawford, but it was another Scot who successfully arranged for members of the Lodge to travel to Washington. As the Commissioners wanted to be sure of recruiting stonemasons they recruited George Walker, originally from Falkirk, as their agent on hearing that he was going to Britain on business. He was in Edinburgh by mid-1793 and soon after at least six members of the Lodge emigrated to the United States, George Thomson, James White, Alexander Scott, Robert Brown, Alexander Wilson and James McIntosh.†

Intriguingly, there is a George Walker recorded as having joined the Lodge in 1783; if this is the same George Walker, merchant, who became the agent for the Commissioners it would explain how he knew exactly where to look for recruits.‡ This means that not only did many of the men employed to build the house for the President know each other well, but they had a special kind of bond that no one else had – the bond of Freemasonry (or the 'Mystic Tie', as described by another Scottish Freemason, Robert Burns (1759–1796)). It shows that erecting this building involved a particular 'type' of Freemasonry, a

* This was a Lodge of stonemasons founded in 1707 and which had broken away from the Lodge of Edinburgh (now the Lodge of Edinburgh (Mary's Chapel), No. 1). Both Lodges continue to meet in the city.

† It is possible that other members of the Lodge also emigrated to the USA.

‡ Although this was a stonemasons' Lodge they did admit a few non-stonemasons.

type that was particularly Scottish (as the connections between stonemasonry and Freemasonry can be traced nowhere else). Scottish Freemasons therefore built the White House and indeed it was a Masonic building from start to finish – even the architect, James Hoban, was a Freemason!

Williamson, who was a stonemason/Freemason, and 'ordinary' Freemasons such as Hoban were present at the foundation stone laying ceremony on 13 October 1792. This too was Masonic.

On that Saturday, people assembled at the Fountain Inn and were formed into a procession led by Freemasons. They were followed by the Commissioners of the Federal District and then gentlemen of the town and area. Bringing up the rear were assorted artificers. The ceremony was performed by Brethren of Georgetown Lodge, No. 9 (Maryland). The Master of the Lodge, Peter Casanave, delivered a suitable Masonic oration and a brass plaque bearing the following inscription was placed on top of the foundation stone:

> The first stone of the President's House was laid the 13th day of October 1792, and in the seventeenth year of independence of the United States of America.
>
> George Washington, *President*
> Thomas Johnson,
> Doctor Stewart,
> Daniel Carroll,
> *Commissioners*
> James Hoban, *Architect*
> Collen Williamson, *Master Mason*

Vivat Republica*

The President's House was not completed until November 1800. It may have been designed and built by Freemasons for a Freemason, but nevertheless it was completed too late for George Washington to move into it – he died on 14 December 1799.

His personal doctor and great friend Dr James Craik (1730–1814)

* William Seale, *The President's House – A History* (White House Historical Association, 1986), p. 36.

attended him in his last illness. Craik was born in Arbigland, near Dumfries, Scotland (where his father employed the father of John Paul Jones, the 'Father of the American navy'– see below). Craik studied medicine at the University of Edinburgh, and served as a surgeon in the British army in the West Indies before landing in Virginia during 1751. In 1754 he accepted a commission as a surgeon in the Virginia Regiment under Colonel Fry. He was with the regiment at the Battle of the Great Meadows (also known as the Battle of Fort Necessity) – the opening shots of the French and Indian War. It was here that he formed a friendship with the President-to-be that lasted until Washington's death. In the American Revolution, Craik rose to become Surgeon-General of the Continental Army and was the first US Surgeon-General. He was active in disclosing the Conway conspiracy of 1777 designed to remove Washington as commander-in-chief. In 1781, when Director-General of the hospital at Yorktown, he was present at the surrender of Cornwallis. He was a Freemason, having been initiated into Freemasonry in Alexandria Lodge, No. 22.[*]

Employed by the father of James Craik, the father of John Paul Jones (born John Paul) (1747–1792) in Kirkcudbrightshire, Scotland was a gardener in Arbigland. The 'Father of the American navy' was initiated in Lodge St Bernard's Kilwinning, Kirkcudbrightshire in 1770.

Part of the reason for the eight years taken to build the President's House was the lack of skilled workmen. Whilst employed at the Aquia Quarry, Williamson had been forced to use slave labour; moreover, he and another Scot, John Reid, were the only trained stonemasons there.[†] But Williamson was 'unable to deal with the hired Negro slaves at the quarry'.[‡] At the building site the stonemasons found it difficult to find anyone with sufficient skill to assist them in their work. It is recorded that they were instructed to train slaves but that they refused. In addition they worked in a traditional, methodical way, as the building they were erecting was intended to last a very long time. However, that very precision ensured that the work progressed slowly.

[*] At the time of his initiation the Lodge was No. 39 under a Pennsylvanian charter.

[†] Little is known of Reid but he too would later join his fellow Scots to work on the President's House.

[‡] Seale, op. cit., p. 60.

Why the Scots refused to use slaves despite their desperate need for assistance has puzzled historians, but the reason lies in the nature of the stonemason–Freemason combination, which was almost certainly unique in the USA. These Scots were stonemasons who were also Freemasons, and probably had a very different attitude towards non-stonemason Freemasons (often called Speculative Freemasons or Free and Accepted Masons). Williamson is known to have looked down on the architect Hoban, a fellow Freemason. As we saw in Chapter 1, there are indications that stonemasons, in Scotland at least, resented the influx of non-stonemasons and that many Scottish lodges refused to have anything to do with the new Grand Lodge 'system', preferring instead to remain independent for as long as possible. Some lodges disappeared before they could come under the wing of the Grand Lodge of Scotland and the last stonemasons' lodge to join the new Masonic system only did so in 1891.* For these men, being a stonemason also meant being a Freemason and therein lay the problem. To train someone as a stonemason meant that they would normally be expected to become a Freemason, but no slave can become a Freemason – a point expressed in Masonic ritual when the candidate is asked: 'As no man can be made a Freemason unless he is a free man and of the mature age, I demand to know if you are free and of the full age of twenty-one years?'

Making a slave a Freemason would mean that the so-called Masonic 'secrets' would have had to be given to someone who did not own their own body and also, theoretically, to someone who was not a Freemason – the slave owner. The Scots therefore refused the plentiful supply of slaves and adopted the more traditional method of taking apprentices.

Interestingly a Masonic Lodge was established in the city soon after. Federal Lodge No. 1, of the District of Columbia, received a charter on 12 September 1793 from the Grand Lodge of Maryland (then Federal Lodge No. 15). It seems that they were aware of the forthcoming ceremony of the laying of the foundation stone of the Capitol Building and wanted to be present as members of their own Lodge. The first Master was James Hoban and the Treasurer was Collen Williamson.

* The Lodge of Melrose St John, No. 1[2].

They were present on 18 September 1793, when their fellow Freemason, George Washington, acting as Grand Master, laid the foundation stone of the Capitol Building in a Masonic ceremony.

John Adams became the first President to take up residence in the building, in 1800. During the war of 1812–1814 between Britain and America British troops burned down almost the entire city; the President's House was gutted and only the exterior walls were left standing. It is a testament to the skill of the builders that much of the stonework survived and remains part of the reconstructed building.

Australia and New Zealand

People from Europe, and especially from Britain, who explored and settled the world in the eighteenth and nineteenth centuries naturally took with them their ways of life, customs and practices. Freemasonry was one of those practices (indeed, for many it is a way of life) to have traversed the world.

Australia was first discovered by Europeans in the eighteenth century, and claimed by Captain James Cook in 1770. Freemasonry arrived in Australia eighteen years later, in 1788, with the First Fleet. It expanded rapidly, with hundreds of Lodges created – at one time there were more than two hundred and fifty Scottish Masonic Lodges in Australia.

Freemasonry arrived in New Zealand somewhat later, in 1842, with the creation of an English Masonic Lodge in Port Nicholson (Wellington). The first Scottish Lodge was founded in Dunedin in 1861 and continues to meet there today.

Africa, India and Asia

Freemasonry spread from Britain to Europe, and from there across the continents. The type of Freemasonry that was exported abroad depended on the nationality of the Freemasons who emigrated. Thus Dutch Masonic Lodges sprang up in parts of the world where people from Holland settled, and there was a similar situation in countries with large immigrant populations from European countries such as France, Germany and Italy. Consequently, whereas Freemasonry in Australia and New Zealand was (and is) heavily influenced by British and Irish Freemasonry, Africa and Asia enjoy a much larger range of national Masonic 'flavours'.

Initially Freemasonry in Africa and Asia was the preserve of Europeans, but indigenous men were very quickly admitted to Lodges. Today, very many African and Asian Lodges no longer have any European members, although the Lodges themselves may still be administered by a European Grand Lodge. For example, there are Scottish Lodges in Botswana, Ghana, Kenya, Malawi, Namibia, Nigeria, Sierra Leone, The Gambia, South Africa, Zambia and Zimbabwe. However, non-European countries can and do form their own Grand Lodges – a process which the older Grand Lodges assist and encourage.

Women and Freemasonry

As we have seen, modern Freemasonry derives from the lodges of the stonemasons. As there were no women stonemasons in medieval times, Freemasonry is simply continuing a centuries-old custom and practice by not admitting women today. Freemasonry is absolutely not anti-women, but merely a gender-specific organization such as a football team.

However, I am sure that many will be surprised to learn that there are indeed women Freemasons – a large number, in fact. In the UK there is one organization that admits both men and women (the International Order of Co-Freemasonry) and there is another that does not admit men (the Honourable Fraternity of Ancient Freemasons). These organizations have a presence outside the UK, and information about them is available on the Internet.

Many of the organizations that admit women, or that are women-only, are often very similar to branches of traditional Freemasonry in terms of what they offer their members, but nevertheless they should not be confused with traditional Freemasonry. These organizations include the Order of the Eastern Star, the International Order of the Rainbow for Girls, Job's Daughters International, Daughters of the Nile and Sigma Tau Alpha. (Only the Eastern Star has a significant presence in the UK, but the others are particularly strong in the USA and Canada.) Most require a Masonic connection for membership.

The Appeal of Freemasonry

Freemasonry is all about equality, regardless of creed, colour, faith or status. Combined with its broad membership from all walks of life, the existence of Freemasonry and its related societies in so many diverse countries, is a testament to the fact that its underlying principles attract good men wherever they might live.

12

A FINAL WORD

> Scottish Freemasonry is Orthodox, English Freemasonry is Reformed and American Freemasonry is Evangelical!*

In *Cracking the Freemason's Code* I have attempted to chart some of the significant developments in Masonic history. This has been from an avowedly Scottish perspective, probably for the first time in a work of this nature. Whilst it has not been a comprehensive account, it is one designed to prompt the reader to think about Freemasonry a little more deeply than through the perspectives afforded by various popular books and novels.

The inclusion of the fairly lengthy chapter on the Free Gardeners was a conscious decision and for the same purpose. By including them, I have attempted to show you that there are more esoteric flavours out there than just Freemasonry! The parallels between the two orders show that these, and therefore others, had similar origins (from the working experiences of ordinary men) and developed in a more or less similar manner.

The idea that Freemasonry has a connection with the medieval Order of the Knights Templar is an interesting one and although the romantic in me is attracted by it, my hard-headed historian side can find no substantial facts to support the theory. That said, I am still of the opinion that Freemasonry remains the most important esoteric

* John J. Robinson, *Born in Blood – The Lost Secrets of Freemasonry* (M. Evans, 1989).

'organization' in existence although I am equally sure that many people (Masons and non-Masons alike) would disagree with me; I am fine with that – everyone is entitled to their opinion so long as they recognize that I have the right to mine!

At the beginning of this book I explained that it is not possible for any one person to speak for Freemasonry, even although many people cite the writings of individual Freemasons to support a particular opinion (those of Albert Pike must be the most abused in this respect).* Here I have tried to chart a little of the most important parts of the origins of the history of Freemasonry by examining the earliest known Masonic ritual, and I have attempted to give some insight into the esoteric world of the stonemasons who were our forebears.

Allegory

I now wish to return to a point previously made about the allegorical nature of Freemasonry, and I do so for emphasis. Many people who have some knowledge of the nature of Freemasonry assume that some of the stories that Freemasons use to convey particular lessons or moral precepts are actually true. However, these stories, including traditional histories, were never intended to be taken literally. They were constructs of stonemasons and early Freemasons to explain their way of looking at certain principles.

This method of teaching is ancient indeed and the story of the Good Samaritan is as good as any with which to make the point. The parable is told in Luke 10:30–38 and is familiar to many, but the point is not whether the Good Samaritan was a real person but what he did. Much of what is written about Freemasonry misses this point entirely and so readers are led into error; they may even find themselves embroiled in a wild-goose chase for the body of a particular individual or the treasure once owned by a particular group! Today, in this much more secular, materialistic world, there is a tendency to take everything at surface value, concentrating on the messenger and not the message. Just like many other organizations, religions and belief

* His book *Morals and Dogma* (1871) is one man's musings as to what Freemasonry means to him, albeit on a grand and heroic scale.

systems, Freemasonry suffers from such superficial treatment and has suffered from those determined to unravel it in the public eye.

Freemasonry and Democracy

Whilst Freemasonry as an institution is, and always has been, strictly non-political and non-religious, it has always had amongst its membership individuals who are active in political life and in the various religions of the world. These aspects of an individual's life are of no consequence to Freemasonry so long as they do not impinge on the Craft. In other words, no Freemason may speak *as a Freemason* on matters of politics or religion.

Democracy and Freemasonry are found together wherever governments believe in tolerance and the right of citizens to a private life, including Freedom of Association.

Many famous men were proud to have been Freemasons, Robert Burns, Sir Walter Scott, Sir Alexander Fleming and Edwin 'Buzz' Aldrin to name but a few. There are very many more (for more examples see the brief list in Appendix 2). These individuals all found something attractive within Freemasonry and that attraction still leads large numbers to knock on the door of the Craft. However, it should be borne in mind that for every famous individual who was, or is, a Freemason there were, and are, many, many more 'ordinary' members drawn from all walks of life.

From time to time there are calls, usually from within the political world, for Freemasons to be 'exposed' and their names made public. Indeed, the suppression of Freemasonry in Hitler's Germany, Franco's Spain, Mussolini's Italy and Stalin's Soviet Union often began with a seemingly innocuous request from the 'authorities' for a list of Freemasons in public service, such as the police, judiciary and the civil service.* It is therefore understandable that Freemasons today remain gravely concerned that some elements within our liberal democracies have actually contemplated forcing Freemasons to disclose their membership.

The Gestapo had a special section to 'deal' with Freemasons, just as

* Not surprisingly none of them was a Freemason.

it had sections to 'deal' with other groups. Whilst Freemasonry was numerically small in comparison to some of those other groups, very many Freemasons were tortured and executed under the Nazis. However, unlike other persecuted groups of that time, Freemasons are seldom mentioned.

All Freemasons are taught that any responsibilities to Freemasonry come a long way behind their duties to their family, their faith, and their employer and their duties as a citizen. The existence of Freemasonry is, I believe, a 'litmus test' of democracy, a test of 'democratic health' if you like. Freemasonry poses no threat to anyone, any government or any faith. In fact the converse is the case: Freemasonry is a force for good in the world.

The Attraction of Freemasonry

So what is the attraction? That, like Freemasonry itself, is difficult to quantify. I for one think that it is simply because Freemasonry has something to offer to everyone. Some become Freemasons for companionship and because they enjoy the various social activities, others because of Freemasons they have known and admired, others because of family associations. Many are attracted by the esoteric and historical aspects of Freemasonry, or the ritual and the role-playing potential. Admirably, some have become members because of the potential to do good in society. In other words there is a niche for nearly every man within Freemasonry.

You might well ask what I have got from my membership. Apart from personal interest in the esoteric and historical dimensions of Freemasonry I can answer that very simply: friendship. I have been fortunate in meeting wonderful people in many different parts of the world and the friendships thus formed are worth more than any treasure.

The Freemason's Code

I have often been asked what the ethos of Freemasonry is, what it stands for and what are its beliefs: what is the Freemason's Code? I have tried to explain that this can be open to interpretation and, indeed, many Freemasons differ in their understanding of the ethos of the Craft. However, there is one explanation that many Freemasons accept: the ethos of Freemasonry is based on brotherly love, relief and truth.

This statement might seem rather old fashioned and so would benefit from a little clarification. 'Brotherly love' means that all Freemasons are expected to treat one another with the respect that one would give to a blood brother. But it is also expected that the Freemason will not only treat fellow Freemasons as if they were blood relations, but also that they must treat everyone else – Freemason and non-Mason alike – in this manner. With the emphasis increasingly placed on the individual in today's world, brotherly love can be a difficult concept for some to grasp and even more difficult for others to apply. But its difficulty does not mean that the attempt should not be made.

'Relief' means charity, but not in terms of giving money to assist victims of a natural disaster. It means charity in the widest possible sense: natural kindness and a willingness to try and understand others' points of view. 'Truth' means that process by which Freemasons may start to improve themselves – by first and foremost being truthful with themselves and then with others.

Cracking the Freemason's Code, the title of the book, is here for all to read but its true meaning may be more difficult for many to 'crack'. A code is, after all, merely a set of guidelines, which in this case Freemasons can choose to follow or not. Assuming that Freemasons understand the 'Freemason's Code', how they apply it, and to what extent, in their lives is a decision for them and no one else. 'Cracking the Freemason's Code' is therefore impossible because every Freemason has a code of his own.

The concept of Solomon's Key, which we have touched upon in this book and which is often referred to in the context of Freemasonry, is something quite different and refers to the existence of 'something'; but whether this is something physical or something abstract is difficult to say with certainty. Personally, I believe that it is both and I have provided sufficient clues in this book for you to discern what the key might be . . .

It is fitting to end with the words of the man I and many others like me call the Father of Modern Freemasonry – William Schaw:

> First . . . that they be true one to another and live charitably together as becomes sworn Brethren and companions of Craft.

This was the first rule that Schaw addressed to all the Lodges in Scotland more than four hundred years ago. If we all followed this simple rule then the world would be a far happier place.

Appendix 1
ORIGINAL MASONIC DOCUMENTS

Schaw Statute of 1598

At Edinburgh the xxviij day of December, The zeir of God V' four scoir awchtene zeiris.

The statutis ordinanceis to be obseruit be all the maister maissounis within this realme, Sett doun be Williame Schaw, Maister of Wark, to his maiestie And generall Wardene of the said craft, with the consent of the maisteris efter specifeit.

Item, first that they obserue and keip all the gude ordinanceis sett doun of befoir concernyng the priviligeis of thair Craft be thair predicesso" of gude memorie, And specialie

That thay be trew ane to ane vther and leve cheritablie togidder as becumis sworne brether and companzeounis of craft.

Item, that thay be obedient to thair wardenis, dekynis, and maisteris in all thingis concernyng thair craft.

Item, that thay be honest, faithfull, and diligent in thair calling, and deill uprichtlie w' the maisteris or awnaris of the warkis that they sail tak vpoun hand, be it in task, meit, & fie, or owlklie wage.

Item, that name tak vpoun hand ony wark gritt or small quhilk he is no' abill to performe qualifeitlie vnder the pane of fourtie pundis money or ellis the fourt pairt of the worth and valor of the said wark, and that by and attor ane condigne amendis and satisfactioun to be maid to the awnaris of the wark at the sycht and discretioun of the generall Wardene, or in his absence at the sycht of the wardeneis, dekynis, and maisteris of the shrefdome quhair the said wark is interprisit and wrocht.

Item, that na maister sail tak ane vther maisteris wark over his heid, efter that the first maister hes aggreit w' the awnar of the wark ather be contract, arlis, or verbail conditioun, vnder the paine of fourtie punds.

Item, that na maister salt tak the wirking of ony wark that vther maisteris hes wrocht at of befoir, vnto the tyme that the first wirkaris be satisfeit for the wark quhilk thay haif wrocht, vnder the pane foirsaid.

Item, that thair be ane wardene chosin and electit Ilk zeir to haif the charge over everie ludge, as thay are devidit particularlie, and that be the voitis of the maisteris of the saids ludgeis, and consent of thair Wardene generall gif he happynis to be pn', And vtherwyis that he be aduerteist that sic ane wardene is chosin for sic ane zeir, to the effect that the Wardene generall may send sic directionis to that wardene electit, as effeiris.

Item, that na maister sail tak ony ma prenteissis nor thre during his lyfetyme w'out ane speciall consent of the haill wardeneis, dekynis, and maisteris of the schirefdome quhair the said prenteiss that is to be ressauit dwellis and remanis.

Item, that na maister ressaue ony prenteiss bund for fewar zeiris nor sevin at the leist, and siclyke it sail no' be lesum to mak the said prenteiss brother and fallow in craft vnto the tyme that he haif seruit the space of vther sevin zeiris efter the ische of his said prenteischip w'out ane speciall licenc granttit be the wardeneis, dekynis, and maisteris assemblit for the caus, and that sufficient tryall be tane of thair worthynes, qualificatioun, and skill of the persone that desyirs to be maid fallow in craft, and that vnder the pane of fourtie punds to be upliftit as ane pecuniall penaltie fra the persone that is maid fallow in craft aganis this ord', besyde the penalteis to be set doun aganis his persone, accordyng to the ord' of the ludge quhair he remanis.

Item, it sail not be lesum to na maister to sell his prenteiss to ony vther maister nor zit to dispens w' the zeiris of his prenteischip be selling y' of to the prenteisses self, vnder the pane of fourtie punds.

Item, that na maister ressaue ony prenteiss w'out he signifie the samyn to the wardene of the ludge quhair he dwellis, to the effect that the said prenteissis name and the day of his ressauyng may be ordlie buikit.

Item, that na prenteiss be enterit bot be the samyn ord', that the day of thair enterer may be buikit.

Item, that na maister or fallow of craft be ressauit nor admittit w'out the numer of sex maisteris and twa enterit prenteissis, the wardene of that ludge being ane of the said sex, and that the day of the ressauyng of the said fallow of craft or maister be ord'lie buikit and his name and mark insert in the said buik w' the names of his sex admitteris and enterit prenteissis, and the names of the intendaris that salbe chosin to everie persone to be alsua insert in thair buik. Providing alwayis that na man be admittit w'out ane assay and sufficient tryall of his skill and worthynes in his vocatioun and craft.

Item, that na maister wirk ony maissoun wark vnder charge or command of ony vther craftisman that takis vpoun hand or vpoun him the wirking of ony maissoun wark.

Item, that na maister or fallow of craft ressaue ony cowanis to wirk in his societie or cumpanye, nor send nane of his servands to wirk w' cowanis, under the pane of twentie punds sa oft as ony persone offendis heirintill.

Item, it salt no' be lesum to na enterit prenteiss to tak ony gritter task or wark vpon hand fra a awnar nor will extend to the soume of ten punds vnder the pane foirsaid, to wit xx libs, and that task being done they sail Interpryiss na mair w'out licence of the maisteris or warden q' thay dwell.

Item, gif ony questioun, stryfe, or varianc salt fall out amang ony of the maisteris, servands, or entert prenteissis, that the parteis that fallis in questioun or debait, sail signifie the causis of thair querrell to he perticular wardeneis or dekynis of thair ludge w'in the space of xxiiij ho' vnder the pane of ten pnds, to the effect that thay may be reconcilit and aggreit and their variance removit be thair said wardeneis, dekynis, and maisteris; and gif ony of the saids parteis salhappin to remane wilfull or obstinat that they salbe deprivit of the privilege of thair ludge and no' permittit to wirk y'at vnto the tyme that thay submit thame selffis to ressoun at the sycht of thair wardenis, dekynis, and maisteris, as said is.

Item, that all maisteris, Inte priseris of wirkis, be verray cairfull to sie thair skaffellis and futegangis surelie sett and placeit, to the effect that throw thair negligence and slewth na hurt or skaith cum vnto ony personis that wirkis at the said wark, vnder pain of dischargeing of thaim y'efter to wirk as maisteris havand charge of ane wark, bot sail ever be subiect all the rest of thair dayis to wirk vnder or w ane other principall maister havand charge of the wark.

Item, that na maister ressaue or ressett ane vther maisteris prenteiss or servand that salhappin to ryn away fra his maisteris seruice, nor interteine him in his cumpanye efter that he hes gottin knawledge yrof, vnder the paine of fourtie punds.

Item, that all personis of the maissoun craft conuene in tyme and place being lawchfullie warnit, vnder the pane of ten punds.

Item, that all the maisteris that salhappin to be send for to ony assemblie or meitting sail be sworn be thair grit aith that thay sail hyde nor coneill na fawltis nor wrangis done be ane to ane vther, nor zit the faultis or wrangis that ony man hes done to the awnaris of the warkis that they haif had in hand safer as they knaw, and that vnder the pane of ten punds to be takin vp frae the conceillairs of the saidis faultis.

Item, it is ordanit that all thir foirsaids penalteis salbe liftit and tane vp fra the offendaris and brekaris of thir ordinances be the wardeneis, dekynis, and maisteris of the ludgeis quhair the offendaris dwellis, and to be distributit ad pion vsus according to gud conscience be the advyis of the foirsaidis.

And for fulfilling and observing of thir ordinances, sett doun as said is, The haill maisteris conuenit the foirsaid day binds and oblisses thaim heirto faithfullie. And thairfore hes requeistit thair said Wardene generall to subscriue thir presentis w' his awn hand, to the effect that ane autentik copy heirof may be send to euerie particular ludge win this realme.

WILLIAM SCHAW, Maistir of Wark.

Schaw Statute of 1599

xxviii Decembris, 1599.

First It is ordanit that the warden witin the bounds of Kilwynning and vther placeis subject to thair ludge salbe chosin and electit zeirlie be monyest of the Mrs voitis of the said ludge vpoun the twentie day of December and that wn the kirk of Kilwynning as the heid and secund ludge of Scotland and yrefter that the generall warden be advertysit zeirlie quha is chosin warden of the ludge, immediatlie efter his electioun.

Item it is thocht neidfull & expedient be my lord warden generall that everie ludge wtin Scotland sail have in tyme cuming ye awld and antient liberties yrof vse and wont of befoir & in speciall, yt ye ludge of Kilwynning secund ludge of Scotland sail haif thair warden pnt at the election of ye wardenis wtin ye bounds of ye Nether Waird of Cliddsdail, Glasgow Air & bounds of Carrik; wt powar to ye said wairden & dekyn of Kilwynning to convene ye remanent wardenis and dekynis wtin ye bounds foirsaid quhan thay haif ony neid of importance ado, and yai to be judgit be ye warden and dekyn of Kilwynning quhen it sail pleis thame to qvene for ye tyme ather in Kilwynning or wtin ony vther pt of the west of Scotland and bounds foirsaid.

Item it is thocht neidfull & expedient be my lord warden generall, that Edr salbe in all tyme cuming as of befoir the first and principall ludge in Scotland, and yt Kilwynning be the secund ludge as of befoir is notourlie manifest in our awld antient writts and that Stirueling salbe the third ludge, conforme to the auld privileges thairof.

Item it is thocht expedient yt ye wardenis of everie ilk ludge salbe answerabel to ye presbyteryes wtin thair schirefdomes for the maissonis subiect to ye ludgeis anent all offensis ony of thame sail committ, and the thrid pt of ye vnlawis salbe employit to ye godlie vsis of ye ludge quhair ony offens salhappin to be committit.

Item yt yr be tryall takin zeirlie be ye wardenis & maist antient maisteris of everie ludge extending to sex personis quha sail tak tryall of ye offenss, yt punishment may be execut conforme to equitie & iustice & guid conscience & ye antient ordor.

Item it is ordanit be my lord warden generall that the warden of Kilwynning as secund in Scotland, elect and chuis sex of the maist perfyt and worthiest of memorie within (thair boundis,) to tak tryall of the qualificatioun of the haill masonis within the boundis foirsaid of thair airt, craft, scyance and antient memorie; To the effect the warden deakin may be answerable heiraftir for sic p(er)sonis as Js qmittit to him & wthin his bounds and jurisdictioun.

Item commissioun in gewin to ye warden and deakon of Kilwynning as secund luge, to secluid and away put furthe of yr societe and cumpanie all p(er)sonis disobedient to fulfil & obey ye haill acts and antient statutts sett doun of befoir of guid memorie, and all p(er)sonis disobedient eyr to kirk craft counsall and uyris statutts and acts to be mayd heireftir for ane guid ordour.

Item it is ordainit be my lord warden generall that the warden and deakyn to be pnt of his quarter maisteris elect cheis and constitut ane famous notar as ordinar clark and scryb, and yat ye said notar to be chosinge sail occupye the office, and that all indentouris discharges and vtheris wrytis quhatsumevir, perteining to ye craft salbe onlie wrytin be ye clark and that na maner of wryt neyther tityll nor other evident to be admit be ye said warden and deakin befoir yame, except it be maid be ye said clark and subscryuit wt his hand.

Item It is ordanit be my lord generall that ye hale auld antient actis and statutis maid of befoir be ye predicessrs of ye masonis of Kilwynning be observit faithfullie and kepit be ye craftis in all tymes cuminge, and that na prenteis nor craftis man, in ony tymes heireftir be admittit nor enterit Bot onlie wthin the kirk of Kilwynning as his paroche and secured ludge, and that all bankatts for entrie of prenteis or fallow of crafts to be maid wthin ye said lug of Kilwynning.

Item It is ordanit that all fallows of craft at his entrie pay to ye commoun bolds of ye luge the soume of ten punds monie, wt x s. worthe of gluiffis or euire he be admttit and that forthebankatt, And that he be not admitit wthout ane sufficient essay and pruife of memorie and art of craft be the warden deacon and quarter mrs of ye lug, conforme to ye foirmer and qrthrow yai may be ye mair answerable to ye generall warden.

Item that all prentessis to be admititbe not admittit qll first pay to ye commoun bankat foiresaid the sowme of sex punds monie, utherwyes to pay the bankat for ye haill members of craft wthin the said ludge and prentessis yrof.

Item It is ordanit that the warden and deakis of ye secund luge of Scotland pnt of Kilwynning, sail tak the aythe, fidelitie and trewthe of all mrs and fallowis of craft wthin ye haill bounds commitit to yr charge, zeirlie that thai sail not accumpanie wth cowans nor work with thame, nor any of yr servands or prenteisses wndir ye paine of ye penaltie contenit in ye foirmer actis and peying yrof.

Item It is ordanit be ye generall warden, That ye warden of ye lug of Kilwynning, being the secund lug in Scotland, tak tryall of ye airt of memorie and science yrof, of everie fellowe of craft and everie prenteiss according to ayr of yr vocations; and in cais yat yai haue lost ony point yrof dvied to thame To pay the penaltie as followis for yr slewthfulness, viz. , Ilk fallow of craft, xx s. , Ilk prentess, x s. , and that to be payit to ye box for ane commoun weill zeirlie & yat conforme to the commoun vs and pratik of the commoun lugs of this realm.

And for the fulfilling, observinge and keping of thir statutis and all oyr actis and statuttis maid of befoir and to be maid be ye warden deaconis and quarter mrs of ye lugis foirsads for guid ordor keping conform to equitie justice & antient ordor to ye makinge and setting doun qrof ye generall warden hes gevin his power and commission to the said warden and yrs abouevrtn to sett doun & mak actis conforme as accords to ye office law. And in signe and taking yrof I the generall warden of Scotland hes sett doun and causit pen yir actis & statutis And hes sybscryuit ye smyis wt my hand eftr ye testimoniale on this syd and on the uther syd.

Be it Kend to the warden dekyn and to the mrs of the ludge of Kilwynning That Archibald Barklay being directit commissioner fra the said ludge comperit in Edr the twentie sevin & twentie awcht of December Instant quhair the said Archibald — in pns of the warden generall & the mrs of the ludge of Edr, producit his commissioun, and behaifit himself verie honestlie and cairfullie for the discharge of sik thingis as was committit into him; bot be ressone of the absence of his Maitie out of the toun and yt thair was na mrs bot the ludge of Edr convenit at this tyme, We culd not get ane satlat order (as the privileges of the craft requyris) tane at this tyme, bot heirefter quhan occasioun sal be offerit we salt get his Maities warrand baith for the authorizing of the ludgeis privilegeis, and ane penaltie set down for the dissobedient persones and perturberis of all guid ordor. Thus far I thocht guid to sgnifie vnto the haill brether of the ludge, vnto the neist commoditie In witnes heirof, I haif subscriuit this pnt wt my hand at Halyrudhous the twentie awcht day of December The zeir of God P"V' fourscoir nynetene zeirs.

WILLIAM SCHAW, Maistir of Wark, Wairden of ye Maisons.

The Oldest Masonic Ritual in the World: The Edinburgh Register House MS. 1696

SOME QUESTIONES THAT MASONS USE TO PUT TO THOSE WHO HAVE YE WORD BEFORE THEY WILL ACKNOWLEDGE THEM

Are you a mason. Answer yes

How shall I know it ? Ans: you shall know it in time and place convenient.

Remark the forsd answer is only to be made when there is company present who are not masons But if there be no such company by, you should answer by signer tokens and other points of my entrie.

What is the first point ? Ans: Tell me the first point ile tell you the second, The first is to heill and conceall, second, under no less pain, which is then cutting of your throat, For you most make that sign, when you say that

Where wes you entered ? An: At the honourable lodge.

What makes a true and perfect lodge? An: seven masters, five entered apprentices, A dayes Journey from a burroughs town without bark of dog or crow of cock.

Does no less make a true and perfect lodge, An: yes five masons and three entered apprentices &c.

Does no less. An: The more the merrier the fewer the better chear

What is the name of your lodge An: Kilwinning.

How stands your lodge An east and west as the temple of Jerusalem.

Where wes the first lodge. An: in the porch of Solomons Temple

Are there any lights in your lodge An yes three the north east. sw, and eastern passage The one denotes the master mason, the other the warden The third the setter croft.

Are there any jewels in your lodge An Yes three, Perpend Esler a Square pavement and a broad ovall.

where shall I find the key of your lodge, yes [Ans] Three foot and an half from the lodge door under a perpend esler, and a green divot. But under the lap of my liver where all my secrets of my heart lie.

Which is the key of your lodge. An: a weel hung tongue. where lies the key. Ans: In the bone box.

After the masons have examined you by all or some of these Questions and that you have answered them exactly and mad the signes, they will acknowledge you, but not a master mason or fellow croft but only as [an] apprentice, soe they will say I see you have been in the Kitchine but I know not if you have been in the hall, Ans I have been in the hall as weel as in the kitchine.

Are you a fellow craft Ans yes.

How many points of the fellowship are ther Ans fyve viz foot to foot Knee to Kn[ee] Heart to Heart, Hand to Hand and ear to ear. Then make the sign of fellowship and shake hand and you will be acknowledged a true mason. The words are in the z of the Kings Ch 7, v, 21, and in 2 chr: ch 3 verse last.

THE FORM OF GIVEING THE MASON WORD

Imprimis you are to take the person to take the word upon his knees and after a great mar y ceremonies to frighten him you make him take up the bible and laying his right hand on it you are to conjure him, to sec[r]ecie, By threatning that if [he] shall break his oath the sun in the firmament will be a witness agst him and all the company then present, which will be an occasion of his damnation and that likewise the masons will be sure to murder him, Then after he hes promised secrecie They give him the oath a[s] follows

By god himself and you shall answer to god when you shall stand nakd before him, at the great day, you shall not reveal any pairt of what you shall hear or see at this time whither by word nor write nor put it in wryte at any time nor draw it with the point of a sword, or any other instrument upon the snow or sand, nor shall you speak of it but with an entered mason, so help you god.

After he hes taken the oath he is removed out of the company, with the youngest mason, where after he is sufficiently frighted with 1000 ridiculous postures and grimmaces, He is to learn from the sd mason the manner of makeing his due guard whis [which] is the signe and the postures and words of his entrie which are as follows

ffirst when he enters again into the company he must make a ridiculous bow, then the signe and say God bless the honourable company. Then putting off his hat after a very foolish manner only to be demonstrated then (as the rest of the signes are likewise) he sayes the words of his entrie which are as follows

Here come I the youngest and last entered apprentice As I am sworn by God and St John by the Square and compass, and common judge to attend my masters service at the honourable lodge, from munday in the morning till saturday at night and to keep the Keyes therof, under no less pain then haveing my tongue cut out under my chin and of being buried, within the flood mark where no man shall know, then he makes the sign again with drawing his hand under his chin alongst his throat which denotes that it be cut out in caise he break his word.

Then all the mason present whisper amongst themselves the word beginning at the youngest till it come to the master mason who gives the word to the entered apprentice.

Now it is to be remarked that all the signes and words as yet spoken of are only what belong to the entered apprentice, But to be a master mason or fellow craft there is more to be done which after follows. ffirst all the prentices are to be removed out of the company and none suffered to stay but masters.

Then he who is to be admitted a member of fellowship is putt again to his knees, and gets the oat[h] administrated to him of new afterwards he must go out of the company with the youngest mason to learn the postures and signes of fellowship, then comeing in again, He makes the masters sign, and sayes the same words of entrie as the app[rent]ice did only leaving out the com[m]on Judge then the masons whisper the word among themselves begginning at the youngest as formerly afterwards the youngest mason must advance and put himself into the posture he is to receive the word and sayes to the eldest mason in whispering

The worthy masters and honourable company greet you weel, greet you weel, greet I you weel.

Then the master gives him the word and gripes his hand after the masons way, which is all that is to be done to make him a perfect mason

[Endorsement]
Edinburgh Register House MS.
Some Questiones Anent [about] the mason word 1696

Note: the punctuation, spelling and layout have been preserved as far as possible. Where there was thought to be a need to clarify spelling or meaning this has been gone by adding details within parenthesis thus [XXX].

Appendix 2
SOME FAMOUS FREEMASONS

Freemasonry is different from many organizations in that it does not care whether or not its members are rich or famous, or both. In fact, it is highly probable that many so-called famous Freemasons will never be identified because the records of their membership are dealt with in the same way as those belonging to anyone else; the word 'famous!' isn't stamped on them in big red letters, and so their names may disappear amongst those of others. They are sometimes only discovered by accident; for example, it has only recently become know that the author and Nobel Prize winner John Steinbeck (1902–1968) was a Freemason. For every famous Freemason there are tens, if not hundreds, of thousands of 'ordinary' Freemasons.

The list below is provided simply to show the diversity of men who have been Freemasons and is not intended to be comprehensive. It contains many Americans as their details are often more readily available.

Abbott, William 'Bud' – One half of the famous Abbott & Costello comedy team.

Adam, Robert – The pre-eminent British architect of the eighteenth century.

Aldrin, Edwin E. – Known as 'Buzz': American astronaut and crew member of Apollo 11. Was the second person to step onto the moon.

Anderson, Robert – Major General US Army in command of Fort Sumter at time of Confederate attack 1861 which marked the start of the civil war.

Astor, John Jacob – A German immigrant to the US who was considered for a time to be the wealthiest man in America. He was Master of Holland Lodge in New York and served as Grand Treasurer for the Grand Lodge.

Audubon, John James – American ornithologist and artist. Famous for his superb and accurate drawings, in colour, of birds of America. In his personal diary he refers to himself as a 'Mason' and 'Brother' but details of his membership have not been found.

Bartholdi, Frederic A. – French sculptor and designer best known for his figure of *Liberty Enlightening the World,* the Statue of Liberty, in New York Harbour.

Benes, Eduard – President of Czechoslovakia elected in 1935 who led his nation's government into exile after the outbreak of World War II. He resigned in 1948 when he was forced to yield to a Communist-directed cabinet.

Bennett, Viscount R. B. – Twelth Prime Minister of Canada, 1930–35.

Berlin, Irving – Entertainer and songwriter who wrote more than fifteen hundred songs including 'Alexander's Ragtime Band' (1911) and several musical comedies, including *Annie Get Your Gun* (1946).

Borgnine, Ernest – Film and television actor who received an Oscar for Best Actor for the film *Marty* in 1955. Known to a generation of television fans for his role as the captain in *McHale's Navy*. Still actively serves Freemasonry and is presently the Honorary Chairman of a programme to support the Scottish Rite Childhood Language Center in Richmond.

Bradley, Omar N. – American general. Played a major part in the Allied victory in World War II.

Brant, Joseph – Chief of the Mohawks 1742–1807. Supported the British in the French and Indian War and the American Revolution.

Brodie, William – Immigrant to the US from Scotland. Grand Master of the Grand Lodge of the State of New York and in that capacity laid the foundation stone of the Statue of Liberty in 1884.

Bruce, James of Kinnaird – Scottish explorer who made an epic voyage to Abyssinia in the eighteenth century. He returned with three copies of the Book of Enoch – the first complete copies in Europe.

that 'title' in a Masonic Lodge. His lyrics, written in the Scots dialect and infused with humour, celebrate love, patriotism and country life. Freemasonry was more important to him than any other institution in Scotland – he was a member of five Lodges.

Carson, Christopher 'Kit' – Frontiersman, scout and explorer.

Chrysler, Walter P. – American automobile manufacturer who founded the Chrysler Corporation.

Churchill, Winston – British Prime Minister (1940–1945 and 1951–1955). His leadership helped Britain survive under the onslaught of Hitler's Nazi war machine.

Cody, 'Buffalo Bill' William – American guide, scout and showman who founded the Wild West Show which toured Europe and America. Cody, Wyoming is named after him.

Cole, Nat 'King' – One of the greatest pianists and ballad singers.

DeMille, Cecil B. – Film director who directed the very first Hollywood film, *The Squaw Man*, in 1914, and who was the creative genius behind Paramount Pictures. He was central in developing Hollywood into the film capital of the world.

Dempsey, (William Harrison) Jack – Became a professional boxer in 1912 and fought in more than one hundred semi-pro and professional bouts before winning the heavyweight championship in 1919, successfully defending his title five times.

Desaguliers, John Theophilus – Inventor of the planetarium and third Grand Master of the Grand Lodge of England.

Edward VII – Prince of Wales and King of Britain.

Edward VIII – King of Britain who abdicated the throne in order to marry Mrs Simpson.

Fleming, Sir Alexander – British bacteriologist, born in Ayrshire, who discovered penicillin in 1928. He shared a 1945 Nobel Prize with Florey and Chain.

Franklin, Benjamin – American printer (published Anderson's *Constitutions* of 1723, the first book to come off the press in the colonies), author, diplomat, philosopher, statesman and scientist.

colonies), author, diplomat, philosopher, statesman and scientist. He held the Masonic title of Grand Master of Pennsylvania and was one of the thirteen Masonic signers of the Constitution of the United States.

Gable, Clark – American actor best remembered for his role as Rhett Butler in *Gone with the Wind.* He received an Academy Award for Best Actor in 1934 for *It Happened One Night.*

Gibbon, Edward – British historian and author of the classic *Decline and Fall of the Roman Empire* (1788).

Gilbert, Sir William S. – British librettist best known for his series of Savoy operas, including *H.M.S. Pinafore* and *The Pirates of Penzance*, written with the composer Sir Arthur Sullivan (who was also a Freemason).

Gillette, King C. – American inventor who developed the safety razor and founded the Gillette Safety Razor Co.

Houdini, Harry (Ehrich Weiss) – American magician and escapologist.

Jackson, Andrew – Seventh President of the United States (1829–1837), who was Grand Master of Masons in Tennessee for two terms (1822–1824).

Jolson, Al – American vaudeville and film performer, who starred in *The Jazz Singer.*

Jones, John Paul – Born in Scotland, he became the 'Father of the US Navy'.

King, Ernest Joseph – Commander-in-Chief of the US Fleet in 1941 and Chief of Naval Operations from 1942 to 1945.

King, Karl L. – One of America's top four march composers (1891–1971).

Kipling, Rudyard – British author of *The Just So Stories* and *The Jungle Book.* Was named one of forty living Fellows of the Philalethes Society.

Kitchener of Khartoum, Herbert Horatio – 1st Earl. Field Marshal.

Lafayette, Marquis de – French soldier and politician who took part in the American Revolution as a close supporter and friend of George Washington.

Lauder, Sir Harry – Music-hall entertainer. Wrote: 'Roamin in the Gloamin', 'I Love a Lassie', 'A Wee Deoch-an-Doris', and 'Keep Right on to the End of the Road'.

Michelson, Albert Abraham – measured the speed of light in 1882 and became the first American scientist to win a Nobel Prize (1907).

Monroe, James – The fifth President of the United States (1817–1825).

Montgolfier, Jacques Etienne – French co-creator, with his brother, of the first practical hot-air balloon.

Mozart, Wolfgang Amadeus – Legendary Austrian composer whose works include the operas *Don Giovanni* (1787) and *The Magic Flute* (1791).

Pickett, General George E. – Commanded the Confederate lines at the Battle of Gettysburg and led the final assault.

Revere, Paul – American silversmith, engraver and revolutionary hero, who on 18 April 1775 was celebrated in a poem by Longfellow. A Grand Master of the Grand Lodge of Massachusetts.

Robinson, 'Sugar Ray' – American prizefighter and six times world champion (once as a welterweight and five times as a middleweight).

Roosevelt, Franklin D. – Governor of New York and thirty-second President of the United States, the only US president to be elected three times.

Roosevelt, Theodore – Twenty-sixth President of the United States and winner of the Nobel Peace prize.

Ross, Sir John – Rear-admiral and Arctic explorer.

Sanders, Colonel Harland – Founder of the Kentucky Fried Chicken fast-food outlets.

Schaw, William – The Father of modern Freemasonry. Wrote the Schaw Statutes and reorganized the stonemasons' lodges in Scotland from which modern Freemasonry is decended.

Sellers, Peter – British actor and comedian.

Sibelius, Jean – Finnish composer of *Finlandia* (1899).

Simcoe, John Graves – Hero of the Revolutionary War, Founder of

Ontario and Lieutenant Governor of Upper Canada. Canadians celebrate Simcoe Day in August.

Shankland, Lt. Col. Robert – Awarded the VC for his heroism during the Battle of Passchendaele in 1917.

Sousa, John Philip – US Marine Band leader from 1880 to 1892, who wrote 'The Stars and Stripes Forever'.

Stratton, Charles ('General Tom Thumb') – American entertainer and circus performer, who was only three feet four inches in height at maturity.

Truman, Harry S. – Thirty-third President of the United States, who served as Grand Master of Masons in Missouri, 1940–1941.

Wallace, Lewis (Lew) – American military leader and author of *Ben Hur.*

Watt, James – Inventor of the first workable steam engine.

Wayne, John – Actor in many Westerns who was known as 'The Duke'.

Ziegfeld, Florenz – Creator of Ziegfeld's Follies in 1907.

SUGGESTED READING

The range of material relating to the subjects covered in this book is truly enormous and so a limited reading list is all that can be offered here. First and foremost I recommend the work of David Stevenson, Emeritus Professor of Scottish History, University of St Andrews. I believe that his books are an essential prerequisite to understand the origins of Freemasonry, and Chapter 9 draws substantially on those books.

Bullock, Steven C. *Revolutionary Brotherhood: Freemasonry and the Transformation of the American Social Order 1730–1840* (Chapel Hill: University of North Carolina Press, 1996).

Coil, Henry Wilson, *et al.*, eds. *Coil's Masonic Encyclopedia* (New York: Macoy, 1961).

Cooper, Robert L. D, 'The Revenge of the Operatives?' in *Marking Well: Essays on the Occasion of the 150th Anniversary of the Grand Lodge of Mark Master Masons of England and Wales . . .*, ed. Andrew Prescott (Hinckley, Leicestershire: Lewis Masonic, 2006).

—, *The Rosslyn Hoax?* (Hinckley, Leicestershire: Lewis Masonic, 2006).

Dyer, Colin. *Symbolism in Craft Freemasonry* (Shepperton: Lewis Masonic, 1976).

Farrah, George. *The Temples at Jerusalem and their Masonic Connections* (Hinckley, Leicestershire: Central Regalia, 2003).

Gould, Robert F. *Military Lodges 1732–1899* (London: Gale and Polden, 1899).

Grand Lodge of Scotland. *Year Book* (Edinburgh, Scotland, 1952–).

Hamill, John. *The Craft: A History of English Freemasonry* (Wellingborough: Aquarian-Crucible, 1986).

Jackson, A. C. F. *English Masonic Exposures 1760–1769* (Shepperton: Lewis Masonic, 1986).

Jones, Bernard E. *Freemasons' Book of the Royal Arch* (London: George G. Harrap, 1957).

Knoop, Douglas, and G. P. Jones. *The Scottish Mason and the Mason Word* (Manchester: Manchester University Press, 1939).

—. *A Short History of Freemasonry to 1730* (Manchester: Manchester University Press, 1940).

—. *The Genesis of Freemasonry* (Manchester: Manchester University Press, 1947).

Knoop, Douglas, G. P. Jones and Douglas Hamer, eds. *The Early Masonic Catechisms* (Manchester: Manchester University Press, 1943).

Lane, John. *Masonic Records 1717–1894*, 2nd edn (London: Freemason's Hall, 1895). First published in 1887. Now available online at http://www.freemasonry.dept.shef.ac.uk/lane/

Lennhoff, Eugene and Einar Frame (trans.) *The Freemasons* (London: Lewis Masonic, 1978).

Lindsay, Robert Strathern. *The Royal Order of Scotland*, 2nd edn (Edinburgh, 1972).

—. *The Scottish Rite for Scotland* (Edinburgh: Chambers, for the Supreme Council for Scotland Ancient and Accepted Scottish Rite, 1958).

McArthur, Joseph Ewart. *The Lodge of Edinburgh (Mary's Chapel), No. 1 – Quatercentenary of Minutes 1599–1999* (published by the Lodge, 1999).

MacNulty, W. Kirk. *Freemasonry – A Journey through Ritual and Symbol* (London: Thames and Hudson, 1991).

Piatigorsky, Alexander. *Who's afraid of Freemasons? – the phenomenon of Freemasonry* (London: Panther, 1997).

Pick, Fred L., and Norman G. Knight. *The Pocket History of Freemasonry* (New York, 1953).

Ridley, Jasper. *The Freemasons* (London: Constable, 1999).

Robinson, John J. *Born in Blood – The Lost Secrets of Freemasonry* (New York: M. Evans, 1989).

Smyth, Frederick. *Brethren in Chivalry* (London: Lewis Masonic, 1991).

Stevenson, David. *The Origins of Freemasonry – Scotland's Century 1590–1710* (Cambridge: Cambridge University Press, 1988).

—. *The First Freemasons – Scotland's Early Lodges and their Members.* (Aberdeen: Aberdeen University Press, 1988).

Tabbert, Mark A. *American Freemasons: three centuries of building communities.* (Lexington, Mass.: National Heritage Museum; New York: New York University Press, 2005).

GLOSSARY

Freemasonry has a jargon all of its own. Like its symbolism, its terms are unique to the organization, with the result that confusion may arise whenever people try to attribute non-Masonic meanings to certain Masonic terms. Here is a concise glossary of some of the more common Masonic expressions.

apron (Masonic) The main item of Masonic regalia (others being jewels, sashes, collar jewels and badges of office). The Masonic apron is almost certainly descended from the stonemason's apron. Now only of symbolic importance. (See Plates 5, 6 and 7.)

ashlar, rough To the stonemason this was an undressed stone as delivered from the quarry. To the Freemason this refers to someone who is not a Freemason or has only recently been initiated.

ashlar, smooth To the stonemason this is a stone dressed and ready to be used in a building. Also known as a perfect or polished ashlar. To the Freemason this refers to a Freemason who has learned and lives by the tenets of Freemasonry.

Brother, Brethren The terms by which Freemasons refer to each other singularly and collectively.

Charter or Warrant The document issued by a Grand Lodge, which authorizes a group of Freemasons to form a Masonic Lodge and to be entitled to confer certain degrees of Freemasonry within it (usually only the first three degrees, i.e. those of entered apprentice, fellow of craft and master mason). Without a charter, a Lodge is not considered legitimate or 'regular', and must be avoided by all regular Freemasons.

Cowan Originally a Scottish word for an untrained stonemason who might be able to do the work of a stonemason but who has not been initiated into a lodge. In Freemasonry, the term refers to a non-Mason.

Degree The ceremony by which a candidate attains a 'degree' such as that of entered apprentice etc.

Entered Apprentice The First degree of Freemasonry.

Exposure A term used by Freemasons to describe the rituals published in the public domain without the authority of other Freemasons. The first of these was published by Samuel Prichard in 1730. The practice of printing exposures continues to the present day, with many now freely available on the Internet (very useful to the Masonic historian!). They are usually made available by anti-Masons in the misguided belief that through allowing non-Masons to read the rituals, both the Freemasons and their rituals will be 'exposed' and people will no longer become Freemasons. The publishers of such exposures fail to realize that the printed rituals are merely words on a page; living as a Freemason in the company of other Freemasons is what is truly important.

Five Points of Fellowship Contained in the earliest Masonic rituals, this is a lesson about relationships between Freemasons. Occasionally symbolized by a five-pointed star.

Grand Lodge A body that has the ultimate authority over any regular Lodges to which it has issued charters or warrants. It is in effect the 'Head Office' of Freemasonry in any particular country or state (each state in the USA has its own Grand Lodge). Some of the older Grand Lodges still administer the Lodges in other countries where there is no Grand Lodge in those countries or when existing Lodges did not wish to move from the existing Grand Lodge to a newly created one. For this reason, Scottish Lodges still exist in some countries in which other groups of Freemasons went on to form a Grand Lodge of their own after those Scottish Lodges were founded. The three oldest Grand Lodges are: The United Grand Lodge of England (1717); the Grand Lodge of Ireland (1725) and the Grand Lodge of Scotland (1736). These are known as the Home Grand Lodges.

Grand Master This is the title of the individual who is the leader of a particular Grand Lodge. The term of office varies from Grand Lodge to Grand Lodge with some Grand Masters serving for one, two or five years and occasionally some serving for life. As every Grand Lodge is an independent sovereign body in its own right, each has the ability to decide the powers, nature and duration of its Grand Master. Therefore some Grand Masters may be mere figureheads whilst others are very hands-on. The correct title of the Grand Master of the Grand Lodge of Scotland is 'Grand Master Mason' as a direct consequence of the link to lodges of stonemasons in Scotland.

Great Architect, The Freemasons avoid direct reference to God as this would offend members of some faiths and religions. Terms such as 'The Great Architect of the Universe' (TGAOTU), 'The Grand Geometrician' and 'The Supreme Being' are used instead. Other non-Masonic organizations use similar terminology; for example, The Great Gardener of the Universe (TGGOTU) was used by Free Gardeners (see Chapter 10).

grip(s) The funny handshake! This is the Freemason's membership card. Used by Freemasons in a Masonic setting, the grip has a symbolic purpose. However, during the Middle Ages it may have been used by a stonemason to prove to other stonemasons the level (or degree) of skill that he had attained.

high(er) degrees An inaccurate term used to describe Masonic ceremonies that were added to the basic Craft Lodge ceremonies of three degrees. More correctly these later additions to Freemasonry should be described as 'side degrees', 'additional' or 'other' orders. The inaccuracy arises because degrees beyond the three Craft degrees are numbered from four to thirty-three, thereby implying that they are 'higher' – but this is descriptive only. The Fourth to Thirty-third degree are part of what is generally known as the Scottish Rite, with other branches such as the Knights Templar falling into the category of the York Rite. These divisions form the structure of Freemasonry in the USA and Canada, but the structure is different again in Europe and Britain.

Installation The ceremony whereby the Master of a Lodge is 'installed' into office. Only Freemasons who are already Masters or Past Masters can attend this ceremony.

lodge (stonemasons) The meeting place of stonemasons where other stonemasons were initiated. Over time, these began to admit non-stonemasons until eventually some became recognizable as modern Masonic Lodges.

Lodge (Masonic) The basic 'unit' of Freemasonry where the first three degrees are conferred. It is not a place.

mason Stonemason.

Mason Freemason.

Master The 'ruler' of a Lodge would be too strong a word, although he has considerable powers because he 'rules' with wardens and the consent of the members of the Lodge. The 'chairman' may be more accurate, but still does not adequately define the position. 'Master' is the written form. Verbally, he is referred to as 'Worshipful Master' (in Scotland 'Right Worshipful Master'). Individuals can become Masters of a Lodge by being elected, having progressed through lesser offices in the Lodge.

office-bearers, officers The collective term for those who perform a specific function in a Lodge. These can be divided into three groups. Ritual office-bearers (master, wardens, deacons and tyler for example); administrative office-bearers (secretary, treasurer, almoner are the main ones) and those members of the Lodge who support the Lodge in a number of ways but have no ritual or administrative duties – they form the largest and arguably the most important group.

passed, passing Having taken the fellow craft degree the Freemason is said to have been 'passed' to the second or fellow craft degree.

preceptory The meeting place of Knights Templar, also the basic 'unit' of the Masonic Order of Knights Templar. In the USA this basic unit is known as the 'Commandery'.

prentice Scottish word for apprentice.

Provincial Grand Lodge In Britain and Ireland this is the intermediate administrative tier between Lodges and Grand Lodges. For that reason, although they meet as a form of Masonic Lodge, they do not initiate individuals into Freemasonry. They can be considered as the bodies that have day-to-day oversight of the Lodges that fall within their geographical area. Members of the Provincial Grand Lodge are drawn from the Lodges over which it has jurisdiction. For example, there is the Provincial Grand Lodge of Ross and Cromarty. The same structure applies to Lodges overseas, but to avoid confusion they are known as District Grand Lodges. There is, for example, the District Grand Lodge of the Middle East – which, Scotland being Scotland, is not in the Middle East at all!

raised Having taken the Third or master mason's degree the Freemason is said to have been 'raised' to the high and sublime degree of master mason – the highest degree of Freemasonry. This has nothing to do with the Resurrection in the Christian religion.

speculative A term used to differentiate a Freemason from a stonemason.

Temple, Masonic The word 'Temple' conjures up images of a place of worship, a place where those of a particular religion gather. However, the word does not have the same meaning within Freemasonry. The oldest rituals such as the Edinburgh Register House MS (see Appendix 1) refer to the first Lodge meeting in the porch of King Solomon's Temple – but the Lodge did not convene there for the purposes of worship any more than Weight Watchers do when they hire a church hall!

Warden, Junior One of the 'three who rule a Lodge' together with the Master and senior warden. He performs an important ritual and symbolic function.

Warden, Senior As for Warden, Junior.

INDEX

Note: page numbers in **bold** show a glossary entry